Becoming Men

*The Development of Aspirations,
Values, and Adaptational Styles*

Perspectives in Developmental Psychology

Series Editor: Michael Lewis
Robert Wood Johnson Medical School
New Brunswick, New Jersey

Becoming Men

The Development of Aspirations, Values, and Adaptational Styles

Daniel A. Hart

Department of Psychology
Rutgers University
Camden, New Jersey

PLENUM PRESS • NEW YORK AND LONDON

Library of Congress Cataloging-in-Publication Data

Hart, Daniel.
    Becoming men : the development of aspirations, values, and
adaptational styles / Daniel A. Hart.
        p.   cm. -- (Perspectives in developmental psychology)
    Includes bibliographical references and index.
    ISBN 0-306-44274-4
    1. Men--United States--Psychology--Longitudinal studies.
2. Social role--United States--Longitudinal studies. 3. Moral
development--United States--Longitudinal studies. 4. Adaptability
(Psychology)--United States--Longitudinal studies. 5. Developmental
psychology--United States--Longitudinal studies. I. Title.
II. Series.
    [DNLM: 1. Adaptation, Psychological. 2. Aspirations (Psychology)
3. Gender Identity. 4. Longitudinal Studies. 5. Men--psychology.
6. Social Values.   BF 692.2 H325b]
BF692.5.H37   1992
155.6'32--dc20
DNLM/DLC
for Library of Congress   92-49929
                                                               CIP

ISBN 0-306-44274-4

© 1992 Plenum Press, New York
A Division of Plenum Publishing Corporation
233 Spring Street, New York, N.Y. 10013

Printed in the United States of America

Preface

This book reports the results of a 20-year longitudinal study of men's development begun by Lawrence Kohlberg. At 3- to 4-year intervals over the course of the investigation, the participants, first as adolescents and then as adults, were interviewed intensively by Kohlberg and his associates. Portions of these interviews had been closely examined by Kohlberg and his colleagues Anne Colby, John Gibbs, Clark Power, and Ann Higgins in order to formulate the moral judgment stages for which Kohlberg is well known; however, many of the data have not been previously analyzed, and it is these that form the basis for this book.

My involvement in this project began with Anne Colby's suggestion that the data collected by Kohlberg and archived at the Henry Murray Center for the Study of Lives, Radcliffe College, might provide an opportunity to extend my previous work on self-understanding (e.g., Damon & Hart, 1988) into adulthood. With Kohlberg's encouragement, and through the grant support of the Henry Murray Center, I began to read the questions in the interviews that pertained to self-understanding.

The interviews proved to be quite exciting to read. One could follow the trajectory of a man's life in a matter of hours by reading through the interviews with him during his adolescence and early adulthood. Change, stability, transformations, self-deceptions, disappointments, aspirations, and achievements were all evident. Once I read the first interview with a man as an adolescent and learned of his goals, dreams, and family, I felt compelled to read the remaining interviews to see how his life changed and matured. The profluent nature of each set of interviews made them read as much like novels as research instruments.

For instance, one 20-year-old, reflecting on the 4 years that had passed since his previous interview, wrote the following:

> I don't know if you will find any great change in my ideas or judgments—there is only one change that I know of, and that is, of course, the feeling I now have toward the other sex.
>
> The girl I am going with now is quite unique. The way she tells it is that she made a play for me, but I thought I won her. She went with me when I didn't have a car (cars seemed important then).
>
> Then I got a job and we drove a sharp car (a '55 Ford, stick-shift, V-8 engine, cherry red). The point is: she stayed with me and we more or less worked our way up from walking to driving. That is just one example.
>
> We are both very stubborn, and yet we never use our stubbornness against each other. We seem to put it together, and we caused quite a commotion among both sets of parents (we are more mature now—I think!).
>
> We will probably become engaged this summer. I want to succeed and be able to take good care of her in the future.

Upon reading this excerpt, I was drawn to the following interviews to answer the questions that immediately arose in my mind: Does he marry his girlfriend? Is success in his future? Can he retain the warmth and humor manifest in his note as he crosses the transition into adulthood? I found myself wanting answers to the questions posed by the lives of the men in the study.

It was clear that the original plan to analyze the interviews in terms of my self-understanding model would need to be modified. Although the model of self-understanding that Damon and I have proposed is more complex and elaborated than other theories, too much of what the men had to say in their interviews could not be captured in terms of a self-understanding model alone.

This book is my effort to describe as fully as possible the paths these men followed. To do so, I have integrated a variety of research approaches. To foreshadow my conclusion, I believe that the complexity of life precludes dependence on a viewpoint based on a single theory or approach. The depth and richness of life demands that the theoretical net be cast widely.

The philosopher Richard Nozick (1981) distinguishes two approaches to philosophy: persuasive and explanatory. *Persuasive* philosophy is aimed at proving that one position is correct and/or that another is wrong. *Explanatory* philosophy, on the other hand, seeks only to examine how certain principles are possible and how they might be related. This distinction is relevant for the work presented here. My goal throughout the book is not so much to validate one hypothesis or invalidate another as to develop a consistent explanation that adequately addresses the commonalities and differences in the men's lives. I hope there are no theoretical straw men set up in order to be neatly opposed by the experimental data. Instead, I try to draw together a variety of perspectives in order to yield a full account of men's lives.

The journey begins in Chapter 1 with a consideration of the central questions to be answered in the study of lives followed over time. These issues are then explored through the answers that have been proposed by the three dominant paradigms of the life course: personality trait, structural-developmental, and crisis-transformational. The best research within each paradigm is examined to determine what the paradigm has to offer for an account of lives. The framework for the investigations presented in this book is based on an analysis of the three paradigms.

Chapter 2 presents the details of the study. The methodological reliance on personal interviews is defended as a means of revealing the meanings that subjects attribute to their lives, meanings that ought to be an important component of every developmental account of adolescence and adulthood. The specific instruments that were used and the types of data that were collected are described in some detail. Considerable attention is devoted to the nature of the sample, including the usual information about subjects (e.g., how they were recruited, social class background) as well as a consideration of the cultural and historical events that make the lives of these men perhaps different from those of adolescents coming of age today.

The social and occupational roles reflected in the ideal self are examined in Chapter 3. Developmental transformations in the ideal self are charted in the longitudinal analyses of the men, as well as in a cross-sectional study of a 1988 cohort of adolescents. Comparisons between the two samples reveal that the development of the ideal self is influenced both by sex roles and historical cohort. The role of the ideal self in the developing life is charted through case analyses of two men: Rick Jenkins and Steve Patton. The close examination of these men's lives demonstrates the importance of the ideal self in development.

Chapter 4 focuses on the development of the ego-ideal, the constellation of values and evaluative criteria with which men judge themselves, their achievements, and their aspirations. Three developmental levels in the ego-ideal are described, and the passage of the men through the levels is charted. The lives of three men—Paul O'Leary, Frank Jones, and Bob Eagleton—are described and contrasted in order to demonstrate the value of the ego-ideal developmental account for understanding the differences among them.

The contributions of personality and parents to the development of moral judgment are considered in Chapter 5 (portions of this chapter appeared previously in a paper on adolescents' socialization and identification as predictors of adult moral judgment development (see Hart, 1988). The goal in Chapter 5 is twofold: (1) to demonstrate how facets of persons may interact (conscience strength with moral judgment development) and (2) to assess the extent to which parents may influence their sons. The role of fathers in fostering moral judgment development receives particular attention.

The gradual movement from the conscious facets of personality (e.g., the ideal self) to the unconscious ones (paternal identification) is completed in Chapter 6, in which adaptational styles, or defense mechanisms, are investigated. How defense mechanisms develop and how they influence the development of other facets of personality are examined in considerable detail. The life of Ronald Brown provides a context within which the role of adaptational style in life can be understood.

Chapter 7 attempts to pull together the various findings to provide a broad overview of the contributions of the study. This overview provides the integrative framework for a detailed inspection of the life of David Vost; this case analysis provides an opportunity to evaluate the strengths and weaknesses of the framework (the weaknesses are also considered in another section).

This project would not have been possible without the financial and logistical support of the Henry Murray Center for the Study of Lives, Radcliffe College. Anne Colby and her staff at the Center have been unfailingly gracious in responding to my requests (even to allowing me to work at the center well into the night). I am deeply appreciative of their faith in this project. Rutgers University provided a supportive environment within which to work and permitted me to assume the position of visiting scientist at the MacArthur Foundation's Program on Conscious and Unconscious Mental Processes, during which time I completed the writing of this book. Finally, research supported by the Lilly Endowment allowed me to understand more fully the contributions of the family environment to moral development (considered in Chapter 5). I am grateful for the support of all these institutions.

This study was begun and guided through its completion by Lawrence Kohlberg. I deeply appreciated his generosity in allowing me to begin this study; I am also indebted to him for his willingness to serve as my mentor in graduate school. I realize more fully now than ever before the influence he had on my life.

My interest in the longitudinal study of lives was deepened by two fine books: *Lives Through Time,* written by Jack Block, and *Adaptation to Life,* by George Vaillant. I hope that I have been able to integrate some of the admirable qualities of those works into this book.

I have had considerable help on various phases of this project. Suzanne Fegley and Susan Chmiel coded much of the data and contributed in many ways to the study. Phil Raimondo, Dave Smith, and William Neveling permitted me into their schools to collect some of the data presented in Chapter 3; Joanne Villa and Dawn Fortune provided valuable assistance in that project. Both Anne Colby, through the Henry Murray Center, and Ann Higgins helped me gain access to the data, the latter by allowing me to search through Lawrence Kohlberg's personal papers. My friends and colleagues Bill Whitlow, David Wilson, Mark Reinhalter, Jonathon Muse, Mardi Horowitz, Melanie Killen, David Hine, John Hart, Rosemary Gorman, Nigel Field, and Karen Anderson helped me refine the ideas presented here. Michael Lewis, Bill Tucker, Bill Damon, Suzanne Fegley, and Rebecca Bauknight (who also coauthored Chapter 4) read one or more of the chapters and offered insightful criticisms (any remaining errors are, of course, mine alone). I am also grateful for the permission of the *Merrill-Palmer Quarterly* to reprint (in Chapter 5) portions of my article, "A longitudinal study of adolescents' socialization and identification as predictors of adult moral judgment development."

I am deeply grateful to the men who shared their lives with the study over the course of 20 years. They graciously agreed to discuss difficult issues, including (at different testing times) morals, aspirations, values, parents, children, marriage, and sex. Their participation is a tribute to their generosity. I have not met any of the men, but I feel as if I know them from reading the interviews; they are a remarkable group, fully deserving of my respect. Perhaps my fascination with their lives is a consequence of my own age; as I write this preface, I am the same age the men were at the completion of the study and my son is the age they were at the beginning of it.

As was true for the men in this study, marriage and children have transformed aspects of my life. I cannot imagine (nor do I wish to) what my life would be like without them. My wife, Deborah, and my children, Matthew and Sarah, have made becoming a man worthwhile.

Contents

CHAPTER 1

The Study of Men's Lives

In this book the lives of a group of men are explored as they pass from early adolescence into early adulthood. The men, all born between 1940 and 1946, became participants in a longitudinal study of development begun in 1955 by Lawrence Kohlberg. At 3- to 4-year intervals for the next 20 years, first as adolescents, then as men, they were intensively interviewed, revealing their values, goals, and perspectives on their lives. In addition, their parents, teachers, and classmates offered information about them through interviews and rating scales. There are literally thousands of pages of information collected from and about these men—transcribed interviews, questionnaires, rating scales, interviewer impressions—and it is possible to follow their lives from early adolescence, when they entered the study, through early adulthood, when the study ended.

The fullness of the men's lives prohibits easy distillation into the small, clear terms favored by behavioral scientists. We know from our experiences with those with whom we have enduring relationships that our understanding of others is both difficult to achieve and continually subject to revision as new information comes to light. I have no such relationship with the men in this book, and consequently I do not claim to know any of them well. While none of the men who participated in the study can be fully understood as individuals, their histories, considered together, can provide a feeling for the contours of development during adolescence and adulthood. One can see the commonalities that the men share, as well as their transformations over time. It becomes possible to ask general questions about the men and to seek answers for them in the variety of data that were collected in this study. It is this goal that guides the various explorations that form this book.

FOUR QUESTIONS IN THE STUDY OF LIVES

What questions pertain to the study of lives? There are many, of course, but there are four interrelated ones that have become central in the field and that guide the investigations presented here: (1) How much do persons change, and how much do they remain the same, across adolescence and adulthood? (2) What are the sources of stability and development in lives? (3) Are lives best understood through the reflections and interpretations of the individual or by reliance on the observations of others? (4) What facets of persons are central in understanding the trajectories of their lives?

Stability and Change

A great deal of theoretical and empirical work has been dedicated to demarcating the limits of stability and change in the course of lives. Surprisingly, there is little agreement on how adolescence and adulthood are best characterized in terms of stability versus change. For instance, some personality trait researchers proclaim that "the search for changes in personality in adulthood does not seem to have been fruitful" (Costa, McCrae, & Arenberg, 1980, p. 798). Others report that, "contrary to what might have been expected by those who view adolescence as a period of great turbulence and stress, we [they] have found a good deal of consistency along dimensions of attitudes, aspirations, and self-concept" (Bachman, O'Malley, & Johnston, 1978, p. 220).

On the other hand, there are researchers who argue that there are regular, predictable transformations in every person from adolescence through adulthood. Levinson (1978, 1986), for one, posits that the life course during adolescence and adulthood is cyclic, with periods of stability alternating with periods of change and development. Levinson suggests that men's "relationships, achievements, failures, and aspirations that are the stuff of life" (1978, p. 6) and constitute a domain broader than that of personality and inclusive of it, a domain that evolves in ways best captured by the metaphor of seasons:

> To speak of seasons is to say that the life course has a certain shape, that it evolves through a series of definable forms. A season is a relatively stable segment of the total cycle .... To say that a season is relatively stable, however, does not mean that it is sta-

tionary or static. Change goes on within each, and a transition is
required for the shift from one season to the next. (1978, p. 7).

The inevitability of periodic change during adolescence and adulthood is a vision quite at odds with the consistency and stability perceived by Costa and associates and by Bachman and his colleagues.
Can such radically different perspectives on stability, continuity, and
change in lives over time be reconciled? If so, how? What theory and
research supports these divergent claims?

The perspective developed in this book is that there is both stability and change in the course of life from adolescence into adulthood.
The evidence presented in the chapters that follow indicates that the
extent to which stability or change characterizes a man depends on:
(1) which man is considered (some men change more than others),
(2) his age (change is more apparent in adolescence), and (3) which
facet of his life is considered. My hope is to do justice to the enduring
and changing qualities of the lives considered in this book.

Sources of Stability and Change

The change and stability evident in lives followed over time inevitably lead to speculation about their sources. Many different explanations have been offered for change and stability in the life course, and
a consensus for the relative importance of each has yet to emerge.
There are, however, a growing number of psychologists who argue
that genetic influence plays a large role in shaping the life course
(Bouchard, Lykken, McGue, Segal, & Tellegen, 1990; Scarr, 1991). Although the evidence for a genetic contribution to the life course comes
from hundreds of different studies, two types of findings are particularly compelling. First, personality and cognitive similarities (as assessed by paper-and-pencil tests) between adopted children brought
up in the same family are difficult to find (Plomin & Daniels, 1987).
Second, identical twins separated in infancy and raised in different
homes are as similar to each other on personality and cognitive tests
as are identical twins raised in the same family (Bouchard et al., 1990).
Together, these findings indicate that there is no uniform home environment that influences the cognitive and personality development of
children in that family similarly. Instead, the evidence points to each
child's unique transactions with the environment as particularly crucial in the formation of personality: "Being reared by the same parents
in the same physical environment does not, on average, make siblings

more alike as adults than they would have been if reared separately in adoptive homes" (Bouchard *et al.*, 1990, p. 227). Many have argued that the twin research also demonstrates that much of the life course—personality, IQ, social class—is determined by genetic factors (e.g., Costa & McCrae, 1987; Johnson & Nagoshi, 1987).

The growing emphasis on the genetic mechanisms of stability has come at the cost of studying the influence of parents and culture. Bouchard and his colleagues conclude that "the diverse cultural agents of our society, in particular most parents, are less effective in imprinting their distinctive stamp on the children developing within their spheres of influence . . . than has been supposed" (Bouchard *et al.*, 1990, p. 226). Similarly, Maccoby and Martin (1983) concluded, after reviewing the literature on the influences of parenting on children's development, that there was little evidence for a powerful effect. Scarr (1991) has argued that parental influence is significant only when it is grossly deficient, and that among "good enough parents"—that is, those past the threshold of pathology—there is little detectable systematic influence of parents on children.

Although the behavioral genetic research has resulted in important revisions of our understanding of development, I believe that it would be a serious mistake to assume that parents and culture have only a small role in shaping lives over time. Certainly, such a conclusion is not in accord with our naive theories of development or with the careful analyses of thousands of biographers who inevitably find deep-rooted connections between parents and their offspring. Furthermore, it is important to note that the paper-and-pencil measures upon which the boldest claims of the behavioral geneticists are based do not comprehensively assess all that is of interest about personality (or cognition).

A more reasonable perspective, and the one followed here, is that parents and culture do influence development, with this influence most evident on particular facets of lives. In several chapters in this book, parents, sex roles, and historical periods are considered in terms of their influence on the life course. An account of the transition to adulthood among the men in this study would be seriously incomplete without a consideration of these factors.

Sources of stability and change also can be found in the interactions that occur among variables within the individual. Particular features within an individual may function to ensure a rigid sameness to the life course over long periods of time; conversely, there may be qualities that result in dramatic transformations in the individual over short periods of time. This too is an issue that is examined in the following chapters.

Conscious and Unconscious Influences on Lives

One emphasis of the book and the studies included in it is a respect for both the subjective, interpretive, constructive qualities of persons as well as the unconscious elements. All too often, researchers have ignored the individual's interpretation and understanding of his own life. Development is seen as determined by genetics, personality, socialization, culture, or some combination of these factors without recognition that these forces intersect in an individual who, in most cases, has an active interest in his own life. Predictions can be made about a person's life without knowledge of his own views of it—for example, educational attainment can be predicted by parental social class—but one cannot, I believe, claim to *understand* that person. One methodological implication is that the study of lives must incorporate instruments that allow the individual's own view to emerge; a reliance on paper-and-pencil tests alone cannot do justice to the individual's life. Demonstrating the contribution of the individual's own understanding of his life is another goal of this book and is a particular focus of many of the case studies presented in succeeding chapters.

A realistic student of human behavior must also acknowledge the influence and prominence of factors of which the individual whose life is studied is not aware. Although the men whose lives are considered in the following chapters are quite insightful about themselves, an observer of them is struck by the biases and self-deceptions that are apparent in each of them. For the most part, the men are not conscious, or but dimly aware, of these distortions in their lives. The blend of conscious and unconscious forces provides a more satisfying and ultimately more accurate depiction of the lives of the men in the study than would conscious factors alone.

Facets of Lives

The course of the men's lives is examined from within a psychological perspective. The fullness of real lives studied over time exceeds the explanatory capacities of theories and even disciplinary approaches, of course, but the data that have been collected bear most clearly on psychological functioning. Although a psychological perspective on the passage of lives through time provides a lens, it does not, by itself, identify the facets of lives that are most important to consider. This raises two issues: (1) To what extent is psychological functioning composed of multiple systems? (2) What domains of psychological functioning are central for understanding lives?

Holism in Psychological Functioning

A perennial issue in psychology concerns the extent to which psychological functioning reflects a single "master" trait or a composite of independent skills and attributes. Researchers interested in the nature of intelligence, for instance, have for the last century debated whether intelligence is a single general ability or is, instead, a concept that is loosely applied to a host of more specific skills that each demand their own investigations (Gardner, 1983). In the study of lives, similar divisions are apparent among researchers. There are those who see the course of lives as determined in large part by the operation of a small number of personality organizations or traits. This group of investigators argues that the study of lives is best accomplished by looking for evidence of the operation of these personality organizations and traits and that a focus on smaller facets of lives risks missing the forest for the trees.

The perspective developed in this book proceeds in another direction and describes men's lives as having many facets. Perhaps the best-established finding in developmental psychology is that the variety of cognitive, social, emotional, and personality characteristics forming the individual develop at different rates along different paths. There is little evidence that an individual is "at" a single stage from which all interesting psychological phenomena can be deduced. Instead, development occurs in spurts and bursts across domains, with attainment in any one predictable only to a small degree from attainment in another. Consequently, I argue throughout the book that development from adolescence through adulthood must be explored along several lines.

A perspective that permits the division of psychological functioning into different components, however, raises the issue of how many components there are. This is a question that cannot be definitively answered. Virtually any psychological function can be broken into subfunctions, which themselves can be divided again and again. The real task, then, is not to identify the irreducibly "real" units of psychological functioning but to identify the composite components that provide the best grasp on human nature studied over long periods of time. In the chapters that follow I describe the components of lives that are central for understanding the men as their lives evolve over the course of 20 years; these components might be too large, however, if the goal was to understand each man's conscious experience over the course of a single day.

Domains of Investigation

What components or topics or domains are essential to an understanding of lives across time? I believe that an account of men's lives would be incomplete without a consideration of their aspirations, goals, morals, values, and styles of adapting to a challenging world. In part, my commitment to these as necessary components for a description of lives arises from my own research and the research of others that is presented and reviewed in the following pages.

The centrality of aspirations, morals, and styles of adapting for understanding lives, however, is not a hypothesis in need of confirmation through psychological research. These are qualities of persons that emerge time and again in novels, drama, myths, and philosophical treatises as well as in psychology. Consider, first, aspirations. Kenneth Burke (1945) has argued that stories would be unintelligible unless the reader understood the characters to be motivated by goals, hopes, and wishes. Similarly, Robert Nozick (1981) has suggested that life plans, which encompass the individual's diverse aspirations, are indispensable elements of philosophical accounts of the meaning of life. According to Nozick:

> A *life plan* [is] an individual's set of coherent, systematic purposes and intentions for his life. These need not be specified fully, they will leave much open for further detailing, they can be revised, and so on. A life plan specifies the intentional focus of a person's life, his major goals (perhaps partially ordering them), his conception of himself, his purposes, what if anything he dedicates or devotes himself to, and so forth . . . a life plan focuses on a person's whole life or a significant chunk of it as a life. (p. 577).

Rawls (1971), like Nozick, suggests that the degree of realization of the life plan is an important contributor to rational happiness and asserts that the possession of a life plan is fundamental to the unity of the self. An account that neglects the teleological qualities of life—aspirations, goals, life plans—that have proven so important in literature and philosophy cannot reflect faithfully how life is experienced.

Values and morals similarly permeate folk psychologies, literature, and philosophy. John Gardner (1985) argued that

> no fiction can have real interest if the central character is not an agent struggling for his or her own goals but a victim, subject to the will of others . . . . We care how things turn out because the character cares—our interest comes from empathy—and though we may know more than the character knows, anticipating dangers the character cannot see, we understand and to some degree sympathize with the character's desire, approving what the character approves (what the character values), even if we sense that the character's ideal is impractical or insufficient. Thus though we can see at a glance that Captain Ahab is a madman, we affirm his furious hunger to know the truth, so much so that we find ourselves caught up, like the crew of the *Pequod*, in his lunatic quest. And thus though we know in our bones that the theory of Raskolnikov is wrong, we share his sense of outrage at the injustice of things and become accessories in his murder of the cynical and cruel old pawnbrokeress. (p. 65).

Accounts in which persons live their lives guided by their values, ever striving toward their goals, are incomplete without some recognition of the psychological adjustments and compromises that are demanded in real life. Consider, for instance, the life of one of the most gifted Americans of his generation, Paul Robeson (for an excellent biography, see Duberman, 1989). The qualities that led Robeson to become a brilliant student, an All-American football player at Rutgers University, and an actor and singer of international renown were all present in him by late adolescence. Unfortunately, as an African-American, he was unable to benefit fully from the wide range of his talents. According to Duberman (1989), the racial atmosphere of the time demanded that Robeson accept the indignity of exclusion from social life at college and pretend to be ill prepared at times in the classroom in order to defuse the envy and jealousy of his white classmates. As with everything else he tried, Robeson was successful in adapting to these insults. In fact, one of his white classmates wrote the following to him: "I will never forget how much you seemed to enjoy watching, though never participating, in any of the social affairs of your contemporaries" (Duberman, 1989, p. 25). Although Robeson apparently fooled many (and, at times, perhaps himself) into believing that the second-class status granted him by white society affected him little, he was later to remember that these events from his adolescence and early adulthood "aroused intense fury and conflict within him" (Duberman, 1989, p. 15). The demands of society required that Robeson restrain (or, as I describe it in a later chapter, repress) resentment and anger, a compromise that allowed him to achieve his educational and vocational goals but whose maintenance cost him a great deal of effort. Surely the story of Robeson's life as an adolescent would be incomplete without an account of his particular means of dealing with the stresses of prejudice.

CURRENT RESEARCH AND THEORY

There are a number of influential theoretical and methodological approaches to the study of lives over time. A consideration of these paradigms provides a context within which the questions posed here can be addressed in the research presented in later chapters. The following review of approaches is selective and is not intended to be representative of all the relevant literature (indeed, such a review would require a book of its own). The studies included here have been chosen because they represent the diversity of views and findings that can be applied to the span of life traversed by the men in this study.

Three broad traditions are represented in the studies that are included in this review: personality investigations, structural-developmental approaches, and crisis-transformational formulations. The traditions differ in their theoretical backgrounds, developmental presumptions, methodologies, and conclusions.

Personality Trait Investigations

One central concern of personality psychologists is the extent to which individual differences persist over time (Buss, 1989; Cronback, 1957). One might be interested in knowing, for instance, whether shyness during childhood is a good predictor of shyness during adolescence or even adulthood. As Block (1971) has pointed out, persistence of individual differences over time can be thought of in terms of stability or continuity. Stable individual differences are those that involve no change over time in the average level of the characteristic among members of the group against which the individual is compared; this is indicated by positive correlations of scores between

testing times, reflecting ordering stability and no significant differences in scores attributable to testing time. Continuity is reflected
by positive correlations from one time to the next and significant average differences between scores of the two testing times. One example
of trait continuity would be shyness in a 10-year-old boy, as compared
to other 10-year-olds, who become less shy by age 13 but is still
considered shy because the average level of shyness in 13-year-olds
also decreases.

Self-Report Inventories

The most frequently employed method of studying personality
traits is the self-report inventory, which consists of a number of items
that correspond to the types of traits of interest to the investigator.
Often, the items consist of short statements that exemplify the trait; for
example, a statement of introversion might be "I would rather spend
time alone than meet new people at a party." Subjects read the different items and judge how accurately each one characterizes them.

There are literally hundreds of studies that have used self-report
inventories to study the course of lives followed over time. Remarkably, virtually all of these studies converge on the conclusion that
individual differences in personality traits (at least as measured by
self-report inventories) are stable over many years. In a very useful review of the literature, Schuerger and his colleagues (Schuerger,
Zarrella, & Hotz, 1989) analyzed the results of 89 different studies that
used common self-report inventories and found stability in individual
differences, as reflected in correlations between testing sessions over
lengths of time varying from 1 week to more than 20 years. The goal
of the reviewers was to identify the factors that influence the magnitude of the stability correlations. Several of the findings emerging from
this inspection are relevant here. First, the reviewers found that the
reported stability is a function of the time intervening between testing
sessions: the correlation between a subject's scores is much higher if
there are only days, not years, between the two testing times. Second,
the analyses suggested that there is higher stability of individual differences in samples of older adult subjects than there is among samples composed of children, adolescents, and younger adults. Third,
and most surprising, Schuerger and his colleagues found that the
extent to which stability is found seems to be largely independent of
the type of self-report inventory that is used. This is a striking finding,
because the various self-report inventories differ in their formats and

theoretical underpinnings. Apparently, it matters little that the construction of one self-report inventory derives from psychodynamic theory and another from psychometric considerations; both measures, when administered to persons followed across time, yield evidence for the stability of individual differences.

Because the accounts of lives over time emerging from studies using self-report inventories are essentially similar, it would be redundant to review a host of these investigations. However, it is informative to consider the best work of this type. McCrae and Costa (1990) are perhaps the leading advocates today of the use of structured personality inventories for research on adult personality development. Because their series of studies have yielded a number of impressive findings, their program of research is worth considering in some detail.

McCrae and Costa (1990) propose a model of personality in which there are five basic dimensions: neuroticism, extraversion, openness to experience, agreeableness, and conscientiousness. Neuroticism, characterized by negative emotionality and susceptibility to stress at the high end of the scale, is perhaps the most important dimension, because it is the best predictor of successful adjustment (McCrae & Costa, 1990, p. 164). Those high in extraversion are affectionate, active, and passionate; openness to experience is characterized by an interest in fantasy and variety; agreeable persons are good-natured and trusting; conscientiousness is reflected in high aspirations and hard work (McCrae & Costa, 1990, p. 3).

As McCrae and Costa describe it, the origins of their model can be traced back to seminal work by Norman (1963). Norman argued that "natural languages such as English would have evolved terms for all fundamental individual differences" (as quoted in McCrae & Costa, 1985, p. 710). The task for the personality researcher, then, is to represent the dimensions of personality inherent in language in as parsimonious a fashion as possible. Although there are a number of attempts to distill the essence of personality differences represented in language—and not all of them yield factors that correspond to those of Costa and McCrae (e.g., Peabody, 1987)—the five factors that Costa and McCrae have proposed have received impressive verification.

To measure a person's personality with respect to the five dimensions, Costa and McCrae use pencil-and-paper inventories. In one study in which they report impressive findings of stability, they used the Guilford-Zimmerman Temperament Survey (GZTS). This survey contains items such as the following: "You start work on a new project with a great deal of enthusiasm . . . Yes or No?"; "You are often in low spirits . . . Yes or No?"; and "Most people use politeness to cover up what is really 'cutthroat' competition . . . Yes or No?" (Anastasi, 1976, p. 507). There are 10 scales on the survey, which together measure the higher order dimensions of extraversion and neuroticism. The survey was administered to 114 men of varying ages on three occasions, separated by 6-year spans. The authors found extremely high correlations from one testing point to another for all 10 scales on the survey. In fact, if the correlations for Time 1 to Time 3, a span of 12 years, are corrected for attenuation due to measurement error, the 12-year stabilities range from .80 to 1.0, with a median of .91. Because there were no changes in the mean scores for the sample over time, these stability figures indicate that there was essentially no change in these men's personalities, as assessed by the GZTS, over a 12-year span. The authors conclude that

> the search for changes in personality in adulthood does not seem to have been fruitful, but the personologist concerned with adult development and aging can profitably turn to other questions. The durability of dispositions despite biological, social, and cognitive changes must result from some form of adaptation; by what mechanisms are we enabled to assimilate the changing experience of a lifetime to our own nature? How do we cope, adjust, adapt, or defend so as to preserve our essential characteristics unchanged in the face of all the vicissitudes and transitions of adulthood and old age? (Costa *et al.*, 1980, pp. 798–799)

Many might object to this conclusion by arguing that personality inventories measure only vague self-perceptions that have no connection to behavior or other facets of the person. Although this argument at one point carried great weight, more recent research suggests that it is simply not so. In one impressive study, McCrae and Costa (1987) asked several hundred men and women to complete a personality inventory assessing the five dimensions. These men and women were then asked to nominate friends who knew them well. These friends were contacted by the researchers and asked to rate the subjects on a version of the same personality inventory (i.e., one that was worded to describe another instead of the self). There was impressive convergence between the self-ratings of subjects and the ratings by friends. This indicates that the personality inventory used in this study is assessing qualities of the person that are apparent to others.

McCrae and Costa (1983) have also found that neuroticism is strongly correlated with negative life affect and that extraversion is correlated with positive life affect. Because the core element assessed by the neuroticism scale is "negative emotionality" (McCrae & Costa, 1987, p. 87), this pattern of results is not totally surprising. Nonetheless, these results indicate that the measures are tapping important qualities of life.

As I hope this review of their work indicates, I believe that Costa and McCrae have contributed quite a bit to our knowledge of personality in adulthood. They have proposed a dimensional model of personality and have demonstrated in terms of the model that personality changes little from late adolescence through much of adulthood. Moreover, Costa and McCrae have demonstrated that the ratings derived from their measures, which tap important characteristics, contrary to common characterizations of personality inventories as measuring irrelevant features of persons, correspond to ratings of the same persons made by their friends and their spouses. These are substantial achievements.

However, there are good reasons to suspect that there may be more to the domain of personality than Costa and McCrae are willing to admit; in fact, there is evidence of this in their own work. Consider first the relationship of Costa and McCrae's neuroticism, extraversion, and openness dimensions to vocational choices, as represented in Holland's (1973) model (Costa, McCrae, & Holland, 1984); persons are likely to be happiest in occupations that correspond to their personalities, Holland (1973) argues. So, for instance, a person with *investigative* vocational interests (one broad type of occupational goals) is more likely to enjoy being a scientist than a car salesman.

One question that McCrae and Costa, in collaboration with Holland, have attempted to answer is the extent to which personality and vocational interests are related (Costa *et al.*, 1984). Large groups of men and women completed a personality inventory assessing neuroticism, extraversion, and openness to experience and also responded to a measure of vocational interests. Correlations among the three personality dimensions and six vocational interest patterns were calculated. For the sample of men the median correlation was .13, three correlations exceeded .30, and seven of the eighteen calculated correlations reached conventional levels of significance (a similar pattern was obtained for women). Although Costa and associates (1984) interpreted the results as indicating that "personality dispositions show strong consistent associations with vocational interests" (p. 397), my own interpretation is that the magnitude of the correlations reported in the study indicates that vocational interests are surprisingly independent of the dimensions of concern to Costa and McCrae. In other words, the very stable personality dimensions of neuroticism, extraversion, and openness to experience appear to have relatively little influence on career interests and, by implication, occupational choice.

In a second study McCrae and Costa (1980) examined the relationship of neuroticism (five scales), extraversion (five scales), and openness to experience (nine scales) to ego developmental level, as assessed by the sentence completion test in Loevinger's (1976) scheme (Loevinger's developmental theory is discussed more fully in a later section of this chapter). This study permitted a direct assessment of the extent to which those dimensions of personality of interest to McCrae and Costa overlap with the focal domains of developmentalists: There was surprisingly little relationship between the personality dimensions and ego developmental level. Only 9 of the 19 calculated correlations were statistically significant, the median correlation was .09, and none of the correlations exceeded .27. This suggests that there is very little relationship between the developmental model of personality of Loevinger and the dimensions of personality posited by Costa and McCrae.

A recent study by McCrae and Costa (1988) attempted to examine the relationship between adult personality and the style of parenting received during childhood in a retrospective study. Men and women who had responded to an inventory assessing all five dimensions of personality were also asked to rate the parenting they received during childhood from their mothers and fathers. The parenting ratings were collapsed to form three dimensions: loving–rejecting, casual–demanding, and attention. Correlations were calculated between scores for the five personality dimensions and the three parenting dimensions. The results for subjects under the age of 55 suggest that there is little relationship between the dimensions of personality and the perceived parenting of mothers and fathers during childhood. Only 13 of the 30 calculated correlations (five dimensions of personality times three dimensions of parenting times two parents) reached levels of conventional significance, the median magnitude of the correlation was .08, and none of the correlations exceeded .30. Because this was a retrospective study, it is not easy to determine how meaningful these findings are (see Halverson, 1988, for a thorough discussion of the interpretative difficulties that arise). Nonetheless, if one assumes with the authors that the retrospective nature of the study is likely to *inflate* the relationship between self-rated personality and perceptions of parenting received during childhood, it seems as if parenting has little significant influence on adult personality. Indeed, recent research with paper-and-pencil personality tests generally finds little evidence for the effects of parenting; many argue that personality factors are more strongly influenced by genetic factors instead (e.g., Bouchard *et al.*, 1990).

These studies suggest, then, that the dimensional model of personality proposed by Costa and McCrae cannot provide a full account of men's lives from adolescence to adulthood because (1) it does not appear to offer much information about men's career aspirations and choices, (2) it has little relationship to the clearly developmental factors in Loevinger's model, and (3) it cannot reflect or capture the influence of parents on their children's lives.

Vocational Interests. Studies that have tracked career aspirations and vocational interests through the use of self-report inventories also find substantial stability in individual differences. According to Holland (1973) there are six basic types of vocations: realistic (involving the manipulation of objects), investigative (involving systematic observation), artistic (involving a desire to create art), social (involving an interest in working with others), enterprising (involving aspirations of economic gain and the achievement of success), and conventional (involving a desire to maintain records and work in highly ordered environments). These basic categories have emerged from Holland's and others' extensive work on vocational interests as assessed by the *Strong Vocational Interest Blank* (SVIB) and similar inventories. The SVIB consists of a number of sections, one of which requires that the subject rate a series of occupations as either desirable or undesirable. Based on the pattern of responses, the subject is then assigned to a personality type and a vocational interest pattern.

Holland (1973) believes that individual differences become increasingly stable during the transition from adolescence to adulthood:

> A child's special heredity and experience first lead to preferences for some kinds of activities and aversions to others. Later, these preferences become well-defined interests from which the person gains self-satisfaction as well as reward from others. Still later, the pursuit of these interests leads to the development of more specialized competencies as well as to the neglect of other potential competencies. At the same time, a person's differentiation of interests with age is accompanied by a crystallization of correlated values. These events—an increasing differentiation of preferred activities, interests, competencies, and values—create a characteristic disposition or personality type that is predisposed to exhibit

characteristic behavior and to develop characteristic personality
traits. (p. 12)

Are individual differences on these scales stable? The answer is
yes, at least for adulthood (see Bloom, 1964, for a thoughtful, if a bit
dated, review of this issue). Over periods of time as long as 30 years,
the correlations of vocational interest patterns range between .56 and
.68 (Strong, 1955). As was the case with personality scores, the stability
of vocational interests is greater among older adults than among adolescents or young adults. Furthermore, the scores derived from vocational interest inventories do allow predictions about an individual's
future: persons are most likely to enter jobs consonant with their
interests and to remain in and be happy with such jobs (Holland,
1973). This body of research, then, indicates that self-report vocational
interest inventories reveal stable individual differences from adolescence into adulthood that have implications for occupations.

There are clear developmental trends in vocational interests (although these are of much less interest to researchers than the evidence
for the stability of individual differences): in his review of longitudinal
studies Campbell (1971) reported that in comparison to older adults
adolescents and young adults endorse more items that suggest an
interest in physical activity and taking risks, suggesting a greater orientation to sensual pursuits and immediate gratification among the
younger age groups.

Although the research tradition on vocational interests has produced a variety of psychometrically sophisticated inventories, which
have led to an accumulation of information about occupations, it
is important not to overestimate what has been accomplished. Indeed, Holland and his colleagues (Gottfredson & Holland, 1975)
have pointed out that the best predictor of the type of occupation
an adolescent or young adult will enter in the future is not one of
the many scale scores derived from the self-report inventories but,
rather, the job the individual believes he will enter. In other words,
asking an adolescent what job he expects to enter as an adult yields
as much (or more) information about his future career as could
be garnered through the administration of a sophisticated self-report
vocation interest inventory. Certainly, an important implication of
this finding is that the value of a person's self-knowledge and aspirations ought not to be underestimated. What people think about themselves, their goals and aspirations, has a real influence on the paths
their lives follow.

Observational Studies of Personality

An alternative to assessing a person's personality through self-reports is to solicit judgments about the person from others. These others might be parents or teachers or the researchers themselves. This type of research has the advantage of avoiding the host of problems inherent in self-reports (the desire to present only the admirable features of self, self-deception, and so on); however, it is far more costly and difficult to collect observational data about an individual's personality than it is to have that individual take a few minutes and answer a questionnaire. For this reason, there are only a small number of longitudinal studies that have collected observational data about personality.

Studies by Block. Probably the most balanced of observational personality studies that have followed adolescents into adulthood is that of Jack Block (1971). Block analyzed the various data that had been collected as part of the Oakland Growth Study, begun in 1932, and the Berkeley Guidance Study, begun in 1929. The subjects in the two studies were tested in early adolescence, middle adolescence, and in middle adulthood. For early and middle adolescence, many different test scores (e.g., IQ, Rorschach, Thematic Apperception Test) were available; information was also obtained from a variety of different sources, including the ratings of teachers, impressions of the research staff, and comments and responses of the subjects themselves. The subjects were extensively interviewed in middle adulthood, with the interviewer's written summary of the interview serving as the principal source of data for Block's analyses.

Because no single test was administered at each of the three testing times, the simple strategy of examining test scores for change and similarity over time was not possible, at least with the data in its existing form. To overcome this hurdle, Block employed a technique he developed that has now become known as the Q-sort approach to personality. In this approach research assistants read carefully all the various materials concerning a subject for one of the testing times in order to form an impression of the subject's personality. The rater then sorts 100 different personality descriptions into different piles, with the piles representing different levels of descriptiveness; for instance, if the rater believes that a particular personality description is characteristic of a subject, the item is put in the very descriptive pile. This process permits the informed judgments of the rater to be reflected in a standard terminology. By having a number of raters examine the materials for each subject, Block was able to obtain average descriptions of subjects and eliminate the biases that would emerge from descriptions by any single rater.

Block found considerable continuity in the group of men in his study. The transition from early to late adolescence was marked by continuity in the extent to which the boys were expressive, compassionate, resilient, and able to rebound from stress and in the extent to which a cognitive orientation toward life was evident. There was also change, with increases in the cognitive, less passionate approach to life and in sexual interests.

The analyses of the second transition, from adolescence to middle adulthood, revealed continuities as well. Individual differences in dependability, impulsivity, and the extent of a cognitive orientation toward life were consistent over this long period of time (and replicate the findings of Kagan and Moss, 1962). Of course, there were changes too, with the men apparently becoming more self-confident and developing greater self-control. Interestingly, Block (1971) concluded that this change in the men from late adolescence to middle adulthood is not without its costs:

> The experience of becoming an adult is not entirely beneficent, but is more a matter of driving a bargain between the self and the world. To meet widening responsibility, our subjects became more effectively controlled and this imposition upon self was evidently rewarded by reduced intrapsychic agitation. However, to an extent, these gains of comfort and competence were at the expense of giving up important qualities of personal expressiveness; accordingly, the reality of orientation of our adult man has a mildly obsessive flavor. (p. 70)

In summary, then, Block found that there is substantial continuity in personality from early adolescence into middle adulthood, as well as important, and not always positive, changes. (Like Block, Bray and Howard [1983] have reported that men followed into middle adulthood become increasingly self-controlled and autonomous but, in the process, become less likable, less friendly individuals.)

Summary of Personality Trait Investigations

The bulk of findings from personality research is consonant with its guiding hypothesis of stable individual differences. Studies employing self-report inventories of personality and vocational interests uniformly find considerable stability over the life course, with this stability increasing with age. Although much of the emphasis of this body of work is on stability, there is evidence for some change as well, particularly in the studies by Block and by Bray and Howard.

To the other questions posed at the beginning of the chapter, personality research offers only implicit responses. There appears to be some agreement that the individual is, in part, aware of his own personality, an assumption that underlies the wide adoption of self-report inventories. The adoption of self- report inventories is, however, a choice of convenience rather than necessity; for the most part, personality researchers believe that peers could provide better information about a subject's personality than the subject himself (e.g., Funder, 1991). This, in turn, implies that the individual's unique interpretations of his own world are not of particular interest.

Although almost all the personality research is based on a model that recognizes different dimensions to personality (e.g., neuroticism, extraversion), there remain many unanswered questions about the number, nature, and interaction of these dimensions. There is also a great diversity of opinion about the origins of personality traits. As I noted earlier, genetic explanations are currently in vogue, but there remain those who stress the roles of parenting (e.g., Vaughn, Block, & Block, 1988) and culture (Elder, 1974) as influences on personality.

Structural-Developmental Investigations

Current structural-developmental investigations have their theoretical origins in the works of Baldwin (1902) and Piaget (1932/1965), although it was Piaget's empirical work that demonstrated the value of this approach and spurred a generation of researchers to embrace it. What makes the structural-developmental approach distinctive is its emphasis on mental structures and their transformations (Gardner, 1981). Mental structures are rules and principles that govern the ways in which the individual understands both the self and the world. The goal is to identify a limited number of mental structures that can be said to generate perception and thought and then to trace the evolution of these mental structures over time.

From the structural-developmental perspective, the course of lives over time is best understood as a process of construction and reconstruction of mental structures, which form the individual's worldviews. The researcher in this paradigm is committed to identifying the structures that underlie the individual's worldviews and to tracing their evolution and transformation over time. The resulting descriptions of development emphasize the differences in the organization of thought that can be identified in persons of different ages and that have implications for thought and behavior.

There are many structural-developmental accounts that are relevant for the age range considered in this book, but only the most important and relevant can be considered here. Piaget's own works tend to focus on the development of logical and mathematical thinking over the course of infancy, childhood, and adolescence, a topic and age range that are outside the scope of the book. However, Piaget did offer some useful insights about the transition from adolescence to adulthood that are based on his research on logical reasoning (Inhelder & Piaget, 1958). According to Piaget, the development in adolescence of a new mental structure, which he called formal operational reasoning, permits the adolescent to reflect on his own thinking. This ability to analyze one's own thought leads to the capacity to develop theories and construct hypotheses. Of course, these new abilities clearly have relevance for the ontogeny of scientific reasoning, with which Piaget was entranced, but they may also be useful for understanding adolescent idealism. Inhelder and Piaget argued that adolescents use their new powers of thought to envision hypothetical worlds in which the problems that beset the real one have been eliminated through the problem-solving abilities of the adolescent. These imaginary worlds, Inhelder and Piaget noted, have too little connection to reality and adolescents carry this idealistic vision of themselves and their worlds forward until they enter the adult world, usually in the context of an occupation. This clash between reality and hypothetical possibility results in a reining in of the dreamy idealism of adolescence, thus producing a better match between cognition and reality. As we shall see, this same sort of argument has been developed along new lines by several investigators. Here, however, it is important to note that Piaget's theory of the transition from adolescence to adulthood is largely speculative, lacking the grounding in replicable findings that makes his theorizing on the earlier stages of life so compelling.

The two most influential structural-developmental theories that bridge adolescence and adulthood (and seek, as well, to address the social and intrapersonal domains that do not receive full attention in Piaget's work) are those offered by Kohlberg (1984; Snarey, Kohlberg, & Noam, 1983) and by Loevinger (1976). Kohlberg and Loevinger are both concerned with what they label ego development. For Kohlberg, ego and ego development "refer[s] to a fundamental structural unity of personality organization, and the concept of a *developing ego* refers to the progressive redefinition or reorganization of the self in relation to the nonself" (Snarey, Kohlberg, & Noam, 1983, p. 305). Implicit in this definition is the traditional Piagetian emphasis on mental structures that are transformed over time. One infers from Kohlberg's description that ego development is an orderly, predictable sequence of changes that are, in large part, cognitive in nature. Loevinger's conception of ego development is more inclusive than Kohlberg's and less sharply defined; in fact, Loevinger (1976) is reluctant to offer a single definition of ego development because of her fear that sharp demarcations of the domain are misleading. For her, ego development is "a complexly interwoven fabric of impulse control, character, interpersonal relations, conscious preoccupations, and cognitive complexity, among other things" (p. 26).

Kohlberg's Theory

Kohlberg is best known for his work on moral judgment development, but in his most recent theorizing (Snarey, Kohlberg, & Noam, 1983) he maintained that his sequence of moral judgment stages is but one thread of ego development. The domain of ego development, Kohlberg argued, can be defined by the intersection of three types of philosophical issues of "meanings" (ethical, epistemological, and metaphysical) with three classes of environments (natural, interpersonal, and numinous, or transcendent). The moral judgment stages, for instance, correspond to the intersection of ethical issues with the interpersonal environment, and Piaget's work on logical reasoning can be viewed as the crossing of epistemology with the natural environment. A fully articulated description of ego development, then, requires the elucidation of the structural stages for each of the nine intersections that constitute the domain of the ego. This is a claim to which we will return in the discussion of Loevinger's work.

The bulk of Kohlberg's (e.g., 1963, 1981, 1984) research has been on moral judgment. His work on moral judgment integrates the Piagetian emphasis on structure and development into a theory with implications for an understanding of lives. For this reason alone, Kohlberg's work warrants detailed exposition; but his work obviously is important for this book for reasons beyond its theoretical force. The men whose lives are described in this book were recruited as children and adolescents by Kohlberg for a study on moral judgment development. Over the next 20 years, these men were regularly interviewed by Kohlberg and his colleagues in order to trace the development of moral judgment into early adulthood. A great variety of data was collected, which permits analyses and findings that have little relationship to moral judgment development; nonetheless, the decisions to collect these various types of data were informed by Kohlberg's theoretical vision. Clearly, then, a description and an assessment of Kohlberg's research program is in order.

Kohlberg (1958) began his work on moral judgment with the intention of extending Piaget's (1932/1965) work on children's understanding of rules and justice. From his reading of Piaget and Baldwin (1902), Kohlberg was convinced that children's and adolescents' understanding of justice evolve through qualitatively distinct phases and that children differ from adults not so much in the sum of knowledge they have about justice (although this may be true) but in the way in which this knowledge is organized. To elicit these different organizations of justice reasoning, Kohlberg adopted the clinical interview format from Piaget and the method of hypothetical dilemmas from philosophers. For instance, in the best known of Kohlberg's dilemmas, children and adolescents were asked to consider the plight of Heinz and his wife:

> In Europe, a woman was near death from a special form of cancer. There was one drug that the doctors thought might save her. It was a form of radium that a druggist in the same town had recently discovered. The drug was expensive to make, but the druggist was charging ten times what the drug cost him to make. He paid $400 for the radium and charged $4,000 for a small dose of the drug. The sick woman's husband, Heinz, went to everyone he knew to borrow the money and tried every legal means, but he could only get together about $2,000, which is half of what it cost. He told the druggist that his wife was dying, and asked him to sell it cheaper or let him pay later. But the druggist said, "No, I discovered the drug and I'm going to make money from it." So, having tried every legal means, Heinz gets desperate and considers breaking into the man's store to steal the drug for his wife. (Kohlberg, 1984, p. 640)

Subjects are then asked a variety of questions such as the following: "Should Heinz steal the drug?"; "Should he steal it if he doesn't love his wife?"; "What difference does it make if it is not his wife but a stranger?"; and "Why should people try to avoid breaking the law?"

It is in their responses to these probing questions that persons reveal the principles that underlie their moral judgment.

Although he had begun with the intention of using Piaget's three-level coding scheme for analyzing the responses to his interviews, Kohlberg found that he needed to enlarge the scheme considerably; he ended up with a model of moral judgment with five stages, a model that can be used for coding interviews. At Stage 1, Heteronomous Morality, the organizing principle for an individual's moral judgment is the avoidance of punishment and obedience for its own sake. A child might argue that Heinz should not steal the drug because if he does he will go to jail. The individual at Stage 1 is incapable of understanding the perspective of another person and consequently cannot genuinely resolve interpersonal conflicts. An awareness of the perspective of another emerges at Stage 2, Individualism. The child or young adolescent at Stage 2 recognizes that persons have different interests and believes that persons ought to be allowed to pursue them. The guiding principle for moral judgment, then, is to do what is best for the self's immediate interests; a child might argue that Heinz should steal the drug to save his wife's life only if he enjoys her company (or her salary or her cooking) and the risks of imprisonment are not too great.

In adolescence, a new organizing principle for moral judgment arises. At Stage 3, Interpersonal Expectations, the individual is aware of shared expectations between persons and seeks to maintain those expectations in moral situations. An adolescent might judge that Heinz should steal the drug because a "good" husband, the kind of husband his wife and family expect him to be, would do so. The Stage 3 individual strives to preserve the esteem of his network of friends and family. The more mature Stage 4, Social System, perspective extends this concern from the interconnections of friends and family to the universe of society. At Stage 4 the individual seeks to maintain the structure of society by fulfilling his obligations as a member of society and by obeying laws that are necessary for its preservation. The older adolescent or young adult might argue that Heinz should not steal the drug because each person has a duty to obey the law in order to preserve the smooth functioning of society.

The capstone of development in Kohlberg's sequence is Stage 5, Social Contract. Underlying and organizing moral judgments is a concern for the relationship of an individual's rights to the rules and regulations of society. Society is perceived as an institution that is intended to serve an individual's interests and protect his fundamental rights; when it fails to do the latter, the rules and regulations can and should be disregarded. An adult might argue that Heinz should break the law and steal the drug in order to save his wife's life because his wife's right to life supersedes society's interest in protecting property.

In his earliest work Kohlberg (1958) believed that the aforementioned stage descriptions were idealized abstractions that bore no necessary relationship to the actual cognitive processes people used in moral judgment. The advantage of this position is that it permits persons to be described in terms of a profile of stages. For instance, a child's moral reasoning might be characterized as primarily at Stage 1 and Stage 2, with some Stage 3 and a dash of Stage 4. This characterization proved unsatisfactory to Kohlberg for a variety of reasons, and he abandoned this "soft stage" description in favor of a Piagetian or "hard stage" (Kohlberg, 1984) model that permitted stronger predictions. According to this model, the stages are accurate descriptions of the actual mental structures used by persons in judging moral issues. Like Piaget, Kohlberg asserted that a person's diverse responses and judgments arise from a single mental structure. Empirically, one expects a person to utilize primarily a single stage in responding to moral dilemmas. A second claim that derives from this model is that the sequence of stages are hierarchical, with each higher stage reorganizing the concerns of the adjacent lower one in ways that permit more a satisfactory resolution of moral conflicts. Because each stage is "better" or more powerful than the adjacent lower one, normal development (in the absence of gross psychopathology or neurological damage) is believed to proceed from Stage 1 toward Stage 5, without regression.

Kohlberg's own longitudinal investigation (Colby, Kohlberg, Gibbs, & Lieberman, 1983) provided solid support for his claims. The analyses of the responses (i.e., the subjects who are followed in this book) provided some confirmatory evidence for Kohlberg's claim that an individual uses a single mental structure (represented by a stage) in making moral judgments; most of the responses offered by an individual during the course of an interview were characteristic of a single stage, although usually there were a number of responses that seemed representative of other stages as well. The analyses resoundingly confirmed Kohlberg's claim for the sequential nature of the stages. Virtually no one in the study showed patterns of regression over the course of the 20 years. In other words, once a person achieved a stage, he did not abandon that stage in favor of a lower one.

There are several other findings from Kohlberg's study that are worthy of note. First, the analyses revealed that there is considerably more change and development occurring early in adolescence than in adulthood. This is indicated by larger average stage differences between, for instance, 10- and 13-year-olds than between 30- and 33-year-olds. Moreover, there are higher correlations between stage scores at different testing times in adulthood than there are among stages scores in adolescence, although even the correlations between early adolescent and adulthood scores are statistically significant. Second, Kohlberg and his colleagues found that high-IQ adolescents were more likely to achieve the higher stages of moral judgement development in adulthood than low-IQ adolescents. Third, there was evidence that those boys from lower social class homes had consistently lower stage scores than the boys from middle-class homes. These findings confirm (at least in part) Kohlberg's claims and also provide information about the sources of moral judgment development.

One of the most interesting phenomena observed in Kohlberg's longitudinal study emerged in the transition from adolescence into adulthood. All of the adolescents in Kohlberg's sample were at Stages 2, 3, and 4 (with most of them at Stage 3); consistent Stage 5 reasoning was evidenced only by men ages 24 and older. For some of the subjects, entry into the adult world resulted in an awareness of the limitations of Stage 4 reasoning but without the compensating acquisition of Stage 5; consequently, some of the men developed *relativism,* a belief that moral judgments are inherently subjective. For instance, one subject claimed:

> Morality is a series of value judgments. For me to say something is morally right means that in my own conscience, based on my experience and feelings, I would judge it right. But it is up to the individual, based on his individuality, to determine if something is right; it need not be right all the time. I guess what I am saying is, I don't think I have a moral right to impose my moral standards on anyone else.

This belief in the subjectivity of moral principles is often accompanied by an awareness that the real world is exceedingly complex and that the ready answers to all questions that one could offer as an adolescent seem less satisfactory in adulthood. Expressing this change in his understanding of the world, the subject just quoted went on to say, "Things are in more shades of gray and are not nearly as black and white as I used to see them in the past."

Kohlberg's initial interpretation of the emergence of relativism and the accompanying sensitivity to the complexity of the adult world was that it was a temporary phenomenon of late adolescence occurring between Stage 4 and Stage 5 (Kohlberg & Kramer, 1969). More recently, however, Kohlberg has suggested that although this relativism still precedes (and therefore is developmentally less mature than) Stage 5, it can become a stable principle of moral judgment for some individuals.

A great deal of related theory and research has addressed the issue of relativism and the accompanying awareness of the world's complexity, with a number of writers claiming that these phenomena constitute a distinctive *dialectical* stage of adulthood development (e.g., Gilligan & Murphy, 1979; Kramer & Woodruff, 1986; Perry, 1968). Contrary to Kohlberg's position, most of these theorists argue that this dialectical stage develops *after* Kohlberg's Stage 5, instead of before it. From the perspective of this group of researchers, the relativism and the heightened sensitivity of complexity characteristic of the dialectical stage emerge as the individual becomes aware of the limitations of Stage 5 reasoning for resolving the difficult and complicated moral issues that arise in adulthood. Because the individual at the dialectical stage is better able than an individual at Kohlberg's Stage 5 to incorporate the particulars of the specific context within which a problem arises, he is equipped to reach a satisfactory solution to the problem.

Much of the research and theorizing on contextual or dialectical stages arose from the perception that many traditional theories portray adolescence as the apogee of development: Piaget, of course, argued that formal operational thought, achieved in adolescence, is the last mental structure to be acquired; IQ researchers have typically found that IQ peaks in late adolescence and early adulthood and then remains basically stable; and personality researchers, like Costa and McCrae report stability and little change in personality traits across adulthood. The contextual/dialectical theorists argue that this description of adulthood omits the many positive changes that occur; their message is that adults do (or at least can) continue to acquire greater wisdom and understanding, resulting in qualitative shifts in their interactions with the world. From this perspective, adulthood is not a period of stasis but, instead, a continuing process of elaborating new mental structures with which to understand the social and physical world.

Although this is an attractive message, there is as yet little evidence that it is true. There has been relatively little research from within the contextual/ dialectical perspective on adult development, and the findings from this body of work are not at all clear (for a particularly good example of research in this area, see Kitchener & King, 1990). It seems safe to conclude, however, that these higher stages of development are reached by only a fraction of adults. In the Kohlberg study, for instance, only a subset of those men achieving Stage 4 (who are themselves a subset of the adult sample) adopt the relativism and contextualism characteristic of this advanced development. This means that the developmental path sketched by the contextual/dialectical theorists is followed by only a small number of adults.

It is impossible to review the various controversies that rage around Kohlberg's work on moral judgment. Kohlberg's focus on justice as the core element of morality has been criticized for excluding more important virtues such as interpersonal responsibility and empathy (e.g., Hoffman, 1976). His description of moral judgment has been assailed as hopelessly biased against women (Gilligan, 1982), political conservatives (Shweder, 1982), and persons from non-Western cultures (Simpson, 1974) and as lacking implications for behavior (Brown & Herrnstein, 1975), and his research methodology and analyses have been criticized as inappropriate and misleading (Kurtines & Greif, 1974).

Refutations and rebuttals concerning Kohlberg's claims appear on a regular basis in philosophical and psychological journals. My own reading of this voluminous literature is that the central tenets of Kohlberg's moral judgment theory, which may contain some flaws, have received impressive support from empirical investigations. The evidence is quite clear that the stages (1) are related to moral action (Blasi, 1980; Kohlberg, 1984), (2) appear in a variety of cultures (Snarey, 1985), (3) are not biased against women (Thoma, 1986; Walker, 1983), and (4) can be measured reliably (Colby et al., 1983). Certainly, this set of findings alone makes Kohlberg's moral stages an important component in an account of lives.

According to Kohlberg, a full account of ego development requires that the description of the sequence of development in the moral judgment subdomain be complemented by descriptions of the developmental sequence in the other subdomains. Kohlberg and his colleagues viewed the stage sequences proposed by Selman (1980) and Fowler (1981) as examples of research and theorizing that could be articulated with the moral judgment theory to yield a complete description of ego development across the life span. Although the relations among the various subdomains are not fully worked out, Kohlberg and his colleagues clearly believe that the stages in one subdomain can be logically related to those in another: "Development in a logically prior subdomain appears to be necessary but not sufficient for the parallel level of development in another subdomain" (Snarey, *et al.*, 1983, p. 308). This theoretical stance has led to assertions that particular stages of logical and social reasoning are prerequisites for attaining corresponding moral judgment stages (Kohlberg, 1984). At a more abstract level, this position suggests that the unity of personality is in large part derived from the logical interrelations among cognitive structures. The cost of adopting this view is the dismissing of the influence of the actual functioning of a real individual in a problematic social environment on the organization of the ego and personality. It is this message that is communicated most clearly in the work of Jane Loevinger.

Loevinger's Account of Ego Development

Loevinger has fashioned a developmental theory of the ego that challenges the basic tenets of contemporary developmental psychology and psychodynamic ego theory. Despite Loevinger's many years of careful empirical work and thoughtful writing (e.g., Loevinger, 1976), her theory has yet to gain wide currency among the developmentalists, clinicians, and theorists for whom it ought to be attractive. Although neither her method nor her theory has been wholly accepted by any group, Loevinger's paradigm serves as a benchmark for other accounts. That is to say, many competing theorists, while rejecting Loevinger's theory, justify their own concepts through a comparison with hers. This is true of this book as well. The position developed here, which proposes that there are relatively autonomous domains of psychological development, is clearly at odds with the holism posited by Loevinger. To draw out this distinction, however, it is necessary to describe Loevinger's theory in more detail.

In many ways Loevinger's approach is the antithesis of Kohlberg's: While Loevinger is extremely reluctant to make generalizations based on her research, Kohlberg endlessly extrapolates from a small body of findings. Loevinger is committed to careful measurement, whereas Kohlberg is more interested in thoughtful theorizing. And most important, Loevinger views the ego as a collection of loosely integrated functions and skills, while Kohlberg sees the ego as the sum of well-demarcated cognitive domains.

Most of Loevinger's own work on ego development has used the Sentence Completion Test (SCT) to collect data. The SCT consists of a series of sentence stems to which the subject responds. For instance, a male subject might be asked to complete the following stems: "If I were king . . . "; "A good father . . . "; or "Usually he felt that sex . . . "Loevinger's assumption is that the meanings that persons project onto these stems, which are revealed by their completions of them, indicate their level of ego development (but there are criticisms of this assumption; e.g., Broughton & Zahaykevich, 1988).

On the basis of years of analysis of responses to these sentence stems, Loevinger and her colleagues proposed ten stages of ego development, seven of which are relevant for the age range covered in this book. At the first or *self-protective* stage, the child is primarily concerned with being caught or blamed, a concern that results in opportunistic, self-protective behavior. This is gradually displaced by the *conformist* stage, in which the individual is concerned with being accepted by others and avoiding the shame that accompanies rule violations. The transitional *conscientious-conformist* stage is characterized by an improved understanding of the relationship of the self to the social context, an advance that results in increased differentiation of personal and social goals. As the conformist elements wane and the individual enters fully into the *conscientious* stage, self-constructed standards as well as concerns for self-respect and personal achievement emerge. At the remaining three stages, other virtues are added to those evident at the conscientious stage: at the *individualistic* stage the person acquires a concern for individuality and dependence; the *autonomous* stage brings a respect for autonomy as well as an awareness of conflicting inner needs and the means to address them; and the *integrated* stage is defined by a concern with personal identity.

Clearly, there are conceptual similarities between Loevinger's sequence and the moral judgment stages outlined by Kohlberg. Because there are clear parallels between the two theories, it is not surprising that moral judgment and ego development scores are associated; by combining a number of studies, Lee and Snarey (1988) were able to estimate that the degree of correlation between the two measures over adolescence and adulthood is approximately .65, which indicates that the two measures are closely related. In both accounts the earliest stages are defined by egoistic opportunism and fear of punishment, the middle stages by an orientation toward social acceptance and social conventions, and the highest stages by autonomous judgment.

Both theories emphasize morals and values, both are concerned with those psychic structures that organize experience, and both suggest that there is change (a tendency to use higher stages with age) in the course of development. As Noam (1988) points out, there is evidence in both paradigms for continuity as well, although this continuity is generally overlooked or de-emphasized. For the most part, the evidence indicates that there is increasing stability and decreasing change as the individual moves from adolescence into adulthood (Lee & Snarey, 1988). Because developmental change is posited, the sources of it have probably received more attention in the structural-developmental paradigm than in the personality trait paradigm. For instance, both Kohlberg (1984) and Loevinger (1976) acknowledge the possibility that development through their sequences might be facilitated by educational interventions in which persons are exposed to the limitations of their current stage and the potential advantages of the next higher one; this sort of artificial development, however, would be very limited in nature. Recent research has demonstrated that both moral judgment and ego development can be facilitated or retarded by particular patterns of family interactions (Dubow, Huesmann, & Eron, 1987; Hauser et al., 1984; Walker & Taylor, 1991).

The two theories diverge in the extent to which an emphasis is placed on unconscious elements. Loevinger's choice of a projective measure suggests that the structures that undergird ego functioning are not easily available to introspection; consequently, one cannot rely directly on the individual's verbalizations about how his ego is organized. Although the stages in Kohlberg's sequence are not based on the introspections of subjects, they are much closer to them; as a means of discerning a subject's stage there is a greater reliance on the subject's conscious efforts to synthesize conflicting goals in the Kohlberg than in the Loevinger system. This emphasis on the subject's conscious attempts to make sense out of dilemmas may be one reason why moral stages are more highly associated with age than are ego stages (Lee & Snarey, 1988).

The high correlation between the two sequences (the correlation is of approximately the same magnitude as that between Kohlberg's moral judgment measure and Rest's measure of Kohlberg's stages; see Rest, 1983) suggests that both are tapping much the same psychological qualities (just as two personality inventories might produce similar scores for neuroticism). Because of the overlap between the two sequences, choosing one over the other is a decision based partly on theoretical grounds. My belief is that the moral judgment sequence is a better choice than the ego developmental stages: the relationship between theory and method is clearer, as is the nature of the stages (Broughton & Zahaykevich, 1988). Furthermore, if one is interested in development, Kohlberg's measure appears to be more sensitive to age changes. For these reasons (and because the moral judgment stages emerged from the study of the very men discussed in the following chapters), it makes good sense to use this well-validated sequence as a major theoretical framework for this book. Nonetheless, Loevinger's emphasis on the functioning of individuals in a real world, as well as her criticisms of Kohlberg's model according to which the facets of the ego are captured by philosophical distinctions (Loevinger, 1983), provides a useful counterbalance to the overly cognitive structuralist bias of Kohlberg.

Crisis-Transformational Theories

Erik Erikson's Theory

Most crisis-transformational theories share a Freudian heritage. Currently, one of the most influential of these theories belongs to Erikson (1956, 1968, 1982). Erikson has constructed a theoretical sequence of eight tasks that challenge each individual in the passage from infancy through late adulthood. The first five of these tasks parallel the Freudian stages of psychosexual development (oral, anal, phallic, latency, and genital) and the last three represent challenges that occur in adulthood, with no direct parallels in Freud's system. Like Freud, Erikson believes that each task has its origins in biological and maturational forces. But Erikson, unlike Freud, sees social and cultural factors as central in the formation of the tasks. Consequently, Erikson believes that the process of development is a predictable sequence of negotiations between the individual and the enveloping social context.

Four of Erikson's tasks have relevance for the period of life considered in this book. The first task, salient in childhood, is to develop a sense of *industry*. The child seeks to become a productive member of a social institution valued by the culture in which he lives. For children in the United States this often translates into a desire to perform well in school (Erikson, 1963), but other pursuits—sports, artistic endeavors, Boy Scouts, to name a few—may offer the same opportunity to develop a sense of competence and productivity. The person who fails to develop a sense of productivity during this period acquires a sense of *inferiority*, which Erikson presumes will interfere with successful adaptation at later points in life.

Puberty brings with it a new set of concerns and challenges. In Erikson's theory the task faced by the adolescent is to develop a sense of *identity*. It is difficult to know precisely what Erikson means by identity because the term includes many facets of personality and self-concept (Hart, Maloney, & Damon, 1987). Achieving a sense of identity as Erikson describes it, however, seems to involve a process of reflection through which the adolescent discerns in himself his true capabilities, interests, and desires. Through this process the adolescent is able to make plans for the future that will allow his unique qualities to be expressed in socially acceptable endeavors. The adolescent who is unable to develop a sense of identity becomes mired in *role confusion*, which is marked by an inability to project the self into particular occupations, relationships, and roles with any certainty. Furthermore, this unsatisfactory resolution of the task of adolescence is likely to impair adaptation at later stages.

The task of early adulthood is to develop *intimacy* in relationships with others. According to Erikson (1963):

> The young adult, emerging from the search for and the insistence on identity, is eager and willing to fuse his identity with that of others. He is ready for intimacy, that is, the capacity to commit himself to concrete affiliations and partnerships and to develop the ethical strength to abide by such commitments, even though they may call for significant compromises. (p. 163).

The failure to enter into intimate relationships with others results in a sense of *isolation*, of being cut off from others, which Erikson believes can result in severe character problems.

The central task of adulthood, Erikson argues, is to develop a sense of *generativity*; the failure to do so results in *stagnation*. Generativity is acquired through many activities, but parenting is the most common. Caring for children and guiding them to maturity is not only necessary for the continuation of society but a valuable opportunity for adults to realize the inner needs to go beyond the self and care for others. Stagnating adults, who fail to form generative relationships, can become self-involved and alienated from the aspects of themselves that reach out toward others.

Erikson's model has inspired a great deal of research. Most of the studies have focused on the task of forming an identity in adolescence. The paradigm for most of this research was contributed by James Marcia (1966), who suggested that the key components to identity were self-selected commitments in the domains of ideology and occupation. Marcia developed an interview methodology for determining which individuals had made commitments in these two domains and whether the commitments resulted from reflective decisions of the self or merely reflected the desires of the parents. An impressive body of evidence has accumulated that indicates that those persons who have made self-chosen commitments to occupations and ideologies are, in general, better off in a variety of ways than those who have not (for a review see Marcia, 1980). Furthermore, there has been research relating identity achievement to a variety of facilitating factors, such as parental interactions (e.g., Grotevant & Cooper, 1985). Although this body of work is impressive, it is not without its critics. Reviewers have noted that the Marcia paradigm does not fully capture the richness of Erikson's conception of identity (Blasi, 1988) and that it leads researchers to the conclusion that identity, once gained, is never lost or reconstructed (McAdams, 1985).

Studies by George Vaillant

The most interesting research on Erikson's tasks in adulthood has been done by George Vaillant (1977). Vaillant has confirmed the importance of successfully resolving the Eriksonian tasks through his analyses of a group of healthy college men followed into middle adulthood. By middle adulthood the paths of the men had diverged; most of the men had succeeded in living reasonably healthy productive lives, but a few had not. Vaillant compared those who had been successful in their adaptations to those who had been least successful on a series of variables that reflected, in part, the tasks proposed by Erikson. For instance, upon entry into the study, each man's "personality integration," a construct similar to identity, was rated by the researchers. Those men who were judged to be successful at mid-life were more likely than those who were unsuccessful to have received high ratings for "personality integration" as late adolescents, which suggests that identity formation is important for later development. Similarly, Vaillant found that the successful men at mid-life were more likely than the unsuccessful ones to have married before the age of 30 (an event corresponding to Erikson's intimacy task) and to have raised healthy, happy children (one means of achieving generativity). Taken together, these findings provide some confirmation of the importance of adequately resolving the Eriksonian tasks.

Vaillant's research led him to propose an additional task, of particular interest here, in Erikson's sequence: *career consolidation*, intervening between the stages of intimacy and generativity. Young men in their late twenties and early thirties, Vaillant found, struggle to achieve both security, through personal and occupational stability, and occupational success. According to Vaillant, the result is a "precarious balance between growing roots in order to settle down and simultaneously striving for the room-at-the-top, which is often somewhere else" (1977, p. 217). Maintaining one's balance is like walking a tightrope, with a fall to either side leading to severe self-recrimination, although the fear of career failure may be more pressing.

The sources of development, Vaillant speculates, are many, but his own findings led him to conclude that interpersonal relationships are the most important and that successful adaptation requires one to *identify* with and to *internalize* the important others in one's life. Vaillant (1977) relates the contrasting cases of two brothers:

> When they were young, their father left home. One brother was six and responded to the betrayal by permanently excluding his father from his life. He subsequently was unable to identify with anyone, and his life became a series of disappointments. The second brother, only four when his father left, continued to reach out greedily for a substitute. In his youth he traveled thousands of miles to rejoin his father . . . . In midlife he has served as an influential, responsible leader of young people. (p. 344)

Identification and internalization of important others allow the individual to absorb their admirable qualities, which, in turn, provide the individual with the strength and ability to successfully resolve the tasks of development.

Although Vaillant found compelling evidence for the value of the Eriksonian sequence, he argues that the sequence by itself is incomplete. Erikson's model does not provide an adequate description of the psychological mechanisms that are employed in adapting to the stresses of day-to-day life. To augment the Eriksonian perspective, Vaillant proposes a hierarchy of unconscious defense mechanisms that range from immature to mature. Immature defense mechanisms such as *acting out*, in which the individual gives in to impulses without reflection or conscious control, are ultimately less successful in resolving the stresses of life. In contrast, mature defense mechanisms such as *suppression*, in which unacceptable impulses are consciously restrained, are more likely to yield healthy adaptation.

Vaillant argues that defense mechanisms are conceptually and empirically distinct from the life crises proposed by Erikson and have their own developmental trajectories. However, there are interactions among the two facets. For instance, Vaillant has found that an individual employing immature defense mechanisms in adapting to stress is unlikely to develop the generativity that is the desirable resolution of the task of middle adulthood. In summary, then, Vaillant has demonstrated the relevance of Erikson's theory for an account of lives and has found that success in mastering these crises is influenced by patterns of defense mechanisms.

Studies by Daniel Levinson

A provocative elaboration and revision of Erikson's model has recently been offered by Daniel Levinson and his colleagues. According to Levinson (1978), there are four major eras in the life span: infancy through adolescence (birth to age 22), early adulthood (17–45), middle adulthood (40–65), and late adulthood (60 to death). The transitions from one era to the next, the periods during which the eras overlap (17–22, 40–45, 60–65), are particularly stressful and involve major reorganization in a person's life. There is also reorganization within each era, and these periods are also stressful, but less so than the transitions. For the period of life considered in this book, adolescence through early adulthood, Levinson has proposed alternating periods of stability and change. In late adolescence, the individual enters the *early adult transition,* which occurs between ages 17 and 22. This transition is the tumultuous period intervening between the relative stability of adolescence and that of early adulthood. According to Levinson two tasks must be accomplished during this transition: the world of childhood must be left behind and a preliminary basis for life in the world of adulthood must be formed.

The first task requires that the adolescent terminate or radically revise relationships from the childhood and adolescent years. This task is seen most clearly in the process of individuation from parents; the fledgling adult must break loose from the expectations that his parents have for him and must develop some level of independence from them as well. Although it is most evident in the context of parent–child relationships, the revision process must occur in relationships with other authority figures and childhood friends. The second task, the construction of a preliminary basis for life in adulthood, may take one or more of several forms: attending college, serving in the military, or working in an apprenticeship are all first steps toward beginning a life in adulthood.

The early adult transition is followed by the phase of *entering the adult world*, which is characterized by relative stability. The young adult works on both exploring the opportunities offered by the adult world and defining himself as an adult with specific goals. It is in this stage of life that the individual forms what Levinson calls "the Dream," a vision of the self in the future as it will be under ideal circumstances. It is the Dream that animates a man's life and gives it meaning. The Dream organizes and guides the choices that give rise to a man's life structure, which is the configuration of self-selected occupations, relationships, values, and activities that defines a man's life.

The calm of the entering-the-adult-world phase ends in the tumult of the *age-30 transition*, which occurs between ages 28 and 33. Entry into this transition is brought on by a man's recognition that the life structure he built during his twenties is no longer satisfactory. Since the choices and decisions during this early phase of life were based on an inadequate understanding of both the self and the adult world, the life structure must be revised and better choices must be made. This transition is marked by a sense of urgency, Levinson claims, because there is the recognition that one is no longer an adolescent; there is considerable pressure to enter fully the world of adulthood.

Emerging from the age-30 transition, the man seeks to establish a secure niche in the adult world. He seeks acknowledgment of his status as an adult; he wants a good job; he wants to establish roots in a particular community; and he desires security and stability in his life. Levinson argues that this set of desires is superseded, to an extent, in the late thirties by a desire to demonstrate special competencies, to "climb the ladder of success." The man still believes that it will be possible to fully realize the hopes and aspirations that constitute the Dream, and he works hard to do so.

The mid-life transition, which stands between early and middle adulthood, is a period of significant reorganization in the life structure and considerable stress. One of the most important changes, Levinson asserts, is that the Dream is deflated. The man recognizes that those facets of the Dream that were realized in his life are not as satisfying as he thought they would be. Moreover, for most men, there is an awareness that most of the goals constituting the Dream will never be accomplished; only a very few of the men who dream of becoming senators or chief executive officers or supreme court justices find that their dreams come true, and this recognition occurs to men as they enter their forties.

To test his theory, Levinson has relied on a single study in which 40 middle-aged men (10 biologists, 10 novelists, 10 hourly workers, and 10 business executives) were intensively studied. Each man was interviewed in depth about his life and how it had changed since adolescence. These interviews permitted the investigative team to construct biographies for each of the men. The analysis of the biographies indicated that the aforementioned periods of stability and change occurred for all the men in the study. Furthermore, Levinson found, the transitions were closely linked to age; for instance, the age-30 transition, marked by instability and revision in the life structure, occurred between ages 28 and 33—not between 25 and 28 or between 33 and 36—for all of the men. The robustness of these findings across all subjects in the study—who differed in social class, educational background, and occupation held at the time of their participation—led Levinson to conclude that the patterns he described constitute a universal sequence that can be found in men in all cultures.

Perhaps the fairest evaluation of Levinson's theory is that it has yet to derive much support from empirical research. On the one hand, Levinson's own data seem to provide strong support for his claims; he found the transformations and age linkages specified by his theory. Even sympathetic critics, however, have noted that his research is problematic for a variety of reasons: (1) The sample does not even approximate a representative sample of American men; few researchers would agree that a description of development derived from such a group is characteristic of men in the United States, much less those in other cultures. (2) Since they were written by Levinson and his colleagues, the biographies may have been influenced by the theory and, consequently, cannot be used to confirm it. (3) The biographies are based on the men's recollections about their lives in their twenties and thirties, and there is substantial evidence that remembering one's life at a later data can be significantly different from one's experience of it at the time (Vaillant, 1977).

While Levinson's own research is of questionable value for confirming his theory, the research of other investigators seems to refute it. For instance, studies by Costa and McCrae (1978; Costa, McCrae, Zonderman, Barbano, Lebowitz, & Larsen, 1986) find little evidence of age-related shifts in negative emotions, occupational and family dissatisfaction, or sense of inner turmoil. This is contrary to the expectation that these variables ought to be related to the phases and transitions posited in Levinson's model. For instance, one would predict that all three (negative emotions, dissatisfaction, inner turmoil) would be high during the age-30 transition and low in the relative calm of the next phase. Yet this hypothesis and similar ones were not confirmed.

The different crisis-transformational theories share an emphasis on the periodic reformulation of life brought on by age-linked tasks in development. Each of these tasks presents challenges that are sufficiently novel as to make new demands on the person; the person must change in order to adapt successfully. This means that these theories envision substantial change in the course of lives. Perhaps owing to their psychoanalytic roots, the crisis-transformational theories include the notion that unconscious factors and family influences play major roles in development.

SUMMARY

What do the three paradigms that have been reviewed contribute to an understanding of development through adolescence and adulthood? The personality trait research program is aimed at demonstrating that meaningful individual differences persist over time. These stable individual differences are presumed to affect the individual's daily life, with cumulative effects. The life span researcher within this paradigm traces the effects of personality differences on the individual's academic achievement, popularity with peers, relationships with parents, occupational decisions and advancement, success in creating a family of his own, and satisfaction with life (e.g., Caspi, Elder & Bem, 1987). The resulting account of the life course emphasizes the host of stabilities and continuities that can be abstracted by a perceptive observer.

Structural-developmentalists begin with different assumptions. Rather than assume the perspective of a perceptive observer seeking stability in the flux of a person's life, theorists in the structural-developmental tradition aim to uncover how the person understands his own life, identify the mental structures that lead to this understanding, and show how these structures evolve over time. Both Loevinger and Kohlberg posited important age differences in the ways in which individuals are presumed to account for different patterns of behavior across the life span. There is a greater emphasis here (particularly in Kohlberg's theory) than in the personality trait paradigm on the contribution to the resulting life course of the individual's active organization of information, aspirations, desires, and psychological resources.

The crisis-transformational theories aim to provide a flexible framework for biographical analyses of individuals. The paradigm is centrally concerned with the intersections occurring between the resources of the individual and the challenges and tasks of life. There is an assumption that these intersections can be mapped onto the life cycle, with certain types of tasks and challenges faced at particular points in life; at each of these points, the individual is thought to draw upon a blend of old and new personal resources to address the task. The crisis-transformational paradigm aspires to capture the richness of an individual's life; personality traits, age-specific competencies, familial influences, societal expectations, and historical circumstances all find a role in the depiction of development. However, the diversity of developmental paths that are apparently consonant with the framework makes it difficult to test the framework in any definitive way; consequently, the credibility of this paradigm rests on its intuitive appeal to a greater extent than is true for either of the other two paradigms.

The relation of each paradigm to the questions posed at the beginning of the chapter are outlined in Table 1.1. The entries in this table reflect the extent of tendencies in the different approaches, not rigid

TABLE 1.1.
*Relative Emphasis on Various Conceptual Elements
in the Three Theoretical Approaches to Lives Over Time*

	Approaches to lives over time		
Conceptual element	Personality trait	Constructive-developmental	Crisis-transformational
Course of life characterized by			
Stability	High	Low/moderate	Low
Change	Low	Moderate	High
Sources of stability and change			
Genetic influences	High	Low	Low
Family influences	Low	Moderate	High
Cultural influences	Low	Low	High
Individual as active interpreter of life	Low	High	Moderate
Facets of lives			
Aspirations	Moderate	Low	High
Morals and values	Low	High	Moderate
Adaptational styles	Moderate	Moderate	High

boundaries. For instance, as noted earlier, there are some personality trait investigators who assign great importance to the formative role of parents; however, this view is uncharacteristic of the representatives of the paradigm reviewed in the chapter (and is therefore scored as "low" in the table). It is worth considering the intersection of paradigm with question in a bit more detail.

Stability

All three paradigms used in the study of lives yield evidence of stability across adolescence and adulthood. The strongest evidence for stability emerges from the personality trait and vocational interests research, particularly those studies that utilize self-report inventories. Individual differences on self-report inventories in personality and vocational interests were found to be meaningful through their relations to occupational careers and other facets of life, although, as noted in the review of these studies, the magnitude of these relations was often quite low. Individual differences also emerged from structural-developmental investigations, although these were characterized by continuity rather than absolute stability. In the domain of moral judgment, for instance, adolescents who were at higher moral judgment stages relative to their peers continued to be at higher stages than their peers into adulthood, even though all subjects were more sophisticated in their reasoning as adults than they were as adolescents. Finally, even the crisis-transformational theories admit to some continuity in the sense that the success with which an individual resolves one life task (e.g., identity formation in adolescence) can affect the resolution of later tasks (e.g., generativity in adulthood).

Not only is there agreement among the paradigms that there is some stability and continuity, but there is convergence among them on the conclusion that stability and continuity are more characteristic of adulthood than of adolescence (only Levinson's theory makes a different prediction). To some extent, the degree to which stability is observed appears to depend upon the type of research methodology that is employed. Self-report inventories, no matter what the underlying theoretical rationale and independent of psychometric properties such as internal homogeneity, yield stable individual differences over time. Apparently, if persons are allowed only to check one of several alternatives in judging the self-appropriateness of a particular statement, they consistently choose the same alternatives. The observational and interview methodologies, which are more sensitive to the subject's interpretations of events, less consistently uncover high stability in the life course.

Sources of Stability

The personality trait paradigm has a number of explanations for the stability evidenced across the life span. Claims of genetic influences on personality traits have become increasingly common (e.g., Bouchard et al., 1990), but references to the enduring effects of parenting and social class have traditionally been made. Because the structural-developmental and crisis-transformational paradigms are oriented toward change, there has been relatively little theorizing within these approaches on the sources of stability and continuity (in fact, high stability would be devastating to the claims of both); there has been some recognition of the mediating effects of social contexts on development, but a satisfying account of the apparent continuity of life courses has yet to emerge from these traditions (although see Caspi, et al., 1987, for an exception). Vaillant's research suggests that pathological stability (e.g., a failure to develop the generativity of middle adulthood) may be a consequence of a profile of immature defense mechanisms.

Developmental Change

It is possible to abstract from the three paradigms general developmental trends in adolescence and adulthood. The opportunism, emotional turmoil, and concern for self-protection that characterize childhood and early adolescence yield gradually during adolescence to increased self-control and a heightened concern for social acceptance and the maintenance of social conventions. Entry into adulthood results in further change toward greater autonomy and emotional control, an increased concern with the relationship of the self to the enveloping society, and, perhaps, an increased awareness of the limitations of cognition. Obviously, describing the developmental changes emerging from the various paradigms in such broad terms results in the loss of important details and qualifications; the goal here, however, is merely to demonstrate some commonalities among the traditions.

Sources of Change

What are the sources of these broad developmental trends? Theorists (e.g., Stewart & Healy, 1989) within the crisis-transformational tradition have developed a well-elaborated framework within which to accommodate the influence of significant life events (like marriage or finding a job) and cultural events. These events or tasks provide the form and structure for the life course, and each of them exerts considerable influence, resulting in developmental change. Even among the personality trait and structural-developmental traditions, there is some acknowledgment of the contributions of life events in producing change. For instance, entering the workplace is generally acknowledge to be a formative influence on personality traits (by requiring greater emotional control) and mental structures (resulting in a greater congruence between thought and reality).

There is also some consensus among the three traditions that parents can influence the course of life. As a whole, the crisis-transformational theories emphasize the importance of family influences to a greater degree than do the other two paradigms; one finds frequent references in the former to constructs like *identification* and *individuation*, which are most meaningful in describing the relationship of child to parents. There is a greater range of opinion among the personality trait and structural-transformational theorists about the nature and extent of familial influences on development. Some see little influence of parents on their children (e.g., McCrae & Costa, 1988), others perceive limited but nonunique influences (e.g., Kohlberg, 1969), and still others argue that parents play a formative role (e.g., Dubow *et al.*, 1987; Walker & Taylor, 1991).

Interpretive, Synthetic Components of Lives

The structural-developmental perspective is committed to the centrality of evolving mental structures for understanding the course of lives and, for that reason, is more concerned than the other paradigms with the forms of reasoning that shape one's interpretation of life. Both Kohlberg and Loevinger viewed their stages as organizing principles for understanding life; a person at a lower stage is presumed to have a conception of himself and his life that is very different from that of a person at a higher stage. The form of an individual's understanding is best elicited, these theorists argue, through open-ended procedures that allow the structures to reveal themselves through their organization and interpretation of information. The person's own understanding of his life is valuable because it reveals the structures that guide his understanding.

Theorists of the other two paradigms accept the concept of self-reflection but are often uneasy in doing so. Personality trait researchers see no special role for the individual's own understanding of his life and, in fact, regard it as potentially flawed. But because self-reports are easy to collect and correlated with ratings made by others, they have become an acceptable methodology.

Crisis-transformational theorists recognize that individuals often have elaborate theories of themselves and worry that these theories obscure the unconscious but more important facets of lives. For instance, an adolescent may occasionally consciously experience identity problems, but identity is considered to be, for the most part, an unconscious phenomenon (Erikson, 1968). Similarly, Vaillant (1977) has argued that defense mechanisms, which are so influential in determining the course of life, are largely unavailable to introspection.

Facets of Lives

To varying degrees, the three approaches are all concerned with the facets of life of interest in this book. Aspirations play a central role in Levinson's account of men's development and are, to a lesser extent, apparent in Erikson's descriptions of the tasks of adolescence and adulthood. Personality trait theorists tap occupational interests through vocational interest inventories, as well as through dimensions of personality related to achievement (e.g., conscientiousness in Costa and McCrae's model). Although little explicit attention to aspirations is evident in Kohlberg's or Loevinger's theory, there are elements in each that are relevant to this facet of life. Furthermore, aspirations play a larger role in structural-developmental accounts designed to augment Kohlberg's theory (e.g., Armon, 1991; Van den Daele, 1968).

The emphasis of the structural-developmental approach is, of course, on values and morals and the ways in which the structures undergirding these are transformed over time. The other perspectives, for the most part, are not explicitly concerned with morals and values, although one can tease these out of personality dimensions (e.g., Costa & McCrae's openness construct) and transitions (e.g., Erikson's phase of generativity). Instead, the personality trait and crisis-transformational paradigms emphasize adaptation and responsiveness to stress. Within the personality trait studies discussed earlier, adaptational styles are subsumed under a single broad construct such as neuroticism (Costa & McCrae) or ego-resiliency (Block). Although the crisis-transformational theorists acknowledge that persons can be characterized as "high in neuroticism" or "low in neuroticism," their own theories attempt to draw out the more specific ways in which success and difficulty in adaptation are manifested. For instance, rather than characterizing a person as neurotic, Vaillant might prefer to identify the specific defense mechanism that the individual is using (e.g., repression), and Erikson or Levinson might point to the specific tasks of a particular life period that have been failed. These theorists would argue that descriptions like "highly neurotic" do not capture the essence of the individual's adaptation to stress.

As we have seen, each of the three paradigms offers its own unique combination of answers to the questions posed at the beginning of this chapter. There are convergences and schisms among the three paradigms in their perspectives on the facets of lives that are relevant to study, the extent to which lives exhibit stability and change (and the sources for each), and the relative importance of conscious and unconscious facets for an account of the life course. My own perspective is that the differences between the three perspectives are not hypotheses to be tested and resolved in favor of one or the other (although claims by the three perspectives certainly should be modified). Instead, the divergences among the perspectives reflect different but potentially complementary views of lived followed over time. In the following chapters the lives of the men studied are examined with approaches drawn from all three paradigms in the hopes of providing a better understanding of them than would be possible from one paradigm alone.

CHAPTER 2

The Methods and the Men

There are relatively few longitudinal studies of development, and each of them is unique. The investigation presented in this book can be distinguished from other longitudinal studies by the developmental periods it spans, its intervals between testing times, and, finally, the types of data that have been collected. The men in this study were followed from early adolescence (some were as young as 10 years of age) into early adulthood (at the termination of the study the oldest men were 36 years old). The men were periodically tested, at 3- to 4-year intervals, for 20 years. There are no other major longitudinal studies that both cover this age range and have such frequent testing (Moss & Susman, 1980).

What makes this study particularly unique, however, is its heavy reliance on interviewing as a means of eliciting information from the participants. At each testing point the men were intensively interviewed by skilled researchers, with the questions and responses audio-taped and later transcribed. The utilization of interviews is consonant with the structural-developmental orientation of Kohlberg, who began the study in 1955. The fundamental assumption of this approach is shared by a range of theorists who believe that "to understand the human condition is to understand what things mean to those we are studying" (Bruner, 1990, p. 345). Well-designed interviews are particularly effective in uncovering the meanings that people construct. By allowing a person to respond to questions in his own words, an interview is less likely than a structured inventory to result in distortions of the individual's own view of the world. As Piaget noted early in his research career, structured tests on which the individual chooses only one from a list of possible answers "falsifies the natural mental inclination of the subject or at least risks so doing" (Piaget 1929, p. 3). Follow-up questioning by a careful, skilled interviewer can further elucidate the subject's meanings, resulting in even greater clarity about how the individual views portions of his world.

The interview is a basic component of clinical work and has been used in intensive case studies. For instance, Robert White (1952) reported:

> By using an abundance of interviews, by evoking strong personal interest in the proceedings, and by giving respectful attention to the subject's self-estimates, his hopes and fears, his plans and daydreams and deepest aspirations, we have been able to learn a great deal about the inner integrations that are so important in giving overall form and direction to a life. (p. 120).

Interviewing as a method for obtaining data is not without its flaws, of course. It is relatively expensive: a researcher must be trained over a period of months in order to become skilled, subjects must be individually interviewed, and the interview sessions must be transcribed. This is one reason for the absence of interview methodologies in other longitudinal studies. Another is that the interpersonal nature of interviewing is believed by many psychologists to introduce biases and measurement error into the testing situation. For instance, the interviewer may like some subjects more than others, which could affect the types of questions that are posed and, consequently, the information that is elicited. Similarly, a subject may not feel comfortable with a particular researcher and may react by responding in nonrevealing ways. Because it is impossible to eliminate these sorts of influences, many researchers reject the interview method altogether. But as Broughton (1978) points out, this line of reasoning reflects an inadequate understanding of what constitutes rigorous social science:

> [A reliance on interviewing] is not the humanist's plea for "freedom" or "spontaneity." It is the structuralist's plea against the logical positivism that exalts measurement and the strict methods of the natural sciences at the expense of a concern for *meaning*. Rigid standardization of questioning ignores the fact that meanings develop through interpersonal understanding in the test situation and leads to a spurious "objectivity" and trivial results. It also leaves us with the possible problem that regularities in our results are entirely a function of specific factors associated with superficial factors of question form. (p. 80)

A final objection to interviews stems from what Bruner (1990) has called "the arrogant error of assuming that the meanings people assign to their worlds are 'mere' rationalizations or symptoms that make no difference in the determination of action" (p. 351). This disparaging of persons' meanings derives from several sources, most notably the psychodynamic tradition in which repression is presumed to remove from consciousness the psychic conflicts that determine behavior (for a discussion of repression, see Erdelyi, 1990) and work in cognitive science that demonstrates that persons are often unaware of the factors that influence their preferences and decisions (e.g., Nisbett & Wilson, 1977). If the meanings people construct about their worlds are but rationalizations or symptoms, eliciting them through careful interviewing would be a worthless endeavor. As I noted in the previous chapter, however, there is good reason to suspect that persons can provide revealing information about themselves through interviews and questionnaires. Several of the chapters that follow are devoted to providing additional evidence. Simply put, I do not think it would be possible to understand the men in this study without an account of the meanings they themselves derive from their lives. What persons think about themselves and their worlds may not be the only elements in the life story, but they are indispensable ones.

Although interviews are a central component of the methodology used in this study, other methods were used as well. Furthermore, the interview was used for several purposes, that is, to elicit different types of data. It will be useful to consider the types of data that were collected within a framework that has been used by a variety of investigators.

TYPES OF DATA

The wide variety of data collected on the men in the study can be usefully classified using the distinctions elaborated by the Blocks (J. H. Block & J. Block, 1980). They identified four basic types of data: life data, test data, self-report data, and observer data. Life data include demographic information about the subjects, for instance, age, social class background, and years of education. Test data are elicited through the use of structured standardized tests. Self-report data (discussed in Chapter 1) are derived from the subject's introspections about his own opinions, personality traits, aspirations, behaviors, and interests. Observer data (Chapter 1) are derived from the observations of the subject by others, including the researchers, parents, teachers, and peers of the subject. All four types of data were collected in this study; the following sections describe the instruments that were used to elicit and organize them.

Life Data

Three interrelated types of life data were collected in this study: social class, years of education, and occupation as an adult. Social class is a broad summary construct that includes the social and economic status of an individual or a family. The social class of each subject as a child and as an adult was recorded. Based on previous analyses (Colby et al., 1983), a dichotomous judgment concerning the boys' socioeconomic class was based on the parents' occupation and level of education, as recorded in school records. Boys whose fathers worked as unskilled or skilled laborers or had white-collar jobs but no college education were considered in the lower middle class. Boys whose fathers had white-collar jobs and a college education were considered to be in the upper middle class.

Each subject's social class as an adult[1] was judged using the more differentiated Duncan Socio-Economic Index (SEI) revised by Stevens and Featherman (1981). (The Duncan SEI is based on detailed analyses of the 1970 United States Census data concerning income and educational level associated with various occupations.) For each 1970 census occupational title, an SEI score was calculated, ranging between 0 and 90. Each man's job as an adult was matched with a census occupational title to obtain his SEI score. The number of years of education each man completed and the exact title of his job as an adult were also recorded; of course, this information is incorporated to a large extent in the SEI score, but it is sometimes useful to look at one or the other independent of the summary construct of social class.

Test Data

At each testing time subjects responded to the Moral Judgment Interview (MJI, see Colby et al., 1983, for this instrument). The MJI consists of nine moral dilemmas, with each dilemma consisting of two values that conflict (one of the actual dilemmas was presented in Chapter 1). The purpose of pitting two values against each other is to elicit the subject's best moral reasoning about the ordering and applicability of moral values. The subject, after being presented with the dilemma, is asked what Heinz ought to do. The interviewer challenges the solutions proposed by the subject in order to elicit the subject's best reasoning concerning the dilemma. These challenges consist of questions like "Should Heinz steal the drug?"; "Should he steal it if he doesn't love his wife?"; "What difference does it make if it is not his wife but a stranger?"; and "Why should people try to avoid breaking the law?"

Responses to the MJI are coded for moral stage using the *Standard Issue Scoring Manual* (Colby & Kohlberg, 1987; Colby, Kohlberg, Candee, Gibbs, Hewer, & Speicher, 1987). A full description of the coding process can be found elsewhere (Colby et al., 1983); briefly, however, all responses were reliably coded by raters unaware of the subjects' ages and performances at other testing times. Two summary indices are used in this book: the Moral Maturity Score (MMS) and the Major Stage. Essentially, the MMS is an average stage score, and it ranges between 100 (indicating only Stage 1 reasoning is present) to 500 (all reasoning is Stage 5). Interrater reliability for the MMS for these data ranges between .92 and .98 (Colby et al., 1983). The Major Stage is the subject's modal stage score for the interview. Percent agreement among raters for the Major Stage is quite high and ranges between 75% and 88%.

IQ scores, based on various group tests routinely administered in the schools (e.g., the Otis and the Thurstone Primary Mental Abilities (PMA)), were taken from school records at Time 1.

Self-Report Data

Throughout the project the subjects were asked to share their perspectives on themselves with the researchers. The most consistently used forum for doing so was the Be-Like Sort. The Be-Like Sort consists of 19 social and occupational roles that subjects were asked to rank, using a fixed 5-point distribution, according to how much they aspired to "be like" each one. The roles are presented in Table 2.1.

The fixed distribution allows for the identification of 2 roles the subject desires to be like very much, 4 roles that are slightly less desirable, 5 or 6 roles that are neutral (at some testing times subjects sorted 17 roles, at others 18), 4 roles that are undesirable, and 2 roles that are very undesirable. This Q-sort type procedure offers a number of advantages (see Block, 1971, for a discussion). One of its great values for this study is that it did not allow subjects to endorse all the

TABLE 2.1.
Roles Composing the Be-Like Sort

1. Someone with a Job Like Your Father's
2. A Judge
3. A Doctor
4. Head of a Company
5. A Pilot
6. A Teacher
7. A Printer
8. An Army Private
9. Someone Who Works Hard to Get Ahead
10. Someone Who Takes After His Father
11. A Good Father
12. A Good Son
13. Someone Who Does Things to Make His Family Proud of Him
14. A Good Friend
15. A Good Sport
16. A Good Leader
17. A Good Ball Player
18. Job Like the One You Have Now

Note. Role 1 (Someone With a Job Like Your Father's) was omitted from the sort at Time 5 and Time 6. Role 7 (Printer) was omitted at Time 5.

socially acceptable roles as desirable and, similarly, to reject all the socially unacceptable roles; instead, subjects made judgments about the desirability of each role relative to each of the others.

All but one of the roles are either occupational or interpersonal in nature. The range of occupational roles is somewhat limited but nonetheless is representative, to a degree, of the diversity of the workplace. Factor analyses have consistently demonstrated that differences and similarities among occupations can be captured by the people–things and data–ideas dimensions (e.g., Cottle, 1950). Based on Hanson's (1974) factor analyses, the occupations in the Be-Like Sort can be described as polar examples of the two dimensions. On the people–things dimension, the items Judge, Baseball Player, and Teacher are at one end and Pilot and Printer are at the other. These occupations are all close to the midpoint with respect to the data–idea dimension. On this second dimension, Doctor is at one end of the dimension and Head of Company is on the other end. Thus, despite the small number of occupations in the Be-Like Sort, the major dimensions differentiating among occupations are represented. Although Army Private and Someone Who Works to Get Ahead in Life are not polar extremes of either dimension, they do differ from each other in autonomy. As noted in Chapter 1, autonomy and achievement are important issues to many adolescents (Lowenthal, Thurner, & Chiriboga, 1975).

The interpersonal items are evenly divided between family and peer roles. The family roles are designed to tap the individual's aspirations with regard to family in general (Someone Who Does Things Which Make His Family Proud of Him), family of origin (Good Son), and the family he creates (Good Father). The peer roles tap dyadic roles (Good Friend) and group roles (Good Sport and Good Leader). Finally, there are two paternal identification items (Job Like Father's and Be Like Father)

As a method for assessing the ideal self, then, the Be-Like Sort is particularly attuned to the roles the individual aspires to; it places less emphasis on assessing the desirability of different personality characteristics. In many ways it would have been desirable to have more occupational and social roles included in the study. More roles would have increased the reliability of the measure and could have broadened its scope as well (for instance, to the domain of romantic relationships). Nonetheless, the occupational and social roles that were included in the study are of interest in themselves and also can be combined in ways that allow tests of a variety of hypotheses.

Following the sorting process, each subject was asked to explain why each of the roles was desirable or undesirable to him. The purpose of this questioning was to elicit each person's framework for assigning value to different occupations and different types of relationships.

In addition to responding to a series of moral judgment dilemmas and explaining their rankings on the Be-Like Sort, subjects were also asked at most testing times to comment briefly about their lives, the changes that had occurred since the previous testing time, and their relationships to their families.

Several self-report measures were used at only a few testing times; because the results are not reported in this book (either because they have been reported elsewhere or because the measures simply did not work), the details of their construction and administration are not presented here. Loevinger's Sentence Completion Test was administered at several testing points in adulthood (the relevant analyses of these data can be found in Lee & Snarey, 1988); the Thematic Apperception Test was administered at one testing point in early adolescence; and questions about sex roles were asked at one testing point in late adolescence.

Observer Data

Four types of observer data were collected on the men in the study. At the first testing time, in 1955–1956, the boys and adolescents were rated by their classmates in terms of their sociometric status, or popularity. In order to determine sociometric status, boys in each of the classes participating in the study were asked to name three boys in their class with whom they would talk intimately. Boys who were never chosen or who were chosen once or twice but never by someone they had themselves chosen were designated sociometric isolates. Boys with at least two reciprocal choices or who were chosen at least three times, with a minimum of one reciprocal selection, were designated as integrates.

At the second testing time teachers provided judgments about each subject's trustworthiness, fair-mindedness, effort, obedience, and peer independence. These judgments were recorded on rating scales on which capsule descriptions were provided for each point on the scale. For instance, the highest score on the trustworthiness scale corresponded to a description of a student as one who "can always be depended on to do whatever he knows is right regardless of what he wants to do at the moment," and the description of a student as one who "is always trying to get away with something" corresponded to the lowest score.

Also at Time 2 each parent was asked to complete a questionnaire. Eighteen mothers and thirteen fathers did so. Most of the items on the questionnaire concerned the parents' perceptions of their own parenting styles (which therefore are self-report, no observational, data), but there were several sets of questions that pertained to the child. One set of questions concerned the parent's perceptions of the strength of his or her son's conscience, and another set focused on the extent of the son's similarity to each of the parents (these question sets are discussed more thoroughly in Chapter 5).

The Q Sort

A third set of "observations" were made by a skilled research assistant who read each of the transcribed interviews conducted with the men. These observations focused on the subject's responses to the questions posed in the interview. Besides assessing the content of the responses, the research assistant also studied the characteristic response styles of the subjects. For instance, some subjects responded to difficult questions forthrightly while others tried to avoid them, some subjects offered such short responses as to appear rude while others had difficulty in letting the interviewer speak, and so on. The research assistant's role was much like that of a biographer writing about a person who cannot be interviewed. In both cases, the goal is to gain a full understanding of a person through a careful inspection of the person's thoughts, feelings, beliefs, and, particularly, the characteristic styles in which these are expressed.

The research assistant's observations were translated into constructs suitable for quantitative analyses using Haan's (1977) Q Sort of Ego Processes. This measure assesses the extent to which various defense mechanisms or adaptational styles are characteristic of a person, as reflected in a transcribed interview at a particular testing time. The Q sort consists of 60 different items, 3 for each of the mature and immature adaptational styles described by Haan. Each item consists of a statement or two describing behavioral characteristic of the defense it represents. The coder sorts these items, following a fixed 9-step distribution, according to how characteristic or uncharacteristic each item is of the individual as manifested in the interview.[2] After the sorting process is completed, the number of the step at which each of the items is placed, ranging from 1 (very uncharacteristic of the person) to 9 (very characteristic) is recorded. The step scores for each adaptational style are summed, which provides an index of its salience in the individual.

Extensive testing of the Q sort prior to beginning this study suggested that some of the items could not be easily sorted by the rater; for these items, additional statements were added, all of them drawn from Haan's descriptions of the defense in question (the modified items are available upon request from the author).

The interviews were coded in random order, and the research assistant was kept blind to the subject's age, moral judgment score, and performance on other interviews. Reading and coding each interview took approximately two hours.

The Q-sort procedure offers several advantages for the purposes of the proposed study. First, because the Q sort results in a description of the relative saliency of adaptational styles within the individual, rather than between individuals, it can be used with persons of widely different backgrounds and developmental statuses, as well as with different sources of data. Haan (1977) has meaningfully applied the Q sort to samples of children, adolescents, and adults, basing the judgments on different types of interviews as well as on observations of moral discussions. As Haan (1977) notes, any data that reveal issues of concern to the subject can serve as a basis for the Q sort; the wide variety of topics considered in the interviews with the men in this study certainly are of concern to them.

LIMITATIONS OF THE STUDY

No longitudinal study can collect all the data that are of interest in a study of lives. This is because longitudinal data are expensive to collect, both financially and in the investment of time required from researchers and subjects. Consequently, the researcher, guided by theoretical orientation and pragmatic considerations, must decide at the inception of a longitudinal study which types of information can and cannot be collected. Much of the value of the longitudinal study at its completion rests upon the wisdom of these initial decisions. Inevitably, by the conclusion of the study, it is evident that the initial choices concerning methodology, measures, and data were flawed; with the benefit of hindsight one sees that some types of data that were collected are of little value and that the failure to collect others was unfortunate.

The study described in this book is no exception. One can imagine a study more closely approximating the ideal, one in which more test data, life data, observational data, and self-report data were collected. Such an ideal study, with a depth and breadth of data never realized in actual investigations, would allow generations of investigators of divergent backgrounds to mine the archived data for new findings. Unfortunately, this study does not realize the ideal. At its initiation the study was intended to reflect structural-developmental presuppositions about transformations in mental structures, and therefore it lacks, in part, the data that might be more amenable to analyses based on different theoretical traditions.

Yet even within the focus of the structural-developmental tradition, the study has its failings. It is clear, in retrospect, that more information should have been collected. One wishes, for instance, that the men's relationships in adulthood had been more consistently evaluated: How well did they get along with their wives? Children? Coworkers? Friends? Similarly, it would have been useful for the account that follows to have more observational data to allow inferences about the ways in which the men's aspirations, values, and adaptational styles were reflected in the context of ongoing life. Although these two are the most unfortunate limitations of the study, others will be noticed by the reader in the following chapters (the limitations of the study will be discussed in more detail in the conclusion). Yet I believe that much can be learned from the study despite its limitations and omissions; the chapters that follow are devoted to an understanding of development that can be drawn from the collected data.

THE SUBJECTS

A study gains form not only through its methodology but from its sample as well. At the beginning of the study in 1955 the sample was composed of 72 boys in a 2 (social class) × 2 (sociometric status) × 3 (ages 10, 13, and 16 years) design. Students were drawn from two schools in suburban Chicago, one predominantly upper middle class, the other predominantly lower middle class.

An attempt was made to equalize intelligence for social class and sociometric groups. Those whose IQs were above 130 or below 100 were excluded from the study. Although complete equalization was not achieved, the IQ differences were small and nonsignificant.

Subjects were first interviewed in 1955–1956 and were retested at 3- to 4-year intervals until 1976–1977 (Time 1 through Time 6). Because testing times were separated by 3 to 4 years, the same span that separates the three cohorts, it is possible to form eight age groups: 10-year-olds, 13- to 14-year-olds, 16- to 17-year-olds, 20- to 22-year-olds, 24- to 26-year olds, 28- to 30-year-olds, 32- to 34-year-olds, and 36-year-olds. For instance, the scores for the 16- to 17-year-old age group are derived from the oldest cohort measured at Time 1, the middle cohort at Time 2, and the youngest cohort at Time 3.

These facts about the subjects are the ones typically found in research reports. Clearly, this was a carefully composed sample. Many questions about it remain, however, with most of these concerning the degree to which the sample is representative of particular populations and, consequently, the extent to which conclusions from this study can be generalized to other groups. For instance, is the sample representative of boys in suburban Chicago in 1955? Of boys in the United States in 1955? Of boys in the world in 1955? Do the various results have any implications for development in girls and women? What about the development of boys in small, communal cultures? Is it the same?

These questions are not answered fully in this book (they are addressed again in Chapter 3). I believe that the developmental trajectories traced in the following pages have relevance for the understanding of boys and men who were not subjects—I sense them in my own life—but it would be foolish to make broad claims about representativeness or universality. The boys who became men in this study are unique in many ways, and it is difficult, if not impossible, to design research that permits an assessment of the contributions of culture, repeated testing, and, most importantly, historical period on the results (Applebaum & McCall, 1983). Rather than deny the influence of these factors on the men in the study, it seems more useful to keep them in mind, to use them as a backdrop against which the results can be understood. Toward this end, Table 2.2 presents a sampling of events occurring during the lives of the men, from 1940, when the oldest subjects were born, through 1977, when the study was completed. The table is not intended to be a serious historical analysis; my hope is that it will activate the reader's memories of the years during which the boys in this study grew into men.

FORMS OF ANALYSES

The variety of data that were collected in combination with the longitudinal design of the study offers a rare opportunity for a genuine personological study. In her classic criticism of personality research, Carlson (1971) noted that too often the person in personality research is ignored. Carlson pointed out that personological investigations attempt to preserve the person as an object of investigation, a goal best accomplished by a number of means, including (1) collecting a wide variety of data, (2) investigating the organization of variables within the individual, (3) utilizing longitudinal designs, and (4) respecting subjects' experiences and frames of meaning. My hope is that these elements, all present in this study, will permit an account of the lives of persons, not simply a description of a variety of variables.

Each of the following chapters presents a variety of analyses on a particular topic. I have tried to strike a balance between statistical and case analyses. Both, it seems to me, are essential for a full accounting of human development. Luria (1979) has contrasted two approaches to science, denoting the first as "classical" (within which an orientation toward statistical analysis would fall) and the second as "romantic" (which would include case studies). He describes scientists in the classical tradition as

TABLE 2.2.

Events Occurring during the Lives of the Men in the Study

1940
  Unemployment, 14.6%
  The oldest men in the study are born.
  FDR is elected to third term.
  Dunkirk
  First color TV broadcast
  You Can't Go Home Again, by Thomas Wolfe, is published.
1941
  Unemployment, 9.9%
  Pearl Harbor
  Declaration of war
  Manhattan Project is initiated (to build the atom bomb).
  Ted Williams hits .406 for Boston Red Sox.
1942
  Unemployment, 4.7%
  Single men ages 18 to 35 and married men ages 18 to 26 are eligible for draft.
1943
  Unemployment, 1.9%
  The middle cohort of men in the study are born.
  Race riot, Detroit, Michigan
  Casablanca wins Academy Award for best picture.
1944
  Unemployment, 1.2%
  United Nations is established.
  D-Day, Normandy invasion
1945
  Unemployment, 1.9%
  Atomic bomb is dropped on Nagasaki and Hiroshima.
  German and Japan surrender; World War II ends.
1946
  Unemployment, 3.9%
  The youngest men in the study are born.
  It's a Wonderful Life, starring Jimmy Stewart, is produced.
  Birth rate surges 20% over the previous year.
1947
  Unemployment, 3.9%
  Jackie Robinson becomes the first black baseball player to play in the major leagues.
  Mississippi blacks vote for the first time.
1948
  Unemployment, 3.8%
  Transistor is invented at Bell Telephone Laboratories.
  Soviet Union blockades Berlin.
1949
  Unemployment, 5.9%
  Polaroid Land camera is invented.

continued

TABLE 2.2 (*continued*)

1950
Unemployment, 5.7%
All About Eve wins Academy Award for best picture.
Korean conflict begins.
1951
Unemployment, 3.3%
Catcher in the Rye, by J. D. Salinger, is published.
Bobby Thomson hits a home run in the bottom of the ninth inning to win the
    National League Pennant for the New York Giants.
1952
Unemployment, 3.0%
The Greatest Show on Earth wins Academy Award for best picture.
"I Saw Mommy Kissing Santa Claus" is a hit song.
The Old Man and the Sea, by Ernest Hemingway, wins Pulitzer Prize.
1953
Unemployment, 2.9%
Rosenbergs are executed for treason.
From Here to Eternity wins Academy Award for best picture.
Science and Human Behavior, by B. F. Skinner, is published.
1954
Unemployment, 5.5%.
Racial segregation in public schools is ruled unconstitutional in *Brown v. Board
    of Education.*
Joe DiMaggio and Marilyn Monroe are married.
Atomic-powered railroad engine is developed at Utah University.
1955
Unemployment, 4.4%
Rosa Parks refuses to yield her seat on a bus to a white man in Montgomery,
    Alabama; a boycott of the buses ensues.
"The Ballad of Davy Crockett" is a hit song.
1956
Unemployment, 4.3%
Arthur Miller and Marilyn Monroe are married.
Elvis Presley (from the waist up) appears on the Ed Sullivan Show.
1957
Unemployment, 4.3%
Black students are prevented from attending a previously all-white high school by
    Arkansas Governor Orville Faubus.
Sputnik is launched by the USSR.
Ford launches the Edsel model.
1958
Unemployment, 6.8%
Alaska becomes a state.
A Coney Island of the Mind, by Lawrence Ferlinghetti, a "beat" poet, is published.
1959
Unemployment, 5.5%.
Ben-Hur wins Academy Award for best picture.

TABLE 2.2 (*continued*)

1960
   Unemployment, 5.5%.
   U-2 pilot Gary Powers is shot down over the USSR.
   To Kill a Mockingbird, by Harper Lee, wins the Pulitzer Prize for fiction.
   Berry Gordy starts Motown Records.
1961
   Unemployment, 6.7%.
   President Kennedy commits country to landing a man on the moon by the end of
      the decade.
   Bay of Pigs invasion of Cuba
   Yuri Gagarin of the USSR is the first person to orbit the earth.
   Roger Maris hits 61 home runs for the New York Yankees.
1962
   Unemployment, 5.5%.
   James Meredith becomes the first black student at the University of Mississippi.
   John Glenn becomes the first American to orbit the earth.
   Wilt Chamberlain scores 100 points in a basketball game.
1963
   Unemployment, 5.7%
   President Kennedy is assassinated.
   Martin Luther King makes his "I Have a Dream" speech in Washington, D.C.
   The TV show "My Favorite Martian" debuts.
   "The Times They Are A-Changin'," by Bob Dylan, is a hit song.
   "I Want to Hold Your Hand" by the Beatles is a hit song.
1964
   Unemployment, 5.2%.
   Gulf of Tonkin resolution passed by the U.S. Congress.
   "Bonanza" is the most popular TV program in America.
   Martin Luther King wins the Nobel Peace Prize.
   Mohammed Ali (Cassius Clay) wins the heavyweight boxing title.
1965
   Unemployment, 4.5%
   Watts riots.
   The Sound of Music wins the Academy Award for best picture.
   Mohammed Ali (Cassius Clay) knocks out Sonny Liston in Lewiston, Maine.
1966
   Unemployment, 3.8%.
   "The Ballad of the Green Berets" is a hit song;
1967
   Unemployment, 3.8%.
   Christian Barnard performs the first heart transplant.
   The first Super Bowl is played between the Green Bay Packers and the Kansas City
      Chiefs.
1968
   Unemployment, 3.6%.
   Martin Luther King is assassinated.
   Robert Kennedy is assassinated.

continued

TABLE 2.2 (*continued*)

1968 (*continued*)

Richard Nixon is elected president.

Bob Beamon wins a gold medal in the Mexico City Olympic Games for his record-breaking broad jump of 29 feet 2½ inches.

1969

Unemployment, 3.5%.

William Calley is put on trial for the My Lai Massacre.

Half a million people go to Washington, D.C. to protest U.S. involvement in the Vietnam War.

Neil Armstrong is the first person to walk on the moon.

Midnight Cowboy wins an Academy Award for best picture.

Woodstock Musical Festival.

1970

Unemployment, 4.9%.

Four Kent State students killed by the National Guard.

A bomb explodes in the mathematics building at the University of Wisconsin.

1971

Unemployment, 5.9%.

The Intel Corporation develops the microprocessor, the heart of personal computers.

1972

Unemployment, 5.6%

Richard Nixon is reelected to a second term by a wide margin.

Watergate break-in

The Godfather wins an Academy Award for best picture.

Mark Spitz wins seven gold medals at the Munich Olympic Games.

1973

Unemployment, 4.9%.

Vice President Spiro Agnew resigns after charges of tax evasion.

1974

Unemployment, 5.6%.

President Richard Nixon resigns following the House Judiciary Committee's vote in favor of impeachment.

Gerald Ford, who becomes president following Nixon's resignation, grants Nixon a pardon for any crimes he committed.

1975

Unemployment, 9.1%

South Vietnam is finally defeated by North Vietnam.

The Godfather II wins an Academy Award for best picture.

Jimmy Hoffa disappears.

Mohammed Ali beats Joe Frazier to win heavyweight title.

Bruce Springsteen appears on the rock music scene.

1976

Unemployment, 8.3%.

Jimmy Carter is elected president.

Richard Nixon is prohibited from practicing law in the state of New York.

1977

Unemployment, 7.6%.

Annie Hall wins Academy Award for best picture.

those who look upon events in terms of their constituent parts. Step by step they single out important units and elements until they can formulate abstract, general laws. These laws are then seen as the governing agents of the phenomena in the field under study. One outcome of this approach is the reduction of living reality with all its richness of detail to abstract schemas. The properties of the living whole are lost, which provoked Goethe to pen, "Gray is every theory, but ever green is the tree of life." (p. 174).

In psychology the classical approach is most clearly reflected in studies in which the relationships of variables within a group of persons are assessed. The goal of such studies is not to uncover how the variables are related within any particular individual but, instead, to discover the laws that relate the variables across many persons. Indeed, many of the procedures routinely employed in psychological investigations, such as randomly assigning individuals to control and treatment groups, are specifically intended to eliminate the contributions of the unique qualities of persons to the results.

There can be no doubt that the classical approach to human development currently holds sway in the field; one need only scan the pages of developmental psychology journals to conclude that most researchers are concerned with "abstract schemas" and not with "the properties of the living whole." This may well be a consequence of the progress and success of classical science in studying human development.

But there must be a place for romantic science. As Luria (1979) describes them, scientists within this tradition

> want neither to split living reality into its elementary components nor to represent the wealth of life's concrete events in abstract models that lose the properties of the phenomena themselves. It is of the utmost importance to romantics to preserve the wealth of living reality, and they aspire to a science that retains this richness. (p. 174).

The distinct contribution of romantic science, as Luria saw it, is in this focus on the variegated richness of phenomena. For the human sciences—medicine, neurology, psychology, and anthropology are the ones with which Luria was familiar—the romantic approach is particularly important. For instance, the classical science approach has yielded the finding that children from lower social classes are less likely to attend college than children from upper-middle-class backgrounds; yet such a statistical connection does not contribute much to our understanding of any particular child from a poor family. It does not reveal the child's parents' interest in education, the aspirations and capabilities of the child, the influences of peers and other adults, and so on. The abstract association between social class and educational attainment provides little grasp on the trajectory of individual lives.

Case studies are one means of infusing the richness of reality into a psychological account of lives. As Runyan (1982) has pointed out, case studies have been used for a variety of purposes; generating ideas, testing hypotheses, and understanding the unique qualities of specific individuals are but a few of the applications. In this book the examination of particular lives is intended to provide a context in which it is possible to assess the extent to which the proposed constructs are useful. According to Allport (1962/1981):

> The commonalities in personality are the horizontal dimensions that run through all individuals. We focus our attention chiefly upon these commonalities: for example, upon the common traits of achievement, anxiety, extraversion, dominance, creativity; or upon the common processes of learning, repression, identification, and ageing [sic]. We spend scarcely one percent of our research time discovering whether these common dimensions are in reality relevant to Bill's personality, and if so how they are patterned together to compose the Billian quality of Bill. Ideally, research should explore both horizontal and vertical dimensions. (p. 67)

The case studies are a means to determine whether the "common dimensions" described in this book are relevant for understanding the course of individual lives. By blending case studies and statistical analyses, romantic and classical sciences, I hope to avoid some of the flaws of the research described in the previous chapter. All too often, biographical analyses, with peculiar samples and anecdotal interpretations, have resulted in seriously flawed accounts of adult development. At the other extreme, descriptions of personality in adulthood based solely on significant findings from statistical analyses of large samples may have little relevance for understanding the course of a particular life.

In each chapter the life of one or two of the men participating in the study is followed from adolescence through adulthood in order to illustrate the function, complexity, and importance of the particular facet of persons under consideration. To protect further the anonymity of the men (the records in the archives at the Henry Murray Center, upon which this study is based, have names and some identifying information removed), the case analyses do not present the actual occupations of the man, his parents, or his wife; other identifying information like educational history, number of children, number of siblings, current hometown, and so forth, has also been changed. In addition to the case analyses, detailed statistical analyses are presented in order to identify patterns of change and stability common to the entire sample.

NOTES

1. Unfortunately, because of lost information, it was not possible to use this scale for childhood social class.
2. The number of items follows this distribution: Step 1, three items, Step 2, five items; Step 3, seven items; Step 4, nine items; Step 5, twelve items; Step 6, nine items; Step 7, seven items; Step 8, five items; Step 9, three items.

CHAPTER 3

The Development of the Ideal Self

Life is not experienced as a succession of moments or days, each existing in isolation from the others. Each individual views himself as evolving in complicated but comprehensible ways over time. A man may remember himself as a shy adolescent and view his current introversion as an extension of the same tendency. Another man might view his interest in biology and chemistry as the foundation for a career in medicine.

Forming a vision of the self in the future is one of the basic tasks of development, one that is particularly important during adolescence and young adulthood. The young male adolescent foresees important transformations occurring in the self in the near future—he will learn to drive, have girlfriends, and hold a job—and the more distant future offers him a tremendous variety of social roles and occupational opportunities. It is through this vision of the self in the future that the adolescent is able to make sense of today's sacrifices and hardships (e.g., working hard in a high school biology class may not be the result of a student's intrinsic interest in the subject matter but may, instead, reflect his desire to become a physician). The projection of the self into the future also serves as a benchmark for the individual, allowing him to ascertain his progress across the life course. To be deprived of a sense of the self in the future is a loss that makes both social life difficult and day-to-day life meaningless (Damon & Hart, 1988).

In this chapter I describe one facet of the projection of the self into the future, the *ideal self*. The ideal self is the representation of one's personal aspirations and goals, including those involving relationships

This chapter was coauthored by Rebecca Bauknight.

("I want to be married"), occupations ("I hope to become a fireman"), desired personality characteristics ("I want to be friendly") and experiences ("I would like to visit California"), to name just a few. The centrality of the concept of an ideal self to an understanding of lives is revealed in the frequency with which some aspect of it enters everyday conversations and in the extent to which the aspirations of others capture our interest. Children, adolescents, and young adults are frequently asked by friends and family to reveal what they hope to become in the future, so much is this information an important component in our folk psychologies.

Picking up where folk psychologies leave off, psychodynamic clinicians and theorists have elaborated upon the importance of the ideal self. Horney (1950) and Winnicott (1971) have reported that grandiose ideal selves, untempered by reality, can underlie neuroses in adulthood; both have claimed that one's ideal self must be integrated into a rational projection of the self into the future. James (1890), who provided the conceptual foundation for so much of the current work on the self-concept, was the first to point out that the ideal self plays a central role in self-evaluation. In James's formulation one's self-esteem is high if the discrepancy between the ideal self and the actual self is low and self-esteem is low if the discrepancy is high. A number of researchers have pursued this seminal idea (see Glick & Zigler, 1985, for a review) and have demonstrated the centrality of the ideal self in shaping self-evaluation.

In this chapter the ideal self is not studied in terms of its influence on self-evaluation. Rather, the focus here is on the ideal self's contribution to an understanding of the paths that men's lives follow. There is now a body of research that convincingly demonstrates that the ideal self influences decisions that affect the life course. One of the strongest of these studies is that of Bachman and his colleagues (1978), who have been following a nationally representative sample of adolescents into early adulthood. Each adolescent periodically responds to a detailed questionnaire that elicits information on a variety of topics. Of particular interest here are the data concerning the adolescents' academic aspirations, that is, whether they plan to finish high school, attend college, and enter graduate school. In addition to these data, academic ability and parental social class were assessed. Bachman and his colleagues (1978) found that one's academic goal "is clearly an important factor in education [al success] .... Even when socioeconomic level and intellectual ability are controlled, it has a major impact" (p. 48). This sort of study, in combination with recent investigations by

Markus and Nurius (1986), implies that the ideal self can influence the life course.

The task of this chapter is not so much to prove that the ideal self is important (although this issue is taken up)—which is better left to studies with large samples like Bachman's—but, rather, to characterize the ideal self at different ages. Curiously, there has been little research on the development of the ideal self (indeed, this fact is revealed by the omission of the topic of the ideal self from a most thorough review of the self-concept research literature by Harter, 1983), and the available studies are not easily synthesized into a single account. This is because there are methodological differences among the studies, reflecting diverse conceptualizations of the ideal self. The approach followed here is to focus on the content of the ideal self, particularly the salience of different interpersonal and occupational roles, because it is of considerable significance whether an adolescent aspires to become a doctor or a lawyer, a loyal son or a good friend, and so on. That is, specific motivations are likely to be generated by the content of the ideal self; as Bachman and colleagues demonstrated, an adolescent may study hard to become a physician or be especially generous in order to be a good friend.

A second reason for the focus on interpersonal and occupational roles is historical, having to do with the research that was available at the study's initiation in 1955. In a 1946 study by Havighurst, Robinson, and Dorr children were asked to describe what they would like to become as adults. Social and occupational roles were frequently mentioned, with young children describing their parents as their ideals, older children listing adults with glamorous occupations, and young adolescents describing realistic adult roles.

The notion that roles are important components of the ideal self has gained support from more recent research as well. From the results of their cross-sectional study of adolescents and adults, Lowenthal, Thurnher, and Chiriboga (1975) inferred that the ideal selves of older adolescents are oriented toward achievement and productivity, concerns that become more focused in early adulthood when career roles are ascendant. Other researchers, while acknowledging that career roles are important to young men, point out that family roles continue to be prominent sources of self-satisfaction (Veroff, Douvan, & Kulka, 1981). Together, these findings suggest that the ideal self during adolescence and early adulthood consists, in part, of both career and family-role aspirations.

THE LIFE OF RICK JENKINS

One useful way to enter into a consideration of the ideal self is to examine the aspirations of one man in the study, Rick Jenkins. Jenkins was interviewed five times between ages 13 and 33; at each measurement point he described his social-role and occupational-role aspirations by means of the Be-Like Sort described in the previous chapter (the details of the Be-Like Sort, taken up in later sections, are not important here).

Rick Jenkins was from a working-class family. His father was an electrician who worked in a shop owned by Rick's uncles. At age 13 what Rick aspired to most was to be the kind of person "who takes after his father" and to have a job like his father's. Provided with just this information about Rick, one gains new insights about him that cannot be deduced from his IQ (which was 120) or from his social class. One can now infer that Rick held his father in high esteem, that he likely had interests in mechanical and electrical machinery, and that his academic aspirations may not have included college. Indeed, all three inferences are supported by Rick's responses to the interviewer's questions. Rick claimed that "some people they don't care what their children do or anything" but that his dad was very concerned about his athletic pursuits and hobbies. Rick liked to go with his father to the electrical shop:

> I like to help fix motors. I like to look at the motors and see what makes them run or something. Lots of times they might have a small motor or lawnmower, and I like to fix them up.

When Rick was asked about attending college, he indicated that he had little interest in it:

> *Have you already decided not to go to college?*
> Yes.
>
> *Have you talked about it with your parents?*
> Well, not too much. My brother didn't go. See, when he was in third year of high school, he used to go to school in the morning and go out to the shop in the afternoon .... He used to get paid for what he did after that. And he works in the shop now; he didn't go to college or anything.

Rick Jenkins's adolescent role aspirations, grounded in his adoration of his father and in his own mechanical interests, shaped much of his early adulthood. The future he foresaw for himself became his reality. Upon graduation from high school, he joined his father in the shop and trained as an electrician. Although he attended an occasional training workshop for electricians, he never returned to school on a regular basis. One cannot but be impressed with the importance of the goals of the 13-year-old Rick Jenkins in determining the path of his life. This is not to say that Rick single-mindedly pursued a career that, in the end, brought him great pleasure and satisfaction. Indeed, in his twenties, he was not happy with his job and ranked it as undesirable or very undesirable; he wished he had gone to college; and he dreamed of having a variety of other careers. But an understanding of Rick Jenkins's ideal self as an adolescent provides a real sense of his life and its future directions. Rick Jenkins's life course testifies to the importance of the ideal self for understanding development from adolescence into adulthood.

Two different studies are presented in this chapter. The first elucidates the development of the ideal self in the men in the longitudinal study. The second study compares the aspirations of adolescents in the longitudinal study who were first tested in 1955–1956 with a sample of adolescents interviewed in 1988. The purpose here is to place the findings emerging from the longitudinal study into a historical context, as well as to examine possible sex differences in the content of the ideal self.

LONGITUDINAL TRENDS IN THE IDEAL SELF

This section charts changes in the salience of various occupational, family, and peer roles at different points in development. What changes might be expected? Research described earlier indicates that children are likely to aspire to roles offering excitement and activity, as well as to roles occupied by their parents. Interest in these roles is likely to wane in adolescents, who are more concerned with interpersonal roles offering popularity and public acceptance. Finally, in late adolescence and in adulthood, it is expected that aspirations of professional and interpersonal roles will become most prominent, reflecting the person's entry into the adult world.

The longitudinal study of the ideal self allows an empirical examination of two important issues: the stability of individual differences and the rate of change in the ideal self. In studies in which subjects' occupational interests (one important facet of the ideal self) are elicited

through their endorsement of various jobs as either desirable or undesirable, there is some stability of individual differences over intervals
of 1 to 10 years during late adolescence and early adulthood (Holland,
1973). The stability of individual differences seems to increase with
age, so that over a 5-year span of time one can expect the young adult
to change less in occupational interests and aspirations than an adolescent (Strong, 1943). These studies suggest that it should be possible to
identify stable individual differences in the ideal self over long periods
of time and that the rate of change in the ideal self should decline from
childhood through adulthood.

The longitudinal study presented here describes the nature of the
ideal self in men during adolescence and early adulthood and maps
the changes and continuities that exist in the ideal self across this age
span. Specifically, it is possible to test three hypotheses: (1) During late
childhood and early adolescence the ideal self is oriented toward activities; during middle adolescence this concern is replaced by a focus
on social relationships; and early adulthood brings with it a focus on
career and occupational development. (2) The rate of change in the
ideal self declines from adolescence through adulthood. (3) Despite
the developmental changes that may occur in the ideal self, relatively
stable individual differences in the ideal self persist over long periods of time.

Methods

At each testing point subjects were asked to complete a Be-Like
Sort, which consists of a number of roles (presented in Chapter 2) each
of which the subject places into one of five piles (following a Q-sort
procedure) according to how much or how little he aspires to that role.
The results in the identification of 2 roles the subject desires to be like
very much, 4 roles that are slightly less desirable, 5 or 6 roles that are
neutral (at some testing times subjects sorted 17 roles, at others 18), 4
roles that are undesirable, and 2 roles that are very undesirable.[1]

Results

Developmental Trends

Because of the multiple testing times (six) of the three cohorts of
subjects, it was possible to form eight age groups (see Chapter 2, The

Subjects). For each age group, an average of the ranks assigned to each role was calculated. These averages were used to order the roles from most desirable to least desirable for each group. Table 3.1 presents the average rank of each role for each group. This table also presents the Spearman correlations between age and rank assigned to each role; 11 of the 18 correlations are significant. Thus, from Table 3.1 it is possible to determine that the most popular role for the 10-year-olds was Ballplayer (1), the least desirable role Teacher (17). For boys and men between the ages of 13 and 22 the role Work to Get Ahead was most central to the ideal self whereas men between ages 24 and 34 aspired most to being a Good Father and the 36-year-olds wanted most to make their families proud of them. An inspection across columns reveals how a role changes in its perceived desirability across the life span. Ballplayer, a desirable role to 10-year-olds, clearly loses its appeal among older boys and men. Also declining in desirability across the age span studied were the following roles: Job Like Father's, Army Private, Be Like Father, and Good Sport. Increasing in desirability from adolescence to adulthood were the roles

TABLE 3.1.
Rank Order Desirability of Roles for Each Age Group

Roles	Age group								r_s
	10	13–14	16–18	20–22	24–26	28–30	32–34	36	
Job Like Father's	9	9	10	14	13	16	10		−.27***
Judge	16	14	13	15	14	11	12	9	.29***
Doctor	12	11	11	11	10	10	11	10	.05
Head of Company	15	13	15	13	15	15	15	12	.13
Pilot	10	10	12	12	12	13	13	14	−.13
Teacher	17	16	14	9	9	12	9	13	.41***
Printer	14	17	16	17	16	17	17	15	−.01
Army Private	13	15	17	18	18	18	18	17	−.42***
Work to Get Ahead	6	1	1	1	4	4	5	5	−.02
Be Like Father	11	8	8	10	11	9	13	7	−.16*
Good Father	2	2	2	2	1	1	1	2	.21**
Good Son	5	5	6	6	6	6	7	6	−.08
Make Family Proud	4	3	4	3	5	2	2	1	.21**
Good Friend	7	6	3	5	2	3	3	3	.21**
Good Sport	3	4	7	8	7	7	8	8	−.28***
Leader with Friends	8	7	5	4	3	5	4	4	.21**
Ballplayer	1	12	9	16	17	14	16	16	−.38***
Job Like Yours	NA	NA	NA	7	8	8	6	11	.00

*p < .05, **p < .01, ***p < .001.
Note. NA: not applicable; role was not included in Be-Like sort for subjects at this age.

of Judge, Teacher, Good Father, Make Family Proud, Good Friend, and Leader with Friends. It appears that paternal identification and interest in active roles (see definition in next paragraph) decline across the life span while social and professional roles increase in desirability.

As a second step toward parsimoniously characterizing developmental trends in the Be-Like Sorts, an Individual Scaling (INDSCAL) (Carroll & Chang, 1970) model multidimensional scaling analysis was conducted on the 15 roles common to the Be-Like Sorts at each testing time.[2] This analysis revealed several clusters of roles: social roles, such as Good Father, Good Son, Work to Get Ahead, Good Friend, Leader, Make Family Proud, and Work Hard to Get Ahead; professional roles, composed of Head of Company, Doctor, Judge, and Teacher; and active roles, such as Army Private, Ballplayer, and Pilot.

Three composite scores, reflecting the clusters of roles revealed in the INDSCAL analysis, were constructed in order to determine if preferences change along these dimensions with age. The first is a social role score, defined as the average of the ranks assigned to the roles of Good Father, Good Son, Work to Get Ahead, Good Friend, Leader, Make Family Proud.[3] Because the roles of Be Like Father and Good Father are separate from the cluster formed by the other social roles, suggesting that the subjects perceived these two roles differently from the others, they are not included in this composite score. The second composite score, the active role score, is defined as the average of the ranks assigned to the roles of Army Private, Ballplayer, and Pilot.[4] Finally, a composite professional role score was defined as the average of the ranks assigned to Head of Company, Doctor, Judge, and Teacher.[5]

The mean scores for each group are plotted in Figure 3.1. At all ages subjects in this study had higher composite social role scores than composite active or professional role scores. These plots suggest a generally linear decrease in the attractiveness of the active roles and linear increases in the desirability of the social and professional roles with age.

Spearman correlations between these composite scores and age group confirm these trends: $r_s = -.45$, $p < .001$; $r_s = .27$ $p < .001$; and $r_s = .36$ $p < .01$ for the active, social, and professional composite scores, respectively.[6]

The relationship of IQ, SES, and sociometric status to each of the three composite scores at Time 1 was assessed in a series of correlation analyses. None of the calculated correlations was significant at the .05

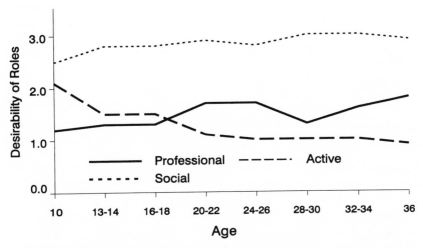

FIGURE 3.1. Desirability of active, professional, and social roles as a function of age.

level. Thus, there appears to be little direct relationship of IQ, SES, and sociometric status to patterns of ideal self development as assessed through the Be-Like Sort.

Change in the Ideal Self from Adolescence to Adulthood

Although it is possible to infer change in the Be-Like Sorts from the aforementioned trends observed in the composite scores, a more direct assessment is possible by comparing changes in ranks assigned to each item from Time n to Time n+1. The summary score used in these analyses is defined as the average of (absolute value of |Time n role 1 – Time n+1 role 1|, absolute value of |Time n role 2 – Time n+1 role 2|, ...). Seven change scores were calculated: 10 to 13, 13 to 16, 16 to 20–22, 20–22 to 24–26, 24–26 to 28–30, 28–30 to 32–34, and 32–34 to 36. These change scores are plotted in Figure 3.2. There is a clear decrease in the amount of change that occurs in Be-Like Sorts between adjacent testing times as the men become older. The correlation between age group and change score is $r_s = -.30$, $p < .001$. This finding suggests that changes in the ideal self become less and less likely between the ages of 10 and 36.

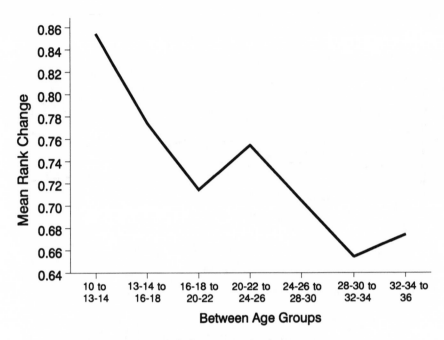

FIGURE 3.2. Mean rank change occurring between age groups.

Stability of Individual Differences

The composite scores used to chart changes in the ideal self can also be used to assess the stability of men's ideal selves, relative to the ideal selves of other men, across the life span. For instance, does the 10-year-old who finds professional roles more attractive than do his peers continue to rank them as more attractive in adulthood? One means of assessing the relative stability of individual differences over time is to calculate correlations between composite scores at different testing times. Table 3.2 presents the correlations among the composite professional and active role scores at the different testing times (because the correlations among composite social role scores are not significant, they are omitted from Table 3.2). The correlations in Table 3.2 indicate that stable individual differences in the salience of active and professional roles in men's ideal selves persist from early adolescence through early adulthood.

Do these individual differences influence the life course? As I noted at the beginning of this chapter, a definitive statistical answer to this question demands large samples. However, some confirming evi-

TABLE 3.2.
Correlations among Composite Professional
and Composite Active Scores for Five Testing Times

	Time 1	Time 2	Time 4	Time 5	Time 6
Time 1	—	.62(42)***	.14(39)	.32(22)*	.54(24)***
Time 2	.36(43)***	—	.17(28)	.27(18)	.42(18)**
Time 4	.31(42)**	.17(32)	—	.10(17)	.32(20)*
Time 5	.13(23)	.24(18)	.52(21)***	—	.38(14)*
Time 6	.37(25)**	.06(19)	.48(23)***	.61(16)***	—

Note. Correlations above the diagonal are among composite professional scores, and those below the diagonal are among composite active scores. Sample sizes are in parentheses. Correlations with Time 4 scores were not calculated because of the small number of subjects participating at that time.
*$p < .10$, one-tailed, **$p < .05$, one-tailed, ***$p < .01$, one-tailed.

dence from this study emerges from the pattern of correlations between the composite scores and adulthood social class. Those subjects who aspire most to hold professional jobs are, one would predict, most likely to attain them. Conversely, those who desire most the active occupational roles will tend to occupy the positions in the lower social classes. The correlations between composite professional and active scores and adulthood social class are presented in Table 3.3. It is apparent that the predictions are supported by the evidence, but only for the scores from late adolescence and early adulthood. In fact, the pattern of results here parallels a trend noted by Bachman and colleagues (1978) in their study of the transition from adolescence to adulthood. The results from both studies indicate that occupational aspirations are greatly affected by entry into the world of work, particularly for those who enter low-status positions. It is during this

TABLE 3.3.
Correlations between Composite Scores
During Adolescence and Adulthood Social Class

	Adulthood social class
Professional scores at ages	
13–14	.14
16–18	.16
20–22	.41*
Active scores at ages	
13–14	.18
16–18	−.13
20–22	−.52**

*$p < .05$, **$p < .01$.

transitional period that crucial decisions regarding occupations are made: those who pursued jobs requiring little formal education beyond high school left school and, consequently, limited their future possibilities. Similarly, those who aspired to professional positions and completed college attained a professional career (a college degree in the 1960s opened more doors than it does in the 1990s).

Summary of the Longitudinal Findings

The longitudinal analyses permit a description of ideal self development in boys and men from ages 10 to 36. At all ages the subjects aspired most to have good relationships with others: to be good sons, good fathers, and good friends and to make their families proud of them. The interpersonal role component of the ideal self, although prominent at all ages, increases slightly in importance across the age range studied. In this respect it is interesting to note that between the ages of 24 and 34, a time of marriage and family formation, men aspired most to be good fathers. One unexpected correlate to the social roles is the role Working to Get Ahead. Perhaps as a consequence of our society's emphasis on achievement, boys and men in this study considered working to get ahead to be associated with the attainment of satisfying relationships with others. Working to Get Ahead also has the highest average rank for boys and men between the ages of 13 and 22, a time period during which the individual typically is preparing to enter the world of work.

For the younger adolescents in this study, the ideal self was also composed of roles that involved action and physical activity, for instance, Ballplayer. From age 20 onward, however, the men in this study were less interested in attaining active occupations and aspired more to professional positions.

Both change and stability were apparent in the longitudinal trends. The rate of change in the ideal self appears to be greatest during adolescence, with steady declines thereafter, as predicted. No evidence was found to support Levinson's (1978) popular claim that the ideal self develops through a cycle of stability and change. This may be due to the nature of the instrument used in this study; for instance, it is possible that a man's ideal self may undergo rapid and significant change in ways not reflected in his occupational and social role aspirations.

Although the ideal self appears to undergo substantial change from adolescence through early adulthood, there is evidence for stable individual differences persisting over the 20-year span of the study. Of course, the stability of individual differences is not incongruent with developmental change. In this study the boys who, relative to their peers, were most interested in professional roles continued to be more interested in professional roles in adulthood despite the general age shift toward these occupations. The stability of individual differences in cases of this sort is a reflection of developmental predictability or continuity, rather than evidence for a lack of change (Block, 1971; Damon & Hart, 1986).

GENDER AND HISTORICAL DIFFERENCES

The development of the ideal self has been explored through a consideration of the lives of men in a longitudinal study. What light does this investigation cast on the nature of development in women? Are men today like the men followed in this study? These questions inevitably beset every study using only men as subjects and every longitudinal study with only one historical cohort. Although they are important questions, they are all but impossible to answer (Appel-baum & McCall, 1983); we can, however, explore their meaning in the context of the results of a cross-sectional study of male and female adolescents conducted in 1988. The cross-sectional study provides insights into the influence of gender and historical cohort on the ideal self, through comparisons of the aspirations of boys and girls in 1988, as well as comparisons between boys in 1955 (when the longitudinal study began) and boys in 1988 (when the cross- sectional study was conducted).

The study of psychological differences between men and women is an area of research fraught with controversy. Some researchers have claimed that there are few well-established psychological differences between the sexes (Maccoby & Jacklin, 1974) or that the extent of such differences is so small as to be virtually meaningless. Hyde and Linn (1988), for instance, have found in their survey of research in the domain of verbal reasoning, in which women have long been judged to be stronger than men, that the difference is nearly invisible in some studies, shows a decline in others, and has no importance for educational planning. Cohn (1991) reports that adolescent females are, on average, about one stage higher in Loevinger's sequence of development than boys of the same age but that this advantage largely disappears by early adulthood. Because they are so difficult to find, and are so small in magnitude when discovered, some authors have suggested that the systematic investigation of psychological differences between the sexes contributes little to science and, in fact, may promote societal divisiveness (Baumeister, 1988).

An opposing perspective is that there are very important psychological differences between men and women and that these have been overlooked by previous researchers. Gilligan (1982), for instance, has argued that women conceive of themselves and their interactions with others in terms of social relationships while men focus more on their individuality and personal principles. The implication for psychology is that we need two streams of theorizing, one for men and one for women. Empirical support for Gilligan's position has been extraordinarily difficult to garner (see, for instance, Thoma, 1986; Walker, 1983). Nonetheless, it is a powerful perspective in developmental psychology.

These two conflicting views on differences between the sexes emerge again in studies of occupational aspirations. It is clear that men and women desire different occupations (Schulenberg, Goldstein, & Vondracek, 1991); the meaning of this difference is not. Some have argued that the tendency of women to favor positions that offer opportunities for interacting with and caring for others is revealing of important psychological differences between men and women. Others suggest that the difference between men's and women's career aspirations merely reflects a tendency for persons to choose jobs that are consistent with cultural stereotypes (e.g., women aspire to be nurses because that is a role that society has endorsed for them).

Whichever explanation for the mechanism underlying occupational aspirations is correct, aspirations may still influence the life course. Predictions to differences between males and females on the Be-Like Sort follow rather readily. We can expect males to favor the active and professional roles and women to favor the social roles.

It is more difficult to envision the effects of the passage of time between 1955 and 1988 on the aspirations of youth. Life in 1955 was different in many ways from life in 1988, with a variety of cultural and economic transformations occurring during that 30-year period (some of these were noted in Chapter 2). There is some convergence among cultural analysts that American society became more individualistic and materialistic between the 1950s and the 1980s (e.g., Bellah, Madsen, Sullivan, Swidler & Tipton, 1985; Lasch, 1979). This shift in cultural values might have influenced the aspirations of youth in the

1980s toward those roles that offer high salaries and away from family roles. Consequently, it might be that the value of professional roles was higher, and that of family roles lower, to young men in 1988 than to young men in 1955.

These predictions are examined in the cross-sectional study presented next. The data in the study were collected in 1988, 33 years after the initial wave of interviewing for the longitudinal study.

Method

Sample

Children and adolescents for this study were recruited from a small school system. Parents of students in Grades 4, 5, 6, 7, 8, 10, and 11 received letters describing the study and informing them that if they did not wish their child to participate in the study, they should return the attached notification slip indicating their decision (no parent did so). Every student in these grades who was in school on the day of testing was invited to participate in the study; the vast majority did so. The final sample is composed only of those students responding to the questionnaire who were 10, 13, or 16 years old at the time of testing. There were 43 ten-year-olds (23 males, 20 females), 34 thirteen-year-olds (18 males, 16 females), and 45 sixteen-year-olds (26 males and 19 females).

Procedure

Students were tested in their classrooms. Each student received a questionnaire that contained the social and occupational roles forming the Be-Like Sort and instructions for rating the desirability of each of the roles. Females received questionnaires on which the items Job Like Your Father's, Someone Who Takes After His Father, A Good Father, and A Good Son were transformed, respectively, to Job Like Your Mother's, Someone Who Takes After Her Mother, A Good Mother, and A Good Daughter. Paralleling the versions of the Be-Like Sort used at Time 1 in the longitudinal study, the role A Job Like the One You Have Now or Will Have was not included.

After students completed the Be-Like Sort, they answered several questions eliciting age, sex, and parental educational and occupational information. The information about the parents' education and occupation was used to assign students to social classes, following the guidelines used in the longitudinal study. There were 72 children and adolescents from middle-class families and 50 from working-class backgrounds, divided approximately equally by sex and grade.

Results

General Age Trends

In general, the analyses of the 1988 sample confirm the age trends emerging from the longitudinal study. There was a significant positive correlation between age and the composite score for desirability of the social roles (with the composite scores formed in the same way as in the longitudinal study) of $r = .51$, $p < .001$, and a significant negative correlation for the association between age and the composite score for desirability of active roles, $r = -.26$, $p < .01$ (but the correlation between the composite professional role score and age was not significant). Significant correlations were also obtained for the relationship between age and the desirability of the following individual roles: Job Like Your Father's (Mother's), $r = -.29$, $p < .01$; Head of a Large Company, $r = -.19$, $p < .05$; Teacher, $r = -.21$, $p < .05$; Army Private, $r = -.18$, $p < .05$; Someone Who Works to Get Ahead, $r = .53$, $p < .001$; Good Leader with Friends and Others, $r = .40$, $p < .001$; and A Good Ball-player, $r = -.22$, $p < .05$.

As in the analysis of the longitudinal sample, there were no significant differences in social, occupational, or active role aspirations between those subjects from middle-class and those from working-class families.

Sex Differences

Table 3.4 presents the means for the composite role scores and for each role taken separately for boys and girls in the cross-sectional study. For the most part, the pattern of results in Table 3.4 is consonant with predictions. Considering first the composite scores, girls are slightly more interested than boys in the social roles but less interested in the active ones. The general tendency of girls to aspire more to the social roles obscures some important differences among the specific items composing the composite score. For instance, boys rank the roles of Good Friend and Good Leader with Friends and Others more highly than do girls, which suggests a greater orientation in boys to peer roles. Girls, on the other hand, are more interested in becoming

TABLE 3.4.
*Average Ranks for Males and Females
for the Composite Roles and for Each Role Taken Separately*

Roles	Males	Females	F Value
Composite for professional roles	1.74	2.15	15.6***
Composite for active roles	1.64	1.03	21.8***
Composite for social roles	2.47	2.58	4.0*
Job Like Your Father's (Mother's)	2.07	1.73	3.6
Judge	1.27	1.51	1.6
Doctor	2.09	2.25	.6
Head of a Large Company	2.66	2.60	.2
Pilot	1.81	1.15	8.2**
Teacher	1.38	1.63	45.7***
Printer	.82	1.24	11.0**
Army Private	1.00	.69	2.5
Someone Who Works to Get Ahead	2.40	2.67	2.9
Someone Who Takes After His Father (Her Mother)	2.16	1.78	5.0*
A Good Father (Mother)	2.69	3.09	8.6**
A Good Son (Daughter)	2.28	2.44	1.7
Someone Who Makes His (Her) Family Proud	2.61	2.55	.1
A Good Friend	2.46	2.75	5.0*
A Good Sport	2.07	1.98	.6
A Good Leader with Friends and Others	2.39	1.98	5.5*
A Good Ballplayer	2.13	1.25	13.7***

$*p < .05$, $**p < .01$, $***p < .001$ (df for all comparisons = 1,110).

good parents than were boys and tended to be more interested in being good children to their parents. This indicates that the ideal selves of girls may be focused on family roles to a greater extent than the ideal selves of boys.

Surprisingly, girls ranked the professional roles more highly than did the boys. This finding may be attributable to the nature of the roles that form the composite professional role score. All of these occupations (Judge, Doctor, Head of a Large Company, and Teacher) involve working with other persons. Perhaps if the roles of computer programmer, molecular biologist, and architect, all relatively nonsocial occupations, were the professions included in the Be-Like Sort, boys might have received higher scores than girls.

Historical Differences

There were a few significant differences between the two cohorts of boys. Only the data from the first testing point in the longitudinal study are included in the analyses here, since the age ranges at that point correspond closely to those in the cross-sectional study. The 1955 cohort of adolescents aspired more to the roles of Working Hard to Get Ahead, Good Son, and Good Sport than did the 1988 group (F values with 1, 123 df = 5.6, p < .05; 9.4, p < .01; and 14.5, p < .001, respectively). The 1988 cohort was much more interested in being the Head of a Large Company than was the 1955 sample (F = 82, p < .001). One can offer cultural and historical interpretations for each of these findings. This should be done cautiously, given that the two cohorts were tested in slightly different ways. Nonetheless, it seems as if teenagers in the longitudinal sample, born in the 1940s, were different from those of the 1980s. As many would suspect, the teenager of 1955 seems to have been more oriented toward the traditional Protestant values of success through achievement, family loyalty, and being a good sport.

Although the adolescent of 1955 had little interest in becoming the head of a company, boys in 1988 saw that role as very desirable. The 1980s was a decade in which the pursuit of money and material goods was endorsed by politicians (e.g., Ronald Reagan) and religious leaders (e.g., Jim Bakker, Oral Roberts). It was a time during which investment bankers received astronomical salaries (indeed, one banker received more than $500 million in one year). Popular culture, particularly television, glorified money and corporate leaders with shows like "Lifestyles of the Rich and Famous" and constant coverage of the affairs of the gloriously wealthy. All of these factors may underlie the salience that the role of *Head of a Large Company* had in the ideal selves of adolescents in 1988. If so, one might predict that the ranking of this role by adolescents will decline during the 1990s as the greed and criminal behavior of many of those famous during the 1980s become evident.

In summary, then the cross-sectional study confirms the basic age trends discovered in the longitudinal study but also suggests that the peculiarities of the sample influence the results. We should expect the aspirations of boys to be different from those of girls, given societal stereotypes and differing patterns of socialization; the results presented here confirm that expectation. Growing up in the 1950s also had an observable influence on the ideal self. The boys in the longitudinal sample were more interested in family roles and success through effort than were boys growing up in the 1980s. Although neither set of findings is particularly surprising, both are valuable insofar as they alert us to the influence of social context on individual development.

STEVE PATTON

In this next section, the life of one of the men is traced through his role aspirations. This offers an opportunity to examine the findings emerging from the longitudinal and cross-sectional studies in the context of a single life followed through time.

Steve Patton entered the study as a very bright 13-year-old. His IQ of 130 placed him near the top of the sample; his grades also were consistently high. He was well liked by other students in his school, and teachers judged him to be reliable and trustworthy. Because his father was a research physician at a major pharmaceutical company, Steve had one of the most advantaged backgrounds, educationally and financially, of any of the subjects in the study.

Steve's ratings for each of the occupational and social roles of the Be-Like Sort at age 13, and at later ages as well, are presented in Table 3.5. The changes in the desirability of the different roles follows the pattern described earlier in this chapter for the longitudinal sample as a whole. There is a decline in the desirability of active roles

TABLE 3.5.
Steve Patton's Be-Like Sorts at Five Ages

Roles	Age				
	13	17	25	29	33
Job Like Your Father's	1	3	1	NA	NA
Judge	2	1	2	1	2
Doctor	3	3	2	2	3
Head of a Large Company	0	1	1	1	2
Pilot	2	1	1	1	1
Teacher	1	1	2	3	2
Printer	0	0	1	1	1
Army Private	1	0	0	0	0
Someone Who Works to Get Ahead	3	3	2	3	2
Someone Who Takes After His Father	3	2	2	2	1
A Good Father	2	4	4	4	3
A Good Son	2	3	3	3	2
Someone Who Makes His Family Proud	3	2	3	4	4
A Good Friend	4	4	4	3	3
A Good Sport	4	2	3	2	1
A Good Leader with Friends and Others	2	2	3	2	3
A Good Ballplayer	1	2	0	0	0
A Job Like the One You Have (or Will Have)	NA	NA	2	2	4

Note. 4 = highly desirable; 3 = desirable; 2 = neutral; 1 = undesirable; 0 = very undesirable. NA: not applicable; roles not included in Be-Like sort at this age.

(Ballplayer, Army Private, Pilot) and an increase in the perceived value of professional ones (Head of a Large Company, Teacher). Like many of the other adolescents, Steve wanted to be well regarded by his peers and therefore aspired to be both a good sport and a good friend. Apparently, he succeeded in becoming accepted by his peers because he was judged by them to be quite popular (according to the socio-metric data).

As a 13-year-old, Steve clearly aspired to be respected by his family. He ranked as desirable the roles of Someone Who Takes After His Father and Someone Who Makes His Family Proud. He felt that one means of achieving his family's loving regard was to plan on becoming a physician, thereby following in his father's and grand-father's footsteps. Patton's age-13 sort indicates that of all the oc-cupations listed, being a doctor was most desirable to him. It is this occupation, which combines his academic talents with parental expec-tations, that shaped his educational career through adolescence.

Steve was aware of his family's influence on his career aspi-rations. When the interviewer asked, "Would your father and mother want you to be a doctor?" he responded, "My father would like me to be a doctor, and I think that my mother would be pleased." Al-though he had not given much thought to the other types of careers he might be interested in, Steve did allow that if he could not be a doctor he "would like an office job of some sort that requires brain work." Steve continued, "Maybe a lawyer because I would like to work in that field."

Little had changed in Steve Patton's career aspirations and the reasons for the by the time he was next interviewed at age 17. He con-tinued to rank highly the roles of Doctor and Job Like Your Father's and also wished to be a Good Son. When the interviewer asked, "What would you like to be if you could be anything at all?" Steve revealed the following:

> I don't know [pause]. I haven't really idealized any profession. I'm interested in medicine. My dad is a physician, and it appeals to me, too. As I said in the beginning, I do pretty well in science, and I enjoy it, and I'm interested in it. This is what I'm really thinking of doing—medicine. This is what . . . I mean I've practi-cally decided already.

In a revealing postscript to this comment Steve said, "I haven't thought about what I'd do if I had my choice . . . I haven't really thought of any other real profession." The lack of exploration of other possibilities is attributable, in large measure, to parental expectations. When Steve's mother was asked to sort the roles on the Be-Like Sort in terms of what she hoped Steve wold become, the roles of Someone with a Job Like Your Husband's and Someone Who Takes After Your Husband were ranked as desirable. Evidently, there was an expectation that Steve would continue the family tradition in medicine.

Between age 17 and the next interview 8 years later, Steve Patton's life veered off the course he foresaw for himself as an adolescent. His entry into college seemed to be a turning point. By going away to school Steve was able to loosen the bonds between himself and his parents, a development that had, from Steve's perspective, improved the relationship. When he was asked how his relationship with his father had changed since the last interview, Steve responded:

> Our relationship now is a lot different than it was when I was in high school. It is much more mature now.

> *How did it change?*
> I feel more at ease when discussing things that are important to me than I did when I was in high school. I suppose it is something most adolescents go through. Certainly, my parents have always been interested in what I was doing. There were a couple of years there where they would want to know what I was doing and I wouldn't tell them. I was asserting my independence or something like that.

Steve's new independence from his parents, gained during the transition from late adolescence to early adulthood, relaxed his need to fulfill his parents' expectations. Although Steve graduated from a prestigious college with a degree in biology, he knew by his senior year that he was not interested in medicine as a career. The interviewer asked Steve to describe the changes that had occurred in his occupational interests:

> The biology and medicine was a decision I guess I sort of made. I couldn't even tell you when. It just sort of evolved. My father is a physician and my grandfather is a physician. Dad works for Smith Pharmaceuticals. I was good in sciences in high school, and I guess it just seemed a natural thing to do. I didn't really stop and think of it that much of the time. I knew that Amherst had a good biology program—my father went to Amherst, too. As far back as

> I can remember, it was that I was going to go to Amherst and be
> a physician. It wasn't a real deep commitment because I hadn't
> really thought it out that far and that has something to do with
> why I am at journalism school right now.

When asked about how his interest in journalism grew, Steve suggested that it had much to do with his friends in college:

> I knew lots of the art students at Amherst. I was in a fraternity
> without a large number of science majors, although there were
> several, but I just started thinking that there was more to life than
> dissecting cats . . . . I think I personally identified with my friends
> who were outside the sciences.
>
> *Any special group?*
> Not really. It was primarily the fraternity because those were the
> guys I knew best. The girls they were dating and the girls I was
> dating were art students and home economics students.

As Steve related it, the period during which he was revising his career
plans was quite stressful:

> At times it was very shaky and the phrase, you have heard it—
> identity crisis, who am I and what am I trying to do?—applied to
> me. I thought about it a lot and at times it was pretty bad.

Steve Patton's adolescent aspirations illustrate the importance of
an account of the development of the ideal self. This subject's ideal self
was a powerful determinant of his life course, influencing his academic efforts and his choice of a college. Revisions of the ideal self—
Steve's decision to become a journalist—were experienced as very
stressful and difficult. Both the life-shaping influence and the phenom-
enal centrality of the ideal self in this case history confirm the importance of aspirations in a description of the life course.

Of course, Steve Patton's life did not end when he entered journalism school. His life continued to evolve in traditional, yet to Steve,
remarkable ways. He got married; he had children; and he became
disillusioned with his work on a large-circulation newspaper. In his
last interview at age 33, Steve revealed that he had returned to school,
this time to pursue a career in law. This was a remarkable turn of
events, because lawyer was one of the jobs Steve had indicated as a
13-year-old that he might like to have 20 years later, with a variety of

intervening educational and occupational experiences, he was realizing this aspiration. This change in occupations had brought him great satisfaction, which was reflected in his ranking the job he would soon have as very desirable.

Steve Patton's ideal self was not only composed of occupational roles, of course, but of social roles as well. The influence of occupational role aspirations on Steve's life is more easily traced than that of his desired social roles because his educational decisions and job choices are all related to the former. But the importance of his social role aspirations were apparent to Steve, even if they do not lend themselves as well to empirical investigation. At age 29 Steve described in very convincing fashion the importance of his goal to make his family proud of him:

> I am close to my family; I care a great deal about them. In my mind one of the greatest responsibilities that I have is that to my children, in particular, and to my wife, too; in terms of bringing up my children to be responsible, intelligent, happy persons, adjusted, whatever else you want to say. I am sure I am as conscious if not more conscious of these responsibilities now as I will be later because with small children it takes a lot of time in helping my wife take care of them now. And it seems to me if you can't do that, if you can't be a close part of the family, then not much else is really worth it.

This brief excerpt compellingly demonstrates the organizing role that family role aspirations played in Steve Patton's view of life in adulthood. Surely we would know much less about him if we were unaware of the components of his ideal self.

SUMMARY

This chapter explored the development of the social and occupational role aspirations forming the ideal self. The statistical analyses of the longitudinal studies provided the book's first insights into the lives of the men followed over the course of 20 years. At all ages subjects aspired most to filling family and peer roles competently; clearly, they were concerned about their relationships with others. Stable individual differences emerged among the adolescents in the extent to which active and professional roles were viewed as desirable. These individual differences at the transition to adulthood predicted the social class the men would occupy 10 to 15 years later. This provides some confirmation that the ideal self is an important component in a developmental account of men's lives.

Findings from the cross-sectional study confirmed the basic age trends revealed in the longitudinal study and also revealed two of the boundaries to generalization from the original sample. A number of significant sex differences emerged between adolescent males and females assessed with the Be-Like Sort in 1988; consequently, we must infer that the patterns traced in this chapter ought not to be considered the path followed by girls as well. Similarly, a few significant cohort differences emerged as well: boys in 1988 were more interested in being a chief executive officer in a large company than were boys in 1955, who placed greater value on hard work and family roles.

The two lives considered in this chapter—Rick Jenkins and Steve Patton—illustrate the value of including the ideal self in an account of development. Both men's lives were shaped by their aspirations: educational, occupational, and social decisions were all influenced by their ideal selves. Without knowledge of their goals and aspirations, we could not provide a coherent overview of their lives.

New issues emerged in the case explorations as well. It seems insufficient to know what a man aspires to be; we need to know *why* such a role is valued and what place this occupation takes in the context of his life. There was evidence, too, that the relationship of the adolescent to his parents has a great deal of influence in orienting him toward the future. In the pages that follow, these issues are explored more directly.

NOTES

1. In a few instances complete sorts are not available for a subject owing to the occasional incomplete recording of data at some testing times. Typically, what happened was that the interviewer recorded the roles ranked as 4 or 3 (very desirable, desirable) and 0 or 1 (very undesirable, undesirable), assuming that with these extremes identified, the neutral roles could be deduced according to the required distribution. However, in some cases one of the roles ranked as a 3 or a 1 was not identified, which made it impossible to deduce accurately the ranks assigned to the remainder of the roles. Because it is only the roles for which the subject was relatively neutral that are missing, we decided to include data from these subjects in some analyses. Our judgment is that the subject's ideal self is revealed primarily through the roles he seeks to become and those he hopes to avoid. When

subjects with incomplete records are included in an analysis, this is so noted.

2. One proximity matrix was calculated for each of the eight age groups. A two-dimensional solution was selected as the most interpretable. The s-stress for the two-dimensional solution is .28, which suggests that the INDSCAL model generally fits these data (MacCallum, 1981).

The weights for each of the two dimensions for each of the eight age groups were inspected. As the subjects in this study became older, they increasingly perceived major differences between roles such as Private and Ballplayer (the left end of Dimension 1) and Good Leader and Making Your Family Proud (the right end of the dimension). Large values for Dimension 2 correspond to major distinctions between professional roles and social roles like Good Sport, Good Son, or Be Like Father. This dimension is especially prominent in the judgments of the younger age groups but is virtually absent from the patterns of preferences of the older age groups. To summarize, the INDSCAL dimension weights indicate that the younger age groups perceive important distinctions between the professional roles and the social roles but do not differentiate greatly between active and social roles. The older age groups show a reverse pattern, with relatively little distinction made between professional and social roles but a major distinction made between active and social roles.

3. At least four of the six roles must have been ranked by the subject in order for him to receive this composite score.

4. Two of the three roles must have been rated by the subject in order for the composite score to be assigned to him.

5. Three of the four roles must have been rated by the subject in order for him to receive this composite score.

6. The effects of attrition were assessed in a series of ANOVAs with age cohort (young, middle, and old) as a covariate. Time 1 social, active, and professional scores for subjects who were interviewed and who were not interviewed at each of Times 2–6 were analyzed in ANOVAs with age cohort (young, middle, and old) as a covariate; only 3 of the 15 analyses (Time 1 social composite scores for those who participated at Time 2 versus scores of those who did not; Time active composite scores for those who participated at Time 2 versus scores of those who did not; with parallel analyses for Times 3, 4, 5) yielded significant effects at the .05 level. At Times 3 and 5 those who participated had slightly higher social scores at Time 1 than those who did not; at Time 4 those who were interviewed had higher active scores at Time 1 than those who were not tested. Generally, however, the small number of significant attrition effects relative to the number of analyses that were conducted suggests that the observed developmental patterns are not a consequence of attrition.

CHAPTER 4

The Development of the Ego-Ideal

Assessing the nature of occupational and social role aspirations from adolescence through adulthood, as described in Chapter 3, provides an entry into the study of men's lives. In this chapter the consideration of men's aspirations continues. However, the focus here is not on the types of roles to which men aspire but on the meaning these roles have for them: Why do 10-year-olds want to be ballplayers? What goals and values are served by the 36-year-old's desire to be a good father? A full account of men's lives must provide answers to these questions.

My purpose in this chapter is to describe the evaluative criteria that men use at different ages to judge the worthiness of their current achievements and future life goals. These evaluative criteria constitute the ego-ideal. The history of this concept originates in Freud's early theorizing. Freud claimed that for the individual the ego-ideal is "an *ideal* in himself by which he measures his actual ego" (Freud, 1914/1957, p. 93).[1] Although Freud apparently lost interest in the ego-ideal construct, more recent theorists have begun to accord it central importance for understanding lives. In particular, the ego-ideal is envisioned as the aspect of personality that binds together disparate aspirations and achievements into a synthetic, motivating whole. For instance, Van den Daele (1968) suggests that it is the ego-ideal that "serves to inspire, guide, and direct behavior" (p. 201) and Westen (1985) writes that it imparts "meaning on existence and provid[es] ideals" (p. 103). As these writers suggest, the value of the ego-ideal to the individual is that it provides meaning, continuity, and direction amid the myriad of failures, successes, and goals that together form much of life.

The ego-ideal is conceptually distinct from the constellation of

99

roles composing the ideal self. This is because the ego-ideal is constituted of value criteria that infuse meaning into achievements and aspirations but does not, by itself, determine them. For instance, a man might be strongly oriented toward success, but this value criterion does not press forcefully toward a career in business rather than in law. Similarly, the meaning that a man derives from (or perceives in) a career in law is not determined by the skills demanded by the position. The quilt of role aspirations forming the ideal self might be imagined as being draped over the framework of value criteria offered by the ego-ideal. There are points of connections between the two systems but no necessary implicative relationships.

The working assumption of this chapter is that the evaluative criteria forming the ego-ideal change during adolescence and adulthood. This is a significant departure from traditional psychoanalytic theorizing on the topic. In its original Freudian formulation the ego-ideal emerged in childhood and, like its related psychic structures, the id and superego, changed little over the course of adolescence and adulthood. But the conception of adolescence and adulthood as a period of developmental stasis has been criticized by recent investigators sympathetic to the psychoanalytic tradition, such as Levinson (1978) and Vaillant (1977). Claims for constancy such as Freud's, Vaillant and Levinson believe, are implausible in the context of the major psychological developments and changes in life structure occurring between childhood and adulthood. Theorists within the cognitive-developmental tradition of Baldwin (1902) have been even more vigorous advocates of the concept that change occurs in the ego-ideal beyond childhood (e.g., Kitchener & King, 1990; Kohlberg, 1969; Van den Daele, 1968). This chapter brings research data to bear on this theoretical debate.

The characterization of the ego-ideal at different points in the course of life is a task more important and more difficult than merely establishing the fact of change in it over time. Fortunately, however, there are clues to the nature of the ego-ideal at different points in the life cycle that are found in several theoretical formulations and empirical investigations. The most solid information concerning the likely nature of the ego-ideal is for the period of middle to late adolescence. The focus on this period is due in large part to the interest generated by Erikson's concept of identity. According to Erikson (1982), "identity must emerge from (1) the selective affirmation and repudiation of an individual's childhood identifications; and (2) the ways in which the social process of the times identifies young individuals" (p. 72).

The achievement of identity, then, requires the adolescent to achieve individuation through a partial separation from the roles adopted as a child and through integration into a social context within which one's commitments to roles and aspirations derive their meaning. As noted in Chapter 1, Erikson's theory suggests that themes of both individuation (or differentiation) and integration should permeate the psychology of the adolescent and, by extension, the ego-ideal as well. Several confirmatory studies have found that when adolescents are asked to explain their reasons for their role aspirations, they tend to respond with references to "being popular" or "fitting in" (Armon, 1984; Hart & Damon, 1986; Van den Daele, 1968). These sorts of explanations reveal the adolescent's concern for integration into a social network. These studies are unclear, however, as to whether there is an individuation component to adolescents' explanations, as Erikson's theory suggests.

Erikson's (1982) theory and Vaillant's (1977) elaboration of it offer insights concerning the transition from late adolescence into adulthood, but it is Levinson's (1978) theory that offers the exposition of development most useful for an account of the ego-ideal during this period. The "Dream," a central construct in Levinson's description of men during their twenties and thirties, is "a vague sense of self-in-adult-world" with "the quality of a vision, an imagined possibility that generates excitement and vitality" (p. 91). This construct seems essentially similar to the concept of the ego-ideal as used in this chapter and by other investigators. Levinson suggests that the Dream is particularly salient during the transition from adolescence into adulthood; during their late teens and early twenties, men project themselves into the future as attaining great personal and occupational success. During the mid-twenties, however, a man's vision of unlimited success must accommodate to the realistic possibilities that are available, a change that might be reflected in the shift toward relativistic or dialectical reasoning described by Gilligan and Murphy (1979; see Chapter 1). For most men this accommodation culminates in a painful period of revision of the Dream during the age-30 transition, which begins at around age 27 and is completed at age 32. As discussed in Chapter 1, Levinson's research support for his claims is hardly conclusive; nonetheless, a tentative hypothesis is that ego-ideal development during the late twenties and early thirties shows some evidence of perturbation.

Finally, there are a few studies that together provide a perspective on the ego-ideal during childhood. Van den Daele (1968) was one of the first to examine in a systematic way ego-ideal development in children. In interviews Van den Daele (1968, p. 247) elicited children's occupational and social role aspirations and then asked them, through such questions as the following, to explain their reasons for those goals: "When you are grown up what two or three kinds of work would you like to do? Which would you like to do the most? Why would you like to do that?" Van den Daele found that most children could be characterized as evidencing an "elementary pragmatism in 'weighing' the utility of behaviors" (p. 252), for example, in seeking to avoid conflict with parents by doing what their parents ask.

Similar findings have emerged in a series of studies by Hart and Damon (Damon & Hart, 1988; Hart & Damon, 1986). In these studies, as in Van den Daele's, children were asked to explain their goals and aspirations for adulthood. Their explanations for their aspirations were categorized according to four developmental levels. For the period of late childhood through early adolescence, immediate consequences and gratification are the value criteria used to judge the life circumstances that are desirable for adulthood.

The theory and research just reviewed suggest that change in the ego-ideal does occur with age and that this change is a qualitative one. The central goal of this chapter is to trace the transformation of the ego-ideal from early adolescence into early adulthood.

A second issue considered in this chapter is the relationships among the developmental paths of the ego-ideal, the ideal self, and moral judgment. If an account of ego-ideal development is to contribute to our understanding of men's lives, it must add new information and not simply echo concepts relating to the ideal self, as discussed in Chapter 3; the conceptual distinctions between the two systems should be reflected in empirical trends.

Similarly, the value criteria forming the ego-ideal must be distinct from those found in Kohlberg's moral judgment stages. Some theorists have argued that the individual's evaluative criteria composing the ego-ideal are primarily moral in nature (Freud, 1923/1961a; Westen, 1985); this would mean that the developmental transformations in the ego-ideal would be identical with the evolution of the moral criteria inherent in moral judgment.

Rather than define the ego-ideal in terms of moral standards, I have allowed a broader connotation. In this chapter the ego-ideal is defined as the set of value criteria with which life aspirations are generated and judged; therefore, its development is not necessarily isomorphic to that of moral judgment. For instance, as they become adolescents, boys may evaluate occupations according to how much fame (a nonmoral criterion) they offer. With this broadened conception, the relationship between the development of the ego-ideal and moral judgment becomes an empirical question. One plausible hypothesis is that early in development, when moral and nonmoral criteria are inadequately distinguished (Kohlberg, 1969), moral judgment and ego-ideal development might be related. With age, however, the two domains might become increasingly differentiated and, hence, less related to each other.

Once a developmental trajectory for the ego-ideal is described and ego-ideal development is differentiated from change in the ideal-self and moral judgment, a third issue arises: are developmental differences between individuals meaningful? This is explored in several ways in this chapter. First, the relationship of adolescent ego-ideal scores to educational and occupational status in adulthood is statistically analyzed. If differences in ego-ideal development among adolescents predict to differences among adults in respect to education and social class, then the ego-ideal construct gains credence as an important component to an account of men's lives.

The value of an ego-ideal account is also examined through a comparison of delinquent and nondelinquent teenagers. In terms of the aforementioned developmental trends, it seems unlikely that delinquent teenagers' ego-ideals share the emphasis on integration into society that may be common to the ego-ideals of their nondelinquent age-mates. Indeed, many of the acts that are labeled delinquent, such as vandalism and theft, inevitably produce societal estrangement. One might hypothesize that the value criteria constituting the ego-ideal of delinquents, like those of children, are likely to focus on immediate personal gratification instead (Damon & Hart, 1988; Wilson & Herrnstein, 1985). Although empirical confirmation of a developmental lag among delinquents would not itself be sufficient to make claims concerning the causal roots of delinquency, such a finding would be one indication of the interpretative value of an ego-ideal developmental description.

Finally, the advantage that an account of the ego-ideal provides for understanding development is assessed through an exploration of two men's lives in the last half of the chapter. Because this sort of analysis is at the level of the individual, rather than statistical comparisons between groups, it is more exacting and ultimately more informative.

THE THREE DEVELOPMENTAL LEVELS OF THE EGO IDEAL

As noted in Chapter 2, at each testing time the men in the study were asked to rank order, from most desirable to least desirable, a host of social and occupational roles. After the roles were ranked, each subject was asked to explain what he found desirable or undesirable about each of them (e.g., "Why would you like to be a good father?" or "Why don't you want to be a pilot?"). It is these explanations that reveal the evaluative criteria underlying the subjects' aspirations concerning occupations and relationships.

In order to characterize the men's explanations of why they found particular roles desirable, three ego-ideal levels were constructed. These three developmental levels are based on the trends in the theory and research described earlier, as well as on an intensive analysis of the interviews of two men from each of the three age cohorts (to allow for the possibility that very young boys might use a distinctly different set of evaluative criteria, which might be labeled Level 1, the levels presented here are labeled 2, 3, and 4).[2]

Level 2

Exchanging favors, experiencing enjoyment, and acquiring material goods are the value criteria constituting the ego-ideal for boys and men at Level 2. Social roles are desirable to the extent that they allow an exchange of favors and material goods. The meaning of peer and family roles for individuals at this level resides in this exchange. Little value is attached to either the societal function of a role or to the potential opportunities it might afford over long periods of time. For instance, two 10-year-olds offered the following definitions of friendship:

What kind of person is a good friend?
Ones that help you when you need help. (age 10)
Well, if you're a good friend, then when you want something done, maybe your friend will do it for you. (age 10)

Not only can friends be identified by their willingness to help, but the adolescent aspires to be a good friend in order to elicit this help:

Why do you need friends in life?
Well, in case you're in a spot, in a predicament, you need, like

you're in a court and say you got a minor traffic violation and you need somebody to testify for you, you can call on a friend to testify. (age 13)

The quality of one's relationships with family members is also defined by a subject at Level 2 in terms of help and obedience, as these responses from 13-year-olds suggest:

What kind of person is a good son?
He does things that his parents ask him to. (age 13)

What kind of person is a good father?
A person who doesn't drink too much and doesn't get drunk and has a good disposition and plays with you. (age 13)

Again, the Level 2 perspective on aspirations emphasizes the advantages that can be drawn from various roles, so it is not surprising that a 10-year-old hopes that being a good father will have its payoff:

Why do people want to be good fathers?
So their sons will be good sons to them. (age 10)

For an individual at Level 2 in the development of the ego-ideal, preferences for occupational roles derive from perceptions of their difficulty, fun, excitement, and time demands; thus, there are a number of jobs that the individual hopes to escape because they seem "stupid," "boring," or just "too hard":

Why wouldn't you want to have your father's job [welder]?
I wouldn't like to be a welder because it gets boring and all. (age 10)

Why wouldn't you want to be a doctor?
Cause every time—sometimes—you always have so many calls to go out on—sick call, and then you have to take care of patients at the shop—it's too busy. (age 10)

Why wouldn't you want to be a private?
Well, I wouldn't like to be an army soldier because it's a lot of hard work and I—and that. I'd like to be in the marines. They're always going out in the ocean, and I like the ocean. (age 10)

Level 3

At level 3, successful integration into the individual's social context and differentiation from the roles adopted as a child are the
dominant value criteria constituting the ego-ideal. Social or occupational roles are desirable insofar as they allow one to become popular
and develop good relationships (integration) or to utilize one's capabilities and eventually achieve success (differentiation). Little value is
attached to the self's own concerns; neither personal pleasures or
advantages (important at Level 2) nor one's beliefs and standards
(important at Level 4) are prominent in considerations of the desirability of various roles. Peer and family roles are portrayed in stereotypical
terms, such as dependable or trustworthy, that reflect concern for
social approval. Boys and men reflect on the congruence between the
self's characteristics and the characteristics needed to fulfill a particular social role. For instance, being a good friend can be important as a
means for achieving popularity:

> Having friends is important, and being a good one shows that
> you can be trusted. Being a good friend, you're bound to make
> good friends. (age 16)

In addition to serving as a means of integration into the social
context, friendships can also contribute to personal success; both facets
of friendship are evident in this adolescent's account:

> I think it's very important to be able to get along with other
> people. If you're a good friend, and I don't think of it as just
> having good friends and other people can see you're good friends.
> It's that you have the characteristics of a good friend and that you
> can get along with other people and you have an understanding,
> you're well liked, your personality is well liked.
>
> *Why do you want to be like that?*
> I want to be well liked and accepted and so on and I think that if
> you have these qualities, these same qualities will also help you
> get ahead in business and enable you to get along with other
> employees and so on . . . well just in general, if you're well liked I
> think you will go far if you have a good personality and good
> qualities and so on. I think you'll be able to get far. You'll be
> accepted and wanted, and so on. Maybe it's a little selfish, but if
> you are a good friend, it'll make you feel important. (age 16)

Of course, good relationships with others need not be valued for their possibilities for integration into a social context; as one young adult described it, aspiring to be a good friend may be viewed strictly in terms of its value for individuation manifested in personal success and social status:

Why is being a good friend important to you?
I think so much of your success depends on getting along with people and respecting and being respected by others. (age 22)

Aspirations for family roles are similarly undergirded by a focus on integration and differentiation. As the adolescent and adult in the following examples emphasize, being a good son means earning one's integration through distinguished achievement:

What is a good son?
I think a person who does the right things. Have meaning behind it, too. If you do something with a certain feeling that you want to accomplish it. Having the right attitude about things. Your family will be more proud of you. "This is my son, and look what he's done." They'll have respect for you. (age 16)

Why is being a good son something you would like to be?
I think if you are raised well by your parents, you will be a good son or daughter, and it is a little harder for me to attach a reason to that, you have to say what is a good son, someone who pleases his parents by doing well, or whatever, is important to them, maybe looking after them when they get older, for example, that's what I would like to do.

What would you say are the responsibilities of a good son?
Look after your parents when they get older, as I mentioned before as an example, doing what might be important to them and an example of that might be being a good citizen or a good American or something like that. (age 36)

Of course, one's sense of integration into the fabric of the family would be threatened by a lack of distinction or objectionable behavior:

Why do you want to be someone who does things to make his family proud of him?
I wouldn't want to do anything that would make my family ashamed, because I would feel like I was letting them down. (age 36)

At Level 3, occupational roles are important because they offer opportunities for achievement, success, social acceptance, and social distinction. Boys and men judge the appropriateness of a role in terms of its potential for attainment of these goals as well as its compatibility with their own personality characteristics. In the following examples adolescents and men make clear that they value roles offering personal distinction:

Why wouldn't you want to have a job like your father's?
Where he is there's no chance for advancement, really. He's been there quite a while, and he hasn't really advanced that much. I want something where I can have an opportunity to move up. (age 18)

To get ahead in life, why is that important?
When you do work to get ahead, you have a sense of accomplishment, and this is where I like, uh, on the way up, things like that I find that exciting. (age 18)

What would you like to do eventually?
Well, I don't really know. I have so many channels to follow I don't really know what I'd like to, actually, I'd like something along the end of prestige, you know like an office job, but without the office. (age 30)

What precisely do you plan on doing?
I'm not really sure yet. All I know is that I want to make a lot of money.
Why is that important to you?
I think that money means quite a lot in this society. (age 20)

Someone with a job like your own, why?
Because I felt that in high school I was a wallflower, shy and everything, and this has got the most of me and done the most for me and I have been greatly rewarded by being out and by being thrust into the public life and the public eye and be forced into dealing with others. It has done the most in the world for me. (age 36)

Level 4

At Level 4 the twin concerns of fidelity to personal beliefs and responsibility to one's society are the value criteria forming the ego-ideal. Desirable roles at this level provide a means for contributing to society and simultaneously living one's life in accordance with personal beliefs. Peer and family roles are viewed as involving commitments to and respect for other individuals. In addition to their importance within the individual's value system, social and occupational roles are believed to serve valuable societal functions. For instance, in the following two responses the men emphasize that friendships are desirable because they offer an opportunity to realize important personal values:

> *How about a good friend and why do you want to be that?*
> I think a person needs friends and the only way that you can have friends is to be a friend yourself, and all too often we get busy and forget our friends and sometimes we treat them rudely and this hurts, this is a human hurt, and I try always to remember to do the things that are best that would help them out. (age 26)

> I think that in life, one of the most important things is not your material possessions, but your friendships that you make with other people. (age 33)

At Level 4 men also aspire to friendship roles because they provide an opportunity to construct patterns of living that are necessary for smooth societal functioning:

> *Why did you choose a good friend?*
> I came back to respect, you can't deal with people unless you can be friends and most relationships are based on friendship and trust, and respect and they are very important to be able to live in a very complex society like we live in. (age 30)

Family roles, like friendship, offer opportunities to be true to one's values, as this 30-year-old explains:

> *What would be the responsibilities of being a person who does things that make his family proud of him?*
> Carrying through what you set out to do, being sensitive to other

people's needs and desires and values, fulfilling obligations which
you incur. (age 30)

For the man at level 4, family roles also provide an opportunity to
contribute to the good of society:

A good father, why is that important to you?
I'll be responsible for my kids, in a general sense responsible for
the younger generation and forming their ideals, and trying to
make them better people. (age 18)

At Level 4, occupational roles are valuable as an avenue to contribute to other people and society and also as an opportunity to act
in accordance with one's personal values. According to the men in the
following three examples, an occupation ought to offer an opportunity
to advance public welfare:

You just can't sit around all day. You have to contribute to the
world somehow; make it a better place to live. Don't just sit
around and twiddle your thumbs; you don't get anything done in
your life and you won't be helping anybody else. (age 18)

You picked teacher first. Why?
That is a loaded question. I guess because I am a teacher and I feel
that as a teacher, I have been able to perhaps make some contribution to the benefit of mankind, through knowledge and
through ideas and to, hopefully, I think a better understanding
among people. I just feel that this is a good way to make a positive
contribution. (age 26)

What would be lacking as a pilot?
It is a very isolated, individualistic kind of thing, interacting primarily with the machine, the plane, and again there are so many
other broader things having to do with human relationships and
following some of the major technological problems in this country that being a pilot doesn't contribute much to. (age 33)

Occupations are seen not only as vehicles for furthering the good
of society but also as opportunities for an integration of personal
values.

Why wouldn't you want to be a judge?
Being a judge seems to be connected with politics in a way, and I don't care much for politics.

Why not?
Politics to me seem kind of phoney. You go in there and if you are idealistic you want to reform this and that and you run up against all these obstacles. I myself want to do what I want to do and I couldn't see myself passing some legislation that my constituents would want and I wouldn't be in favor of. (age 20)

These three levels capture the major developmental trends I perceive in the ego-ideal between ages 10 and 36. The construction of any developmental sequence requires judgments about what distinctions should be captured and which should be ignored; consequently, one can always question the number of levels and stages proposed in a stage model. With only three levels, the ego-ideal sequence presented here makes fewer distinctions than many stage theories. Perhaps if a sample of young boys had been included in this study it would have been possible to describe a level that is developmentally earlier than Level 2; similarly, there might well be a form of the ego-ideal more sophisticated than Level 4 (e.g., the dialectical perspective that some theorists argue emerges in adulthood; see Chapter 1). However, I hope to demonstrate in the following pages that the three levels presented here have much to recommend them.

LONGITUDINAL ANALYSES

The nature of the levels and their corresponding examples conform to expectations about development. Although their congruence with intuitions about change over the life span in men's lives is a powerful source of confirmation, statistical analyses can provide information about the levels not apparent from casual inspection. In the following sections statistical analyses are directed toward four general questions: (1) In explaining the meaning they perceive in different social and occupational roles, do the boys and men make consistent use of one level of ego-ideal development or is a mixture of levels more typical? (2) Do the levels form a sequence? In other words, do the boys begin at Level 2, move to Level 3 during adolescence, and attain Level 4 during adulthood? (3) How is ego-ideal development related to the context of men's lives? In particular, is ego-ideal development related to juvenile delinquency, level of education, and occupational status during adulthood? (4) Does the path of ego-ideal development diverge from those followed by the ideal self and moral judgment?

Method

A coding manual containing criteria for the three ego-ideal developmental levels was constructed. A developmental level code was assigned only to the explanations for the roles ranked as desirable. This is because explanations for the roles judged undesirable were occasionally cursory and unelaborated (e.g., in answer to the question "Why don't you want to be a printer?" a subject might respond, "It doesn't interest me" or "I don't know anything about it"), and it was difficult to determine whether the answer reflected fairly a man's value criteria. The average number of scored responses per interview session was 5.9. To assign the developmental level code, the coder matched the explanation offered by the subject for a particular role with a prototypical example of an explanation for the same role in the scoring manual. After the entire interview was coded, two summary scores, collapsing together responses to the social and occupational roles, were calculated: a modal level score and an average level ego-ideal (ALEI) score (the sum of the level scores assigned to an interview divided by the total number of scores). The high levels of internal consistency for both summary scores suggest that little information is lost by combining developmental scores for the two types of roles: for all testing times combined, 78% of a man's responses are at his modal level, and at Time 1, when the sample was largest, the alpha coefficient (a measure of internal consistency) for the ALEI score is .65. These findings suggest that a single ego-ideal level is representative of the value criteria evident in a person's explanations for his occupational and social role aspirations. These are relatively high levels of internal consistency and compare favorably with the results reported by Van den Daele (1968) and Armon (1984, 1991).

In order to assess interrater reliability for the ego-ideal developmental coding manual, two cases were randomly selected from the eight different age groups described in Chapter 2. Two raters coded these 16 interviews and agreed on the modal level of an interview for 87% of the cases. The correlation between the ALEI scores of the two raters for the 16 interviews was .85, $p < .001$. These results represent about the same degree of interrater agreement found in other studies using developmental coding manuals (e.g., Hart & Damon, 1986; Loevinger & Wessler, 1970).

Responses to the Moral Judgment Interview were coded according to the *Standard Issue Scoring Manual.* An average stage score (Moral Maturity Score, MMS) was calculated to represent the subject's overall performance on the Moral Judgment Interview.

Both the ego-ideal and moral judgment interviews were coded by scorers blind to a subject's scores on the same interviews at other testing times.

Results

In Chapter 2, I described the problems related to attrition in this study. Some men were interviewed at all six testing times, others were interviewed for many of the testing times, and some dropped out of the study after the first, second, or third testing time. In considering longitudinal trends, then, it is necessary to distinguish as far as possible between changes attributable to age and those deriving from particular members of the sample dropping out of the study. To assess the impact of attrition, Time 1 ALEI scores for subjects who were interviewed and those who were not interviewed at each of Times 2 to 6 were analyzed in t tests; no significant differences were found for any testing time between those who did participate and those who did not. This suggests that those who dropped out of the study were not systematically different from those who remained in it. It seems safe to conclude that any trends that emerge are therefore developmental in nature.

Developmental Trends

The level of ego-ideal reasoning used by boys and men was closely related to their age, with boys, as expected, using lower levels than men. There were moderately strong correlations between age group and developmental level scores, as indexed by both modal level ($r = .58$, $p < .001$) and by ALEI ($r = .52$, $p < .001$). These correlations and the averages presented in Table 4.1 provide strong confirmation for the general developmental qualities of the levels (Table 4.1 presents the number of subjects at each modal level as well as the average ALEI score for each age group).

TABLE 4.1.
Modal and Average Level Scores for Each Age Group

	Age							
	10	13–14	16–18	20–22	24–26	28–30	32–34	36
Number of subjects at modal level								
2	17	8	1	2	0	0	0	0
3	5	29	48	7	7	17	17	7
4	0	0	1	2	8	13	2	2
Average level score (ALEI)	2.2	2.7	2.9	3.0	3.4	3.3	3.1	3.3
SD ALEI	.43	.42	.20	.63	.51	.50	.31	.35

Most 10-year-old boys are at Level 2, as Table 4.1 indicates, but this level rapidly becomes less common among adolescents and men. Between the ages of 13 and 22, almost all of the boys and men in this study received modal scores of Level 3, indicating that the issue of finding one's place in society occupied the central focus of the ego-ideal. Not until ages 24 to 30 did a substantial number of men become concerned about their responsibilities toward society and themselves as manifested by the presence of modal scores of Level 4.

The longitudinal analysis of the modal level scores supports the claim that the levels form a sequence. Sequentiality means that at adjacent testing times $Time_1$ and $Time_{n+1}$, every subject should be at the same level for the two sessions or one level higher at $Time_{n+1}$. For all the adjacent testing times, there were no instances in which a person skipped a developmental level (went from a modal score of Level 2 to a modal score of Level 4).

Regression to a lower level from $Time_1$ to $Time_{n+1}$ never occurred in adolescence but did occur during adulthood in five cases (all of them from Level 4 to Level 3 and all occurring between age groups 24–26 and 28–30). Up to early adulthood, then, the levels appear to constitute a developmental sequence, but entry into adulthood results in the reemergence of lower level concerns, at least in some men.

The regression from Level 4 to Level 3 among five men in their late twenties was not expected; interestingly, however, this regression reflects a general decline in ego-ideal scores among the men in early adulthood. In fact, if the correlations between ALEI scores and age is calculated for the four oldest age groups, there is a significant decline with age, $r = -.34$, $p < .01$ (versus $r = .55$, $p < .001$ for the four youngest age groups).[3] Figure 4.1 depicts the average percentage of re-

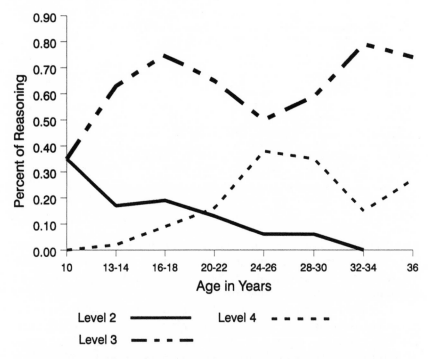

FIGURE 4.1. Percentage of ego-ideal reasoning at each level as a function of age..

sponses at each of the three levels at the different ages, which also suggests some regression. This means that men in their thirties retreat from the Level 4 ego-ideal criteria they had constructed during their twenties. This pattern raises at least two questions: Does this abandonment reflect some sort of general reorganization in men's ego-ideals? What factors in their lives are related to this change?[4]

Stability of Individual Differences

These questions cannot be answered definitively, but findings suggest that there is genuine reorganization in men's ego-ideals. The pattern of correlations among ego-ideal scores (ALEI scores) at the different testing times presented in Table 4.2 indicate that there is considerable developmental or ordering stability, as indicated by moderately strong correlations for all but the last two testing times, when the men had all entered adulthood (at Time 5 the men ranged in age

TABLE 4.2.
Correlations among MMS and ALEI Scores at the Different Testing Times

	Time 1	Time 2	Time 4	Time 5	Time 6
Time 1		.80(27)***	.51(28)**	.51(24)*	.01(23)
Time 2	.53(27)**		.81(14)***	.68(14)**	.46(13)
Time 4	.45(28)*	.78(14)***		.68(17)**	.35(13)
Time 5	.08(24)	−.13(14)	.19(17)		.87(18)***
Time 6	−.20(21)	−.13(13)	.03(13)	.29(18)	

Note. Correlations above the diagonal are between MMS scores; correlations below the diagonal are between average level ego-ideal (ALEI) scores. Correlations between Moral Maturity scores (MMS) for the same subjects are provided in this table for comparison purposes. Because of the small number of subjects participating at Time 2, no correlations were calculated with scores at that point. Only subjects for whom both ALEI and MMS scores were available at the two testing times were included in the correlational analyses. Degrees of freedom are in parentheses.
*$p < .05$. **$p < .01$. ***$p < .001$.

from 26–32; at Time 6, 30–36). This means that the extent of ego-ideal development up through age 26 is predictable from earlier scores. This predictability and continuity in development is disrupted, however, once men enter their late twenties.

It is interesting to note that although developmental stability for ego-ideal development and that for moral judgment development are approximately equal for late childhood through the beginnings of adulthood, ego-ideal development becomes unpredictable at that point while moral judgment scores retain some relationship to earlier scores.

Developmental Level and Life Circumstances

What relationship do ALEI scores have to life circumstances? Answers to this question are interesting in their own right but can also contribute to an understanding of the apparent regression and reorganization occurring during the late twenties.

There are several facets of these issues that are of interest. One worth considering is the extent to which knowledge of ego-ideal development in adolescence allows predictions to characteristics of interest during adulthood. As described in Chapter 2, men's level of educational achievement and their social class at the end of the study are two outcome variables of significance. Is the adolescent's ego-ideal level a predictor of educational attainment in the succeeding years of late adolescence and early adulthood? The correlations between ego-ideal level (ALEI score) at ages 10, 13, and 16 and years of education are, respectively, −.25 (n.s.), −.03, (n.s.), and .47, ($p < .01$). This means that 16-year-olds who have, relative to their age-mates, developmentally advanced ego-ideals are likely to pursue more education.

Similarly, 16-year-olds evidencing higher developmental levels for the ego-ideal are more likely to be in the higher social classes by the conclusion of the study than the less advanced adolescents. This pattern can be seen in Table 4.3, in which correlations between adulthood social class and ALEI scores from ages 16 to 36 are presented.

The correlation of ego-ideal scores at age 16 to level of educational attainment and adulthood social class suggests that a concern with integration and differentiation, Level 3 value criteria, leads adolescents to make plans and position themselves in ways that facilitate their later occupational success. Those adolescents whose ego-ideals continue to be oriented toward excitement and immediate material advantage may begin to fall behind their age-mates (further evidence for this pattern will be presented in a later section concerning the delinquent adolescents).

The pattern of correlations in Table 4.3 also suggests that entry into the adult world leads to a decreased concern with Level 4 issues of fidelity to personal values, at least temporarily. This is indicated by the negative relationship between ALEI scores and adult social class during the late twenties, with men in the highest social classes receiving ALEI scores no higher—and at ages 28–30 actually scoring lower—than men in the lower social classes. At age 36 those men in the higher social classes are once again receiving higher scores. Thus, it seems that once men enter high-status positions, their concern with responsibility to others and fidelity to personal values declines, at least initially.

Ego-Ideal, Ideal Self, and Moral Judgment Development

To this point the statistical analyses have suggested that the ego-ideal levels proposed in this chapter are related to age, allow interesting predictions to adulthood characteristics from ego-ideal status

TABLE 4.3.
Correlations between ALEI Scores at Different Ages and Adulthood Social Class

	Age					
	16–18	20–22	24–26	28–30	32–34	36
	.38*	.50	−.13	−.41*	.05	.87**

*$p < .05$. **$p < .01$.

during adolescence, and evidence an unusual relationship to job status during adulthood. The significance of these findings rests in large part upon their uniqueness. If the ego-ideal scores merely duplicate other sources of information, their relevance for an account of adulthood development in men is severely limited. One way to assess the extent to which this is true is to calculate correlations between ego-ideal scores and indices for other potentially related domains.

The evidence suggests that ego-ideal development is generally independent of development in other domains. In Table 4.4 there is no consistent pattern of a relationship between ego-ideal scores and the composite ideal self scores, confirming that the two domains are independent. The correlations between the ALEI score and MMS are also presented in Table 4.4, but here there is evidence of a relationship between domains. Four of the eight correlations are significant, suggesting that there is a relationship between the development of the ego-ideal and moral judgment. The magnitude of the relationship is generally low to moderate, which indicates that the two domains, although related, are also partially independent. The relationship between moral judgment and ego-ideal development is generally strong from childhood through late adolescence and also at age 36. Entry into early adulthood, however, is accompanied by an apparent divergence of the developmental paths of the ego-ideal and moral judgment, as indicated by a lack of significant association between the two from age 24 to age 34.

Ego-ideal level is also unrelated to IQ and sociometric status, a finding consonant with the general pattern of results of Van den Daele's (1968) study of ego-ideal development in childhood and adolescence. To assess these relationships, correlations were calculated between ALEI scores and IQ and between ALEI scores and socio-

TABLE 4.4.
Correlations of ALEI Scores to Composite Ideal Self
and Moral Maturity Scores for the Eight Age Groups

Ideal self composite scores	Age							
	10	13–14	16–18	20–22	24–26	28–30	32–34	36
Professional	.24	.27	.15	.56	.01	−.02	.16	−.62
Active	−.26	−.39*	−.11	−.51	−.61*	−.15	−.23	.23
Social	.23	.04	−.09	−.02	.11	−.14	−.17	.06
MMS	.57*	.37*	.29	.71*	.32	.28	.28	.91*

*p < .05. **p < .01.

metric status for the eight age groups. None of the sixteen correlations were statistically different from zero. These null findings confirm the uniqueness of the information about men's lives conveyed by the ego-ideal developmental account.

Comparisons with Delinquent Youths

Statistical analyses. The ALEI scores of the delinquent youths interviewed by Kohlberg in 1955 and the 16-year-old subjects at Time 1 were compared. The latter group was chosen for this purpose for two reasons: First, it is the only group composed of persons 16-years-old (because testing times were separated by 3–4 years, the 13-year-olds at Time 1 were 17 years old at Time 2). Second, because both groups were tested at Time 1, differences attributable to minor variations in the testing procedure from time to time were eliminated. As predicted, the delinquent youth had a lower level of ego-ideal development, with an average of 2.5, than did the nondelinquent 16-year-olds, with an average of 2.85 ($t[31] = 2.16$, $p < .05$). Given the small number of subjects (33) in this comparison, the attainment of statistical significance suggests a large effect. The magnitude of the difference between the two groups is approximately one-third of a level. A comparison with the means for the different age groups presented in Table 4.1 reveals that the delinquent group has a lower mean ALEI score than the 13- to 14-year-old group as well. Thus, although the differences do not appear large, the lower average score of the delinquent group represents a significant developmental lag.

Case analysis. The significance of the lag in ego-ideal development for understanding juvenile delinquents can be grasped in the context of Paul O'Leary's life. Paul O'Leary was first interviewed as a 16-year-old and, like the other delinquents in the study, was living in a home for delinquent boys at the time. Paul was typical of the delinquents in his use of Level 2 ego-ideal value criteria. To be a good father to one's children, for instance, meant to Paul to "be nice to them and stuff like that" and "buy them a lot of things." His interests in becoming a ballplayer and an army private were derived from the enjoyment and fun these roles appeared to offer. Paul rejected working hard to get ahead ("I'd just like to go along gradually, I guess") and thought that being the head of a company would involve "too much responsibility."

Why is it that Paul and the other delinquents fail to develop an orientation toward integration and individuation like their age-mates? In part, the delinquents' developmental lag may be a consequence of the failures they experienced in their initial attempts to join the network of social relationships and achieve distinction within it. The pain of rejection and failure may have led them to give up, to envision a future of alienation and lack of recognition. This history of failure is reflected in Paul's poignant response to a question about his desire to be a good leader:

> When I used to go to school, that's one of the reasons I quit; I could get along with the kids in school; it's just the teachers that got me mad.
>
> *What did they do?*
> I don't know; they just never could get along with me, they say. And the other thing, I couldn't get along with them; but then when I'd try to get along with them, they wouldn't even listen to me or anything like that.

The lack of concern with age-typical values on social integration and advancement means that the delinquent does not fear the estrangement from society that accompanies theft, property destruction, and so on. Once the adolescent is involved in delinquency, he is farther away from social integration and social success. As a consequence, Level 3 value criteria become more difficult to reach, which in turn leads to more antisocial behavior and distance from integration. Four years later, when Paul was interviewed in the state prison, his sense of isolation was evident:

> When I first got in trouble, I got put in jail for about six months. I was in jail all that time, and I didn't even get a letter from my parents; I didn't get nothin' from them.
>
> *Do they care about you?*
> Evidently not. Because my father is a big lawyer—he's got his own firm and everything—and my mother, she is the president of the chamber of commerce. My mother doesn't care; she won't even write a letter because she's afraid someone will see the envelope and figure out she's got a kid in jail. She's got a surprise coming 'cause when I get out, because they're going to know I was up here.

In this interview Paul's sadness and resentment run deep. He no longer feels a need to blend into his family and earn their respect. He seeks only to make them suffer for the alienation he endures.

TWO LIVES

The results presented in the earlier sections of the chapter demonstrate that there are regular age-related changes in the nature of men's ego-ideals. The general pattern, I claimed, is from a concern with enjoyment and an exchange of favors in early adolescence to an orientation towards integration into and differentiation from the network of relationships and roles in late adolescence and early adulthood, with some men developing further and evidencing a focus on fidelity to personal values and responsibility to others. What purchase does this description provide on an understanding of development in men?

In this section of the chapter, the relevance of the development of the ego-ideal is embedded in the context of the lives of two men, Frank Jones and Bob Eagleton. Jones and Eagleton are similar in many respects: both were born into upper-middle class families, have deeply ambivalent relationships with their fathers, and become highly successful professionals as adults. Yet their lives differ in ego-ideal development in significant and meaningful ways.

Frank Jones

Frank Jones was 10 years old when he was first interviewed in 1956. He was both a popular boy, as judged by his classmates and teachers, and a smart one (with an IQ of 124). His father was a well-respected architect, who had achieved considerable professional success. Frank's personal characteristics and family social position made him one of the most advantaged boys in the study.

In his interview at age 10, Frank responded to questions about his aspirations with age-typical Level 2 ego-ideal notions. For instance, when asked about his desire to become a baseball player, Frank answered, "I like sports, and baseball is my favorite sport, and I want to be good at it." His interest in activity and the enjoyment that results was further evidenced in his lack of interest in becoming the president of a company:

All he does is give orders and stuff like that. He doesn't really do the work. Lot of people working for him; they do the canning, stuff like that.

You'd rather do the work than give the orders?
Yeah.

Why?
A lot of money for sitting around talking.

What Frank aspired to most at age 10, however, was to become an architect like his father. It is in his responses to queries about this issue that there is an indication that Frank was beginning to elaborate a premature Level 3 understanding of his life's goals. For instance, although he aspired to a job like his father's, Frank also indicated that there were limits to his desire to be like his father; he did not want to be a clone. At age 10 this issue is evident in his response to the interviewer's question about why he wanted to be like his father:

> Well, it's nice, but you really shouldn't take after somebody unless he's real good. You should have your own mind and your own feelings; if you act exactly like your father, you just sort of get the habit of following other people . . . I want to be an architect like him. Yeah, but not in the way he walks, or something like that. Like if he stoops over when he walks, that doesn't mean I have to.

It seems likely that Frank's developmentally premature Level 3 concern with individuation from his father was a consequence of Mr. Jones's deep involvement in his son's life. For instance, Mr. Jones expected Frank to attend college. This expectation was firmly implanted in Frank in the course of a ritual he and his father shared. As Frank related it:

> I buy savings bonds, and I've got about four hundred dollars saved up.

By yourself?
Yeah. Well, my father takes a little bit out of his check and buys one every two months for me and then when I save enough in my bank, then I buy an extra one. I have about nine or ten and that's making twenty-five dollars, and you pay eighteen seventy-five for twenty-five dollars it's pretty good.

Did your father go to college?
They were kind of poor—they lived on a farm in New Hampshire.

My father worked ten years going to school part-time during the day and working at night; he had to work awfully hard. He still didn't get enough education that he would if he went in the daytime full-time for four years.

According to Frank's telling of the story, his father was certainly a classic American success, a boy from a poor farm family who made good by attending school part-time. It is no surprise then, that Frank had a great deal of respect for his father. By making a ritual of buying savings bonds for Frank's future education, Mr. Jones communicated to his son the importance of education and planning ahead for the future.

Four years later, there were vestiges of Level 2 ego-ideal reasoning in Frank. When asked why he wanted to be a good son, for instance, Frank answered, "Well, your parents put a lot of work into raising you so I should try to be a good son so it pays them back." This orientation toward concrete, reciprocal rewards is further reflected in his reasons for avoiding the role of teacher; Frank argued, "[It is] too much of a drag on a person; you have to yell at people, and you'd get tired." However, much of Frank's ego-ideal reasoning was then at Level 3. He still aspired to become an architect like his father, but his reason for doing so had evolved into an ambition to stand out, to become a success:

If you don't have any cause to get ahead, then I don't think you should work. But if you work and try to get ahead, that's worthwhile; if you just work and don't try to get ahead, you're not doing much good. But if you work and get ahead, try to be president or make the highest salary, then you're making something out of yourself.

Frank's parents continued to make the task of individuation from the family more difficult, maintaining high expectations for his success and an evident desire to have him continue in his father's footsteps:

What would your parents like you to be?
Well, my father wants me to be an architect. And I think, my mother does, too.

Eight years later, when Frank next participated in the study, he was attending a college noted for its architecture program and majoring in that area. His ego-ideal reasoning was firmly consolidated at

Level 3. Frank wanted both to feel a sense of integration into a network of friends and to achieve success and independence, as shown in the following discussion about his social life in college:

You're in several clubs?
Ya, right.

How do you like them?
I like it. I think it's, well, as far as the university is concerned, it's the only way to go as far as that goes. Because everybody lives off campus, and it's hard to meet girls.

Is that why you brought your girlfriend with you today?
Ya. Well, anyway, it's the only way you meet them. Yeah, if you don't join something, you can't meet girls. That's just a fact. I like the social life. And I wanted a social life. I just didn't want to be a student all the time, you know. So I really enjoy it.

You get along well with most of the people in your clubs?
Real well. In a lot of ways it's, it broadens your outlook. Not restricting whatsoever.

In what ways does it broaden your outlook?
Well, you have to learn to work with people, you know. And you meet all types of people, from all over the country. All personalities and everything, and if you get along with them, you know, you get along with people out in the world, really.

Frank's desire to fit in and belong was balanced by his continuing desire to achieve success and separation, particularly with respect to his family. When he described his first major separation from his family, which occurred when he entered college, Frank made the following claims:

It didn't really affect me at all, I don't think. I was never homesick. And I like getting away. I like being on my own. I suppose I'm independent. But I enjoyed it.

There was little apparent change in Frank's developmental level of ego-ideal reasoning between college and his next interview at age 26. His responses indicate that he remained at Level 3 and that his relationship with his father continued to be ambivalent. In his Be-Like Sort, Frank now ranked being like his father as undesirable, for which he offered this explanation:

The only thing I would disagree with, my father actually is a brilliant architect . . . and the only thing that I don't like that he did
was he didn't personally gain from a lot of the things that he did.

Gain in what way?
Well, right now, he is near retirement and is making less money
than I am, and yet he's responsible for many innovative buildings
and he just never pushed anything from himself to gain from it
and I don't agree with that.

You mean monetarily.
Yah.

You feel that is important?
Yes I do.

Why?
Well, I am not just defining it as an occupation, but I admire
people who are aggressive and constantly strive to better themselves, better their lives, their family, achieve.

In this excerpt the depth of Frank's desire to achieve individuation
through success is quite evident, and, as the interviewer noted at the
conclusion of the session, at age 26 Frank was "particularly concerned
in his own development with his occupation, and financial and professional status."

The final interview with Frank occurred when he was 30 years
old. He was by then an architect, as he so accurately forecasted as
a 10-year-old in fifth grade. His ego-ideal reasoning remained characteristic of Level 3, with a particular focus on individuation through
achievement and success. One of Frank's chief complaints concerning his firm was that his attempts to earn recognition often were
overlooked:

The one problem that really strikes home is the one that if you do
a bad job nothing is done about it and if you do a good job
nothing is done about it. Of course, that is relative, but that blows
the merit system or the work ethic or whatever. What are you
bucking your ass for?

This failure to receive recognition was not a minor irritation for Frank;
indeed, success was the goal of his life.

I want to get ahead in life. I like to achieve, I like to live well, I like success. And, of course, I am measuring these things in the units that I think everyone measures them in, so that is what I am doing.

What satisfactions would you expect?
I want to live well, I want to feel self-satisfied, I want to get recognition, all the pluses . . . . My job is the majority of my life.

Frank's attempts to achieve occupational success and distinction were very successful. However, he had to compromise in other areas of life in order to achieve this success. He noted that he had failed to spend as much time with his children as he wanted, and he also acknowledged that he needed to do more with his wife:

> There are a lot of things that need to be improved. I guess I would like to be more supportive or stimulating to Ellen. Ellen has a tough dilemma on her hands right now, it is a tough dilemma, and I am not helping her with the situation. Her dilemma is one of not feeling particularly fulfilled in her motherly role; it is wearing thin now. And she wants to do something else. But she is locked in at the same time.

Finally, it is worth noting that Frank drew back from opportunities to consider the responsibilities and personal fidelity that are characteristic of Level 4 ego-ideal development:

> *Do you feel in your job that you are making any kind of contribution to society?*
> I doubt it. In fact, I don't worry about it too much. Yah, I am doing something; we are keeping a lot of people employed, kept a lot of construction workers off the street.
>
> *What do you think is an appropriate philosophy for someone in a job like yours to have?*
> I guess that is my philosophy. I don't really know what the work ethic is. I characterize it as work hard and get ahead.

The ego-ideal developmental scheme provides an interpretative framework for understanding the transformation that occurred in Frank's value criteria during adolescence. He changed from a boy who valued occupations and roles that offer excitement and enjoyment to a young man who sought to achieve individuation and individual distinction, the typical pattern for most of the men. This, by itself, is not sufficient to describe the changes that occurred in Frank's life over the span of 20 years. Yet the value of an account of ego-ideal development for understanding Frank's life is substantial; this account permits some interesting comparisons to be made with the life of Bob Eagleton, who is discussed next.

Bob Eagleton

Bob Eagleton also had a socially privileged background as the son of a very successful lawyer. Bob received consistently high grades in school, even though his IQ at the time of his entry into the study was a rather undistinguished 104. Like Frank Jones, Bob was considered by his classmates and teacher to be a popular boy.

At age 10, Bob's social and occupational role value criteria were characteristic of Level 2 ego-ideal development. When asked, for instance, why he wished to make his family proud of him, he responded as follows:

> Well, maybe your parents will give you something to do. If you win, like, the good citizenship award in your room. I got it in third grade—good citizenship. But not this year—I came so close, but it's hard to do.
>
> *Was your family proud then?*
> Yeah. They give you something. Most of the time they give me something.

This focus on the material rewards that derive from particular roles is a common characteristic of Level 2. Bob not only used Level 2 value criteria but he also seemed to reject those characteristic of Level 3. When the interviewer asked him about working hard to get ahead, Bob explained his own lack of interest in personal distinction by reference to his father:

> My father works hard but he isn't trying to get ahead in life; he's just trying to make a living.
>
> *What does trying to get ahead mean?*
> To beat the others. To get more money.

As this passage suggests, Bob had a great deal of respect and admiration for his father and he desired to be like him. When he was asked about his, Bob responded,

> Yeah, I guess I would take after my father.
>
> *Like how?*
> Be a lawyer.
>
> *Any other ways?*
> Most likely when I'm thirteen, I'll be a meat salesman like my father was as a teenager. Well, he would go to the market and they would give him the meat to sell to the people. In Los Angeles. He was born there. He sold meat to get money to go to law school.

When Bob Eagleton was interviewed as a 14-year-old, his determination to become a lawyer had become stronger. Becoming a lawyer had also acquired new meaning for Bob, who had begun to elaborate Level 3 conceptions of the ego-ideal. He now viewed the role of lawyer as an opportunity to become a full member of his family, through carrying on a tradition:

> *Why do you want to be a lawyer?*
> My father's one and I just would like to be a lawyer.
>
> *Why?*
> Well, mainly I guess because of all the lawyers in my family . . . . Everybody's been a lawyer, so I guess I would like to be one, too.

Not only did Bob desire this for himself, but his mother had similar aspirations for him. In her sort of the Be-Like items in terms of what she hoped her son would be like, Mrs. Eagleton rated highest the role of Someone with a Job Like Your Husband's. Both parents had a clear vision of what Bob's life would be like and wished to guide him in that direction.

When interviewed at age 22, Bob was still committed to a career in law. In response to questions about his future career, Bob replied as follows:

> *What are you majoring in there?*
> I'm majoring in sociology—pre-law.
>
> *So you are primarily interested in going to law school?*
> Yes.

Do you have any idea where you want to go?
Yes, possibly Yale.

Where did your father go to law school?
Yale

That both Bob Eagleton and Frank Jones decided to pursue the career of their father is not simply a coincidence but is, instead, a consequence of the deep emotional bonds both boys felt to their family. Since his last interview at age 14, Bob's parents had divorced and his mother had moved to Europe. Bob believed the divorce had a tremendous influence on his life. In particular, he felt that his relationship to his father had changed:

> I never brought any problems to my dad [before the divorce]. It was always my mother . . . . We always, all our emotions always went out to our mother. My father was busy all the time, and he was always the cruel, harsh father, but you know, but he, there has been an amazing switch ever since the divorce. He's a lot more liberal.

The improvement in his relationship with his father did not, however, free Bob from the commitment to become a lawyer. Indeed, his father's growing emotional dependence on him prohibited any other career focus:

> My dad lets me bear my own responsibilities. He still yells once in a while, and I think he would be greatly upset if I didn't become a lawyer. I've always wanted to become one and it just so happens that I'm interested in it anyway, but I've always wondered what if I decided not be become one at this stage, what would happen. He would go through the roof, psychological trauma or something, because—I think he is just living for me to become a lawyer now.

> *Why is that?*
> I suggest it once in a while. Well, maybe my aptitude isn't for law. Maybe I should take an aptitude test. He says no, no, you want to become a lawyer. Very affirmative.

Although Bob claims some ambivalence about a career in law, his grades over the next few years did not evidence it; he distinguished himself by graduating at the top of his class.

As Bob entered his mid-twenties, he began to articulate Level 4 ego-ideal conceptions. He discussed his feelings about making money and the relationship of money to his personal goals and values:

> The thing is, even with a family, you are still not going to be hurting, really. The average fee is thirty-five thousand dollars in this country now [1970], the average lawyer is making; you can live on fifteen or twenty thousand dollars. Sure, you maybe can't make four trips to Europe a year or something, but that is not everything in life; it all depends, like I say, what is your meaning in life, to accrue a fortune? Basically, that was what my father's goal in life was, I swear to God it was, and I think maybe that is why I have been turned off about it; maybe that is one reason why I don't worry about it either . . . . I have seen it, you know. How money can ruin a man, and, really, he never spent any time with the family; he was always in the office.

Bob was particularly interested in working with people who were poor, people who did not have his social advantages:

> What I hope to do is, I am going to try and incorporate a couple of things, and I want to be in academia, too; I love to teach. And I will hook up with a law school somewhere and just teach a couple of classes, just clinical law; I love to teach. I'd love to have a practice, too. I am going to have one or two days where I work in the ghetto, a five- or six-day workweek and take two days out and just devote it to these people.

Bob's aspirations, although noble, sounded naively idealistic. When the interviewer challenged these goals, Bob acknowledged that there was considerable social pressure, particularly from his family, to retreat from idealism:

> *What happens when you get married and have the house payments and the babies and you lose this idealism?*
> . . . That is what I was telling you, you know, you've got to do this and your wife says, "Aw gee"; it's amazing, some of the guys are very idealistic, but talk to their wives. One wife said, "Skip will be out in four years, and then I will be able to move into a two hundred thousand dollar house." I look in sheer disbelief that Skip would go along . . . Skip has no desire to go out into practice, none.

It was Bob's goal, if he married at all, to find a woman who would nurture his strivings to integrate his concerns for the poor with his life's work as a lawyer.

Did Bob's values, evident in his age-26 interview, shape his life over the succeeding years? Or did he regress to Level 3 ego-ideal criteria, as did many of the men in the study from the higher social classes? The answer is not simple. His full entry into the world of work by age 30 resulted in a life in which he was less concerned with saving the poor than he had been 4 years earlier. His vision of himself simultaneously running a law firm 4 days a week, practicing law in the ghetto 2 days a week, and teaching at a law school had yielded to the more modest reality of practicing law. Bob's marriage had also effected change in him. At age 26 he was concerned that women might exert a corrupting influence on their idealistic spouses; 4 years later, in the context of his own relationship, he was aware that the challenge of marriage is not in steadfastly maintaining personal goals but in achieving openness to negotiation and collaboration:

> *When you have discussions, what do you do to try and make them go well?*
> I try and view it from her perspective and I really do. At times I apologize and I'm wrong and that is all there is to it, and other times I will tactfully take her position, though I am reluctant and I can see that there is no right or wrong, it is just one way or the other.

Thus, at age 30 there was a softening of the idealistic principles Bob had held for himself at age 26; although this softening process did not result in a relativistic or dialectical perspective (discussed in Chapter 1 in connection with Kohlberg's theory), it was in the direction of it.

Although Bob's life was less idealistic at age 30 than he had hoped at age 26 that it would be, he retained the Level 4 concern for fidelity to personal values and responsibility to others that characterized him at the previous interview. He manifested these values in his daily interactions with clients:

> It is very interesting, I am dealing with clients as a personal philosophy. I tend to go in with a very positive attitude and I tend to be very open, I tend to be very warm, and these are not just qualities that I perceive but that everyone has perceived about me. I tend to be very personable and I am convinced that the best way

to attain a person's trust is to have these attributes and to take time and spend an extra five or ten minutes with a client. And once you have won their trust, you have won their respect most of the time, too . . . it makes it a lot easier to deal with clients and explain things and they come to accept your opinion. I am often a consultant rather than a lawyer handling the case, and the client will often tell me later, "You are the first lawyer who has ever actually spoken to me like a human being and a friend, and I will trust you and take your word now." My clients are very, very loyal, they are very trusting, and they believe me.

Bob attempted to fashion the same sort of relationship with his friends and family. When he was asked about the importance of friendship, he responded as follows:

This is something I value and trust. I think that [a good friend] is one of the most important things you can be in life, to be someone that people can turn to and trust and if you let them down you are not being honest with them and for me, it is all aspects of my life, professionally or anything, to befriend everyone.

Contrasts Between Two Lives

The lives of Frank Jones and Bob Eagleton have followed similar paths in many respects. Both men were from upper-middle-class families, met with academic success from grade school into professional school, and were popular as boys. As 10-year-olds, the two aspired to the careers they would eventually enter as adults. This stability in a specific occupational desire from childhood into adulthood is quite striking. It is clear that the impressive accuracy with which these two subjects predicted their future occupation is not a consequence of an unusually precocious awareness of their talents during childhood but is attributable to their deep emotional bonds to their fathers. Both Frank Jones and Bob Eagleton entered their father's occupation and received explicit encouragement to do so from their families across the adolescent years. Both men were successful in their careers and, at the point at which the study ended, were married. These two cases are powerful examples of the continuity that can exist from childhood through early adulthood.

Despite their commonalities, however, Frank Jones and Bob Eagleton differed during adulthood in terms of their ego-ideal development. Frank Jones is typical of the men in the study, reaching Level 3 during late adolescence and remaining at that level during early adulthood. The centrality of Level 3 value criteria in Frank's life is reflected in his emphasis on differentiation from others through success: "I want to get recognition, all the pluses . . . . My job is the majority of my life." Frank's concentration on achievement paid off: he was a very successful architect, and his rise in the firm had been remarkable. As Frank noted in his last interview, his meteoric success had been at some expense to his family. Nonetheless, he found his life generally meaningful, and in the context of Level 3 ego-ideal value criteria he judged himself to be a success.

Bob Eagleton's life followed a different course of ego-ideal development. During the transition from adolescence into adulthood, Bob's value criteria evolved to include concern with personal fidelity and responsibility to others, characteristics of Level 4. In their preliminary forms these value criteria sounded unrealistic: Bob wanted to find a selfless wife, teach law school, run a law firm, and volunteer his services to the poor. To his credit, however, Bob was partly aware of the unrealistic nature of his goals. He also sensed that there would be considerable pressure on him to give up his Level 4 criteria and retreat to Level 3 concerns of integration and differentiation. It seems that he achieved an equilibrium of sorts by age 30: the shape of his life by then was more conventional than he had envisioned during his mid-twenties, yet he was able to remain true to his personal values concerning the treatment of others and to derive great satisfaction in the context of his commitments and responsibilities to others.

The lives of these two men are significantly different, I believe. Yet without an account of ego-ideal development, this difference could not be specified; this is because along other dimensions (such as background, education, childhood popularity, and even moral judgment—both men's reasoning was predominantly at Stage 4) the two men are essentially identical. In fact, given the many commonalities of their lives, it is difficult to argue that Bob Eagleton's use of Level 4 ego-ideal criteria made him more successful in a conventional sense. My deep respect for the life of Frank Jones prohibits a claim that Level 4 ego-ideal reasoning is logically or universally better; it develops later and is particularly susceptible to abandonment upon entrance into the world of work, but perhaps the judgment of better or worse in this case cannot be made on the basis of psychological findings alone.

CONCLUSION

In this chapter I have described the predictable, age-related changes in the evaluative criteria composing the ego-ideal. As children, the subjects in the study valued occupations and social relationships for their potential for immediate excitement or advantage of some sort. This orientation of the ego-ideal declined steadily between the ages of 10 and 24, at which point it totally disappeared. For the adolescent the dominant motif for the ego-ideal was integration into and differentiation from the surrounding social context. Adolescents who were most advanced in ego-ideal reasoning were more likely than their peers to attend college and graduate school in early adulthood; developmental lags in the ego-ideal were associated with juvenile delinquency. Although the Level 3 themes of integration and differentiation remained the most common ones in even the older age groups, some men in this sample became more concerned, beginning at age 24, about their responsibilities toward themselves and toward their society. Interestingly, this orientation waned, with average ego-ideal levels declining through the late twenties and early thirties, with some evidence for a reemergence of Level 4 themes among 36-year-old men.

What gives rise to the developmental patterns presented in this chapter? It is clear that the passage of time is not sufficient for development to occur; many of the juvenile delinquents had not achieved age-typical Level 3 and not all men in the study reached Level 4. Unfortunately, a definitive description of the sources of ego-ideal development cannot be offered at this point. It seems likely, however, that the meaning boys and men perceive in their lives is influenced by those with whom they live and work. Ego-ideal development in both Frank Jones and Bob Eagleton seems to have an important connection to their relationship with their father (this issue is taken up in Chapter 5 and 6). Similarly, the negative correlation between ALEI scores and social status during early adulthood means that the desirable professional jobs may demand that men abandon, at least temporarily, their concerns for society and their personal values. But these associations provide only the vaguest answer to an important question that must await future research.

Although the research presented here does not address every issue or answer every question, it does have several important implications. One is that the developmental patterns of the ego-ideal traced in this chapter demonstrate that early adulthood in men can be a period of considerable change and, consequently, a topic of interest to psychologists, despite a tendency among many researchers to describe it in unfavorable terms. A common theme of current conceptions of early adulthood is that the young man in his late twenties and thirties becomes narrowly focused on success and social integration. In his insightful study of adult development, Vaillant (1977) describes the task of this era as one of "career consolidation." As a consequence, men in this age are characteristically "materialistic," "dull," and "crass" (pp. 218–219). Not until they become older, Vaillant claims, do men separate themselves from the tyranny of their need to find a distinguished niche in society. This same claim is echoed by Levinson (1978), who writes that prior to age 40 a man has two central tasks: "(a) He tries to establish a niche in society: to anchor his life more firmly . . . . [and] (b) he works at making it: striving to advance, to progress on a timetable" (p. 59). The developmental pattern traced in this study provides support for these claims. It is true that many men in this study, during their twenties and thirties, explained their occupational and social role aspirations in terms of their desire to "fit in" or to "succeed." Furthermore, only among the men leaving this time period, the 36-year-olds, was there a systematic relationship between their moral stage and ego-ideal criteria.

But it is important to qualify the broad generalizations about this era in the life cycle in light of the findings in this chapter: there are a significant number of men in their twenties and thirties who consider their career and role aspirations as reflections of their responsibilities to personal values and to society. Even if these men lack the wisdom that characterizes generativity, their idealistic concerns for fidelity to personal values and responsibility to others warrant recognition as observed traits of men in young adulthood besides those of narrowness, crassness, or materialism.

A second implication, and a theme that is developed in this book, is that development in men consists of partially independent systems, each following its own developmental trajectory. In Chapter 3 it was shown that the roles that men aspire to have considerable stability from early adolescence well into early adulthood. That pattern of findings, I noted, is consonant with much of the research literature using vocational interest and personality inventories. A consideration of only the findings in Chapter 3 suggests that personality is essentially formed by early adolescence, with little significant change occurring in later developmental periods.

In contrast to the ideal self, as presented in Chapter 3, the ego-ideal undergoes considerable development in late adolescence and early adulthood. This means that the goals of becoming a lawyer, doctor, or good father may remain stable from ages 13 to 20 but the meanings men infuse them with change systematically. Many researchers may be tempted to dismiss the transformations in men's understanding of their lives as mere epiphenomena and argue that the study of development should focus instead on the more tangible stabilities evident in men's occupations, relationships, and beliefs. Such a strategy would be a mistake. The ego-ideal developmental scheme presented here allows predictions from adolescence to adulthood of such characteristics as educational attainment and social class, variables that are of interest to most personologists. Further, the ego-ideal levels provide a powerful framework for understanding the lives of men such as Frank Jones and Bob Eagleton.

Conceptually and empirically distinguished between personality systems can also provide a resolution to the debate about continuity and stability in early adulthood. The results presented in this chapter, particularly those concerning a return to Level 3 ego-ideal criteria among men in their late twenties and early thirties, are consonant with studies by Gilligan and Murphy (1979), Jessor (1983), and Levinson (1978). These investigations report that this era is one in which there is a growing concern with the context of life, a return to conventional values, and a disequilibrium in one's understanding of one's commitments and choices. If these changes are viewed as changes in one facet of the life course, rather than in the whole of it, they become reconcilable with findings of stability. Men's lives offer both continuity and change, and our accounts ought to recognize them both.

NOTES

1. Freud later merged the concept of the ego-ideal and its ideal standards with the punitive irrational superego. Currently, theorists generally believe that the fusion of the superego and the ego ideal was unfortunate because it does not fully acknowledge the distinctive qualities of the latter (Sandler, Holder, & Meers, 1963, p. 148).
2. The coding manual for assessing ego-ideal developmental level from an interview is available upon request.
3. Further confirmation of this trend is obtained by calculating n (the correlation ratio): the value of n for ALEI scores and age groups is .67. The degree of nonlinearity in the relationship between ALEI and age group can be

calculated as $n (.67)^2 - r (.52)^2 = .15$. This value confirms the existence of a nonlinear trend in the data.

4. As noted in Chapters 2 and 3, the changes in these men occur during the late 1960s and early 1970s, a historical context exerting its own unique influences. One might speculate that the apparent regression observed in some of the men is a reflection of the broad disillusionment with American society shared by many young adults, particularly well-educated ones, at the time.

CHAPTER 5

Moral Judgment Development in the Context of the Family

Moral judgment and its development were the research issues that led to the longitudinal study of men that has been explored in this book. In Chapter 1 the findings of Kohlberg and his collaborators concerning moral judgment and its transformations over time were described and evaluated. In brief, the contribution of this line of research to an understanding of development has been enormous.

The purpose of this chapter is to consider the development of moral judgment in one social context, the family. Research on the process of moral judgment development has consistently focused on its cognitive prerequisites or its facilitation through peer interaction (see reviews by Maccoby, 1980, and Rest, 1983). The interest in the cognitive precursors to moral judgment development derives from Kohlberg's (1976) claims that specific logical abilities are necessary, but not sufficient, for the attainment of different stages of moral judgment development. The peer interaction research follows the lead of Piaget (1932/1965) in hypothesizing that it is because interactions with one's age-mates are characterized by mutuality and equality that such relationships foster the process of construction and reconstruction of moral principles that constitutes development (e.g., Damon, 1983). Beyond their theoretical relevance, cognitive precursor and peer interaction studies are attractive to researchers following Kohlberg and Piaget within the structural-developmental paradigm because they offer clear evidence that development is not directly due to adult influence. This proof is especially desirable because the two major alternative paradigms propose adult-mediated mechanisms for moral judgment development *socialization of emotions,* by which the natural tendencies to experience empathy and guilt are sculpted by adult caregivers to yield moral character, and *identification*, resulting in similarity between child and parent. Through cognitive precursor and peer interaction research, then, constructivist researchers have provided convincing evidence for the mechanisms of development proposed in their theories.

There is no necessary reason, however, why the constructivist theory of moral judgment development must be counterposed to socialization and identification theories. As Gibbs and Schnell (1985) make clear, it is possible for different accounts to meaningfully complement each other. The value of complementarity among the various theories of moral development is that it does not, of necessity, limit the empirical examination of sources of development. Thus, one can entertain the possibility that developmental processes postulated within the socialization and identification paradigms are also relevant for an understanding of moral judgment growth. Indeed, it is difficult to imagine that parents, as the adult models with whom children are most familiar, serve no role in the development of morality (Hoffman, 1971). The process of moral development would also seem to involve some elements of moral sentiment and character (Saltzstein, 1976). The introduction of personality factors and parental influences as determinants of structural development might result in a more powerful explanation of change than is possible with peer interaction alone. To my knowledge, however, such an integrative approach has not been attempted in empirical research.

The research presented here is one demonstration of how the socialization and identification paradigms might contribute to an understanding of observed patterns of moral judgment development without distorting the theoretical system undergirding Kohlberg's constructivist approach (Colby *et al.*, 1983; Kohlberg, 1984). As noted earlier, the development of moral reasoning proceeds through five stages, with each higher stage more adequate than the previous one. Because of the nature of the sample in this study (males between the ages of 10 and 30) only Stages 2, 3, and 4 in Kohlberg's system need to be discussed here. At Stage 2 moral behavior is defined as action that serves to advance one's own interests while allowing others to do the same. At Stage 3, what is right or just is behavior that ensures that important others continue to judge the individual as "good." Finally, at Stage 4, moral judgment is concerned with maintaining society and enabling the "imperative of conscience to meet one's defined obligations" (Kohlberg, 1987, p. 285).

How can socialization and identification theories contribute to an explanation of movement through these stages? The products of socialization and identification—conscience and the emulation of parental standards—serve to motivate the individual's search for appropriate moral principles with which to guide behavior in conflictful social interactions. Consider first the motivating role of conscience. Socialization theory, as presented in its most sophisticated version by Hoffman (1976, 1982), posits that infants are born with social emotions, such as empathy, that are precursors to conscience. The child's natural tendency to experience vicariously the emotions of others is encouraged by parental rearing practices that sharpen the child's awareness of the distress of another; and by pointing to the child's role in producing the other's distress, parents encourage the emergence of a sense of guilt in their child. It is the tendency to experience guilt that is the basis for what is commonly referred to as conscience. Those who experience guilt most strongly are most likely to act morally, Hoffman argues. Finally, he suggests that differences in conscience strength, as measured during adolescence by teacher and parental reports, can be traced, in part, to the parenting styles exercised by parents (Hoffman, 1982; Hoffman & Saltzstein, 1967).

Guilt or conscience strength is hypothesized to be related to moral judgment development. There is likely to be relatively little relationship between conscience strength, as described by Hoffman, and development into Kohlberg's Stage 2. This is because the moral principle the child constructs at Stage 2 allows him to consider only the self's interests as long as others are permitted to do the same. As a consequence, the child's guilt is irrelevant to developing the moral rule of Stage 2. Conscience strength begins to play a role in the transition from Stage 2 to Stage 3, which occurs in adolescence. The moral principle to be constructed at Stage 3 attempts to balance the concerns and feelings of self and others in ways that preserve the group's esteem for the self. Those who experience guilt most readily and are high in conscience strength will construct this rule earlier than others because they are likely to experience emotional disturbance at causing distress in others, which serves to sensitize them to the limitations of Stage 2 and the strengths of Stage 3 moral principles. It is in the transition from Stage 3 to Stage 4 (usually during early adulthood), however, that conscience strength is likely to play its biggest role. To achieve Stage 4 reasoning, the individual must find inadequate as the criterion of morality the socially defined " goodness" or acceptance characteristic of Stage 3. The individual who feels guilty for contributing to the injury of another even though peers and adults endorse that action (e.g., the young adult who feels troubled by his anti-Semitic conversations, even though his family and friends encourage such thoughts) is likely to search earlier for a new moral principle and with more fervor than others of the same age who experience little guilt. Thus, the degree of conscience strength developed in childhood and adolescence is hypothesized to influence the progress of development through the moral judgment stages in adolescence and adulthood. Empirically, then, one might expect little correlation between childhood and adolescent measures of conscience strength and childhood and adolescent assessments of moral judgment. However, there should be a meaningful association between childhood and adolescent conscience strength, and the developmental level of moral judgment achieved in early adulthood.

Identification has been used by developmental theorists to refer to a variety of features: the child's emotional dependency on the parents, similarity to the same-sex parent, vicarious self-esteem deriving from the parents' achievements, and conformity to parental expectations, to name the most common (see Kohlberg, 1969, for a synthesis of different definitions).[1] Kohlberg (1984) proposed that identification is the product of the child's continual striving to achieve competence by assimilating the behaviors of models that are similar to the self. For instance, boys are likely to imitate their fathers because fathers are males (similar to the self) and have a variety of capabilities (thus making them models worthy of emulation). It follows that fathers who are involved in their sons' lives and who model a wide variety of competent actions will be identified with strongly. The result of continued imitation is that the child and adolescent develop a sense of mutuality joining self and other that is the basis for an emotional bond. Through close attention to the behavior of the adults with whom he identifies, particularly the father, the child discerns the moral rules that restrain even their behavior (Hart, Kohlberg, & Wertsch, 1987a). Because these moral rules are especially salient in the competent father, they form an ideal toward which the child strives. For this reason, then, paternal involvement and identification are predicted to foster development out of the egoism of Stage 2 into the stereotypical good citizen of Stage 3 and the societally oriented individual of Stage 4. Measures of maternal involvement and identification should be less related to moral judgment development in sons because of the dissimilarity between son and mother should prohibit a strong identification relationship from emerging.

The hypothesized relationships among structural development in moral judgment, socialization, and identification are similar to those proposed by Maccoby (1980, p. 343) and Hoffman (1982, pp. 99–103). Although Kohlberg never clearly articulated on a theoretical level the types of interactions that might occur among the different sources of development (Gibbs & Schnell, 1985), there is little reason to think that he believed that such interactions were implausible. As discussed in Chapter 2, the numbers of subjects for some of the following analyses are rather small. However, the high quality of the moral judgment data and the longitudinal design of the study permit many facets of these issues to be addressed.

LONGITUDINAL ANALYSES

Method

Sample

This study's sample is composed of the subjects from the two youngest cohorts in the longitudinal study who remained in the study at the second testing time (Time 2). The sample is restricted in this way because the socialization and personality measures of interest were administered only at Time 2 and only to the subjects in the two youngest age cohorts, their teachers, and their parents. At Time 2 the two age cohorts were formed by twenty-one 14-year-olds and by seventeen 17-year-olds.

Procedure

Moral Judgment. Subjects in this study responded to the Moral Judgment Interview (MJI) at 3- to 4-year intervals over 20 years (Time 1 to Time 6). Because all subjects were not interviewed at each time, the actual composition of the sample differs slightly from one testing session to the next. Previous analyses have indicated no effects of attrition, however, as noted in preceding chapters. In the analyses reported in this study, moral judgment scores from the six age groups are considered in relation to the socialization and identification measures administered at Time 2.

Responses to the MJI were coded according to the *Standard Issue Scoring Manual* (Colby *et al.*, 1987). All interviews were coded blind by coders who were unaware of subjects' ages, scores on interviews at other testing times, and ratings by parents and teachers. The index of overall performance on the MJI used in this study is the Moral Maturity Score (MMS), essentially an average of the different stage scores on the MJI. The minimum possible score is 100, representing an MJI in which only Stage 1 is evident, and the maximum score is 500, corresponding to the exclusive use of Stage 5 in response to the MJI. Because the analyses of the moral judgment data have been presented elsewhere (Colby *et al.*, 1983), these data are only considered here in relation to the socialization and identification measures.

Teacher Ratings. At Time 2 homeroom teachers of the subjects were asked to rate them along five polar personality scales: (1) trustworthiness, (2) fair-mindedness, (3) effort, (4) obedience, and (5) peer independence. For each scale, capsule descriptions of the five different points on the scale were provided. For instance, the highest score on the trustworthiness scale would be received by a student who "can always be depended on to do whatever he knows is right regardless of what he wants to do at the moment," and a student who "is always trying to get away with something" would receive the lowest score.

Parental Questionnaires. Also at Time 2 each parent was asked to complete a questionnaire. Eighteen mothers and thirteen fathers did so. Three of the questions on the questionnaire were designed to assess the parent's perception of his or her involvement with and affection toward the son:

> When your child was small, did you ever find time to play with him for your own pleasure? Choose one answer: not very often; sometimes; fairly often; almost every day; and every day, if possible, and usually for fairly long periods.

> How about now? Do you spend much time doing things with him or does he do things on his own or with his friends? Choose one answer: Do things seldom; sometimes; every week or two spend part of an evening or day with him; spend an evening or day together at least once a week; often spend a day together; go on frequent trips together; spend most of our leisure time together.

> Some people believe in showing lots of affection, and some believe in being more reserved. How have you and your child been in this regard, particularly when he was younger? Choose one answer: Quite restrained; refrain from showing much affection; affectionate but restrained; very affectionate.

Items were summed so that a high score corresponds to high levels of involvement and affection.

Each parent was also asked three questions about the strength of his or her son's conscience:

> To what extent is your child guided and controlled by his conscience? Choose one answer: Untrustworthy—is always trying to get away with something; unreliable—can only be depended on to follow rules if someone is around to check up; conforming— follows rules mostly in order to keep out of trouble or to win approval; reliable—usually does what's right even with no one around to check up on him; completely trustworthy—can always be depended on to do what he knows is right, regardless of what he wants at the moment.

> When your child has done something wrong (something he knows you don't want him to do) at a time when your are not there to see it, how does he act with you? Choose one answer: Tries to hide it from me and denies it if I ask him; doesn't mention it but usually admits it if I ask; sometimes mentions it to me and usually admits it if I ask; usually mentions it to me; always tells me about it.

> How does he feel when he has done something wrong? Choose one answer: Doesn't seem to feel bad; feels somewhat sheepish; feels bad, really wants to fix things up; feels miserable, really needs to be forgiven.

Ratings on these items were summed to form each parent's estimate of the strength of the son's conscience. Finally, each parent was asked to estimate the degree to which the subject resembled the parent as well as the spouse:

> To what extent does your child take after you (your spouse)? Choose one answer: Not like me; like me in some small things (some ways or mannerisms of mine) but different in most ways; like me in some small things and in some important things; like me in a number of important things, in important attitudes, and character; very much like me.

The sum of the parents' ratings for the similarity of their son to each parent was used as an index of parent-judged maternal and paternal identification.

To briefly summarize the design, moral judgment data were collected on the subjects at six different times, separated by 3 to 4 years. The two cohorts of subjects were combined to form six age groups, ranging in age from 10 to 30. Various assessments of conscience strength, parental identification, and parental involvement during adolescence were collected at the second testing time. It is possible, then, to examine the relationships of these socialization and identification scores to moral judgment at earlier ages, the current age, and at older ages.

Results

Age Trends in Moral Judgment

It is possible to infer the developmental tasks faced by the boys and men in this study by considering the average MMS for each age group: age 10, 188; ages 13–14, 245; ages 17–18, 308; ages 20–22, 330; ages 24–26, 357; and ages 28–30, 378. Thus, as a group, the 10-year-olds are relinquishing the last vestiges of Stage 1 in favor of Stage 2 reasoning, while the 13- and 14-year-olds are in transition from Stage 2 to Stage 3. Both hypotheses considered in this chapter predict relationships for transitions from Stage 2 to 3 and from Stage 3 to 4, but not from Stage 1 to 2. This means that there should be more relationships between the socialization and identification factors and moral judgment for the adolescent and adulthood ages.

Conscience and Moral Judgment Development

The results provide substantial evidence for an interaction between the strength of the adolescent's conscience, as estimated by both the teacher and parents, and moral judgment development. Correlations among the five teacher rating scales were first calculated in order to determine if it was possible to increase the reliability of the teachers' evaluations by combining scores. These correlations are presented in Table 5.1. The correlations presented in Table 5.1 indicate that

TABLE 5.1.
Intercorrelations among Teacher Rating Scales (n = 38)

	Trustworthiness	Fair-mindedness	Effort	Obedience
Trustworthiness				
Fair-mindedness	.71*			
Effort	.69*	.70*		
Obedience	.59*	.68*	.65*	
Peer independence	.24	.34*	.47*	.28

*$p < .05$.

the five scales were all interrelated. An index of conscience strength was formed by summing the teacher's ratings.[2]

Teachers' estimations of the subjects' conscience strength were independent of the subjects' intelligence as measured by IQ tests. The correlation between IQ and conscience strength scores was a nonsignificant .22. This suggests that teachers' estimations of conscience strength were not mere reflections of the subjects' general intelligence.

Correlations between the teachers' ratings of conscience strength and MMS at different ages, for each cohort taken separately and for the entire sample, are presented in Table 5.2. For Cohort 1, the teachers' assessment occurred when subjects were 14 years old. As can be seen from Table 5.2, the correlation between teacher's ratings of conscience strength and subjects' moral judgment development at that same measurement point was not significant ($r = .39$). Similarly, moral judgment maturity at age 10, the preceding measurement point, was not significantly associated with teachers' ratings at age 14 ($r = .34$). Teacher ratings at age 14 are statistically significant predictors, however, of adult moral judgment at ages 24 and 28. The same general pattern of findings appears for subjects in Cohort 2 (i.e., subjects who were 17 years old at the time of the teacher assessment), although the smaller number of subjects in this group may prevent the correlations from reaching conventional levels of significance.

To increase statistical power, the two cohorts can be combined and the teacher ratings can be considered as teacher ratings of adolescents 14–17 years of age. One rationale for collapsing the two cohorts on this index is that the teacher ratings appear to assess a personality, rather than a developmental, dimension. A comparison of the teacher ratings for the two cohorts revealed no significant difference ($t[36] = 1.01$). With this increased statistical power, a significant association emerges

TABLE 5.2.
Correlations between Teachers' Ratings
of Strength of Conscience and MMS at Different Ages

Subject	Age					
	10	13–14	17–18	20–22	24–26	28–30
Cohort 1	.34(20)	.39(20)	.32(14)	.33(17)	.57(12)*	.69(10)*
Cohort 2		.26(14)	.32(14)	.75(5)	.53(10)	.43(12)
Sample	.34(20)	.30(34)	.27(28)	.41(22)*	.52(22)*	.46(22)*

Note. Values for *n* are in parentheses. Cohort 1 was composed of 14-year-olds when rated by their teachers; Cohort 2 was composed of 17-year-olds when rated by their teachers.
*$p < .05$, one tailed.

between the teacher's ratings of the adolescent and the adolescent's MMS at that time (both assessments occur at Time 2); the correlation is $r = .40$, $p < .05$, which indicates that teacher's ratings of conscience strength reflect in part the adolescent's moral judgment maturity. The increase in sample size also reveals significant relationships between teachers' ratings of adolescents' conscience strength and all three measurement points in adulthood considered in this study.

One question raised by this pattern of findings is whether the relationship between conscience strength ratings in adolescence and adulthood moral judgment reflects only the ordering stability (positive, moderately high intercorrelations) in moral judgment scores over this time period (for one example of this pattern of results, see Colby et al., 1983). To examine this possibility, partial correlations were calculated between the conscience strength ratings and MMS at the three adult ages (20–22, 24–26, 28–30), controlling for MMS at Time 2. These partial correlations are $r = .29$, n.s.; $r = .38$, $p < .05$ (one-tailed); and $r = .47$, $p < .05$ (one-tailed) for the three age groups, respectively. The partial correlations indicate that conscience strength, as rated by the teachers, makes its own unique contribution to the prediction of adult moral judgment.

A similar pattern of results emerges from a consideration of the correlations between parents' ratings of their sons' consciences. The intercorrelations among the three items for the mothers' questionnaires were $r = .14$, n.s.; $r = .30$, n.s.; and $r = .57$, $p < .05$. For the fathers' questionnaires, the intercorrelations among the conscience strength items were $r = .31$, n.s.; $r = .04$, n.s.; and $r = .04$, n.s. The generally low intercorrelations among these items are difficult to interpret but may indicate that the three items on the questionnaire tap slightly different aspects of conscience strength, at least as judged by the parents. Nonetheless, because all three items clearly ask for estimations of conscience strength, ratings on the items were summed.

The relatively small number of parents who completed the questionnaires prohibits the separate consideration of each cohort; nonetheless, a relatively consistent pattern of results emerges. As Table 5.3 reveals, mothers' and fathers' estimations predict their sons' moral maturity during adulthood and also relate to moral judgment development during adolescence. Mothers' estimations of conscience strength are clearly better predictors of moral judgment development than are fathers'; four of six correlations are significant for the mothers' estimations, but only one of six for those of the fathers. It is noteworthy that the estimations of conscience strength by mothers and

TABLE 5.3.
Correlations between Parents' Ratings
of Adolescent Conscience and MMS at Different Ages

Parental rating	Age					
	10	13–14	17–18	20–22	24–26	28–30
Mother's rating	.21(8)	.50(17)*	.51(15)*	.20(11)	.76(12)*	.64(12)*
Father's rating	.51(9)	.28(13)	.56(10)	.51(10)	.71(10)*	−.10(7)

Note. Values for n are in parentheses.
*$p < .05$, one tailed.

teachers are significantly correlated ($r = .57$, $p < .05$), but the fathers' judgments are not related to those of the teachers ($r = .39$, n.s.). Moreover, mothers' ratings (but not fathers'), like those of the teachers, are related to MMS measured at Time 2 ($r = .71$, $p < .001$). Partial correlations between mothers' ratings of conscience and adult MMS, controlling for Time 2 MMS, again confirm the unique contribution of conscience ratings to the prediction of adult moral judgment scores: $r = -.16$, n.s.; $r = .62$, $p < .05$ (one-tailed), and $r = .81$, $p < .001$ (one-tailed), for the age groups 20–22, 24–26, and 28–30, respectively. The corresponding partial correlations, controlling for Time 2 MMS, for the fathers' ratings and MMS scores were $r = .39$, n.s.; $r = .61$, $p < .05$ (one-tailed); and $r = -.16$, n.s. Together, these findings indicate that adolescents who are rated by their teachers and parents as high in conscience strength are likely to exhibit the most advanced moral judgment in early adulthood. In addition, the correlations are generally higher for the age groups of 24–26 and 28–30. This suggests that conscience strength serves to promote moral judgment development into adulthood.

Identification and Moral Judgment Development

The analyses of the identification measures confirm the importance of the boy's relationship to the father for moral judgment development. Parents were asked to judge the similarity of their son to themselves and to their spouse; if the father judged that his son was similar to himself and the mother judged that the son was similar to her husband, the boy received a high rating for paternal identification as judged by the parents. Neither the paternal nor the maternal identification score was related to the son's MMS at Time 2 (when paternal and maternal identification were measured). However, the correlations between parent-rated paternal and maternal identification and MMS at the different ages suggest that identification may be a predictor of childhood and adulthood moral judgment.

The pattern of findings in Table 5.4 suggests that identification with the father, but not with the mother, is associated with higher levels of moral judgment development even into adulthood. Controlling for MMS at Time 2 confirms that paternal identification makes its own unique contribution to the prediction of moral judgment development at ages 13–14 and 28–30, with correlations between parental identification and MMS of $r = -.73$, $p < .05$ (one-tailed), and $r = .87$, $p < .05$ (one-tailed), respectively.

Parental Involvement and Moral Judgment Development

A second source of confirmation for the importance of the father's role in fostering moral judgment development emerges from a consideration of parental reports of involvement and affection with their sons. As described earlier, each parent responded to three items requiring a rating of the degree to which he or she participated in joint activities with the son and was affectionate toward him. The intercorrelations among the mothers' ratings on the three items were $r = .60$, $p < .01$; $r = -.01$, n.s.; and $r = -.03$, n.s. The corresponding intercorrelations for the fathers' ratings were $r = .52$, $p < .07$; $r = .60$, $p < .05$; and $r = .74$, $p < .01$. These correlations generally indicate that the different items are tapping the same domain, although this domain may be more differentiated for the mothers, an interpretation suggested by the lack of correlation between several items. As reported earlier, the ratings on each questionnaire were summed to form one measure of affection and involvement for each parent.

The correlations between the mothers' and fathers' scores on this measure and their son's moral maturity at different ages are pre-

TABLE 5.4.
*Correlations between Paternal and Maternal Identification
as Judged by Parents and MMS at Different Ages*

Identification	Age					
	10	13–14	17–18	20–22	24–26	28–30
With father	.39(7)	.61(13)*	.34(10)	.05(9)	.47(10)	.87(8)*
With mother	.26(8)	.18(14)	−.08(11)	−.37(10)	.08(11)	−.18(9)

Note. Values for n are in parentheses.
*$p < .05$, one tailed.

sented in the first two rows of Table 5.5, in which the two age groups are combined.

An inspection of Table 5.5 makes clear that it is the degree of involvement with the father that has importance for moral judgment development from childhood through early adulthood. The pattern of correlations indicates that subjects whose fathers reported more involvement and affection are at higher levels of moral judgment from childhood through early adulthood. Mothers' degree of involvement with and affection toward their son was unrelated to moral judgment development. This finding is not the result of a ceiling effect (i.e., in which mothers might be reporting the highest levels of involvement and affection allowed by the questionnaire, resulting in a lack of variance): the mean scores and standard deviations for mothers' and fathers' ratings on these scales are very similar ($M = 10.5$, $SD = 3.5$, and $M = 10.5$, $SD = 4.1$, for mothers and fathers, respectively).

Discussion

Developmental relationships among moral judgment, socialization, and identification are documented in the findings of this chapter. First, adolescents' conscience strength, as rated by teachers and parents, was found to be correlated with adolescents' moral judgment level. Because these ratings reflect in part subjects' behavior, the findings confirm the relationship between adolescent behavior and moral judgment development, replicating results of others (e.g., Gibbs *et al.*, 1986).

Unique to this study is the finding that conscience strength measured during adolescence is a predictor of adulthood moral judgment development. This by itself is quite remarkable. Consider the teachers' ratings. Given only five rating scales, teachers were able to provide estimations of subjects' moral judgment maturity that were predictive

TABLE 5.5.
Correlations between Parental Involvement and MMS at Different Ages

Parental involvement	Age					
	10	13–14	17–18	20–22	24–26	28–30
Mother's involvement	−.15(10)	.09(18)	.37(15)	−.18(13)	.39(12)	.31(12)
Father's involvement	.79(7)*	.56(12)*	.66(9)*	.48(9)	.74(9)*	−.07(7)

Note. Values for *n* are in parentheses.
*$p < .05$, one tailed.

10 to 15 years later. Importantly, these estimations were independent of subjects' IQ and were still significant predictors even after partialling out the effect of adolescent MMS. The similar findings from the analyses of the parents' judgments of conscience strength indicate that adults are capable of discerning some aspects of moral character. From a developmental perspective, the pattern of these findings suggests that conscience strength serves to facilitate progress through the moral judgment stages, especially during adulthood.

Paternal identification and involvement also were found to be related to moral judgment development. These findings are congruent with those of Hoffman (1971), who found that the degree to which boys aspired to be like their fathers was related to their tendency to respond to hypothetical moral dilemmas with "internal" responses which Hoffman claimed reflected advanced moral reasoning. What is particularly interesting about the present set of findings is that paternal identification and involvement, as measured during adolescence, are related to sons' moral judgment development during childhood, adolescence, and adulthood.

One interpretation might be that fathers who are more involved with their sons and are identified with most strongly are the fathers who also encourage the most democratic discussion in the family. Because democratic family discussion is known to facilitate children's moral judgment development (Parikh, 1980), such an interpretation would argue that it is parenting style, not identification, that is the determining factor in the findings of this study. However, the claim that fathers have particular influence on their sons' development draws further support from recent longitudinal investigations that indicate that paternal involvement is a predictor of empathy in adulthood (Koestner, Franz, & Weinberger, 1990) and that parental identification in childhood is a predictor of ego stage in adulthood (Dubow, *et al.*, 1987). These findings, together with the pattern of null findings concerning the influence of maternal identification and involvement and the consistent relationships of paternal identification and involvement with moral judgment development, seem most parsimoniously explained by an interpretation according to which the father-son relationship is central.

At the beginning of the chapter, I predicted that the relationship between conscience strength and identification to moral judgment development would become stronger at the higher stages. This prediction received only weak support. For instance, the adolescent measures of conscience strength and identification were significantly related to moral judgment for 6 of the 12 comparisons for the three youngest age groups, in which Stage 2 was either dominant or just yielding to Stage 3. However for the comparisons involving the three oldest age groups, in which Stage 3 reasoning was firmly consolidated and Stage 4 reasoning was emerging, 8 of the 12 calculated correlations were significant. It is also interesting that the correlations of conscience strength and identification with moral judgment assessed concurrently is no higher, and in some instances is lower, than with moral judgment measured 10 and 15 years later. Together, these two trends provide some tentative evidence that socialization and identification factors are most important in energizing adulthood moral reasoning development.

NOTES

1. Identification in the context of psychoanalytic theory can also refer to a particular defense mechanism. This connotation is not included within the construct of developmental identification considered here.
2. The internal consistency or homogeneity of this index was assessed by calculating Cronbach's (1951) alpha; for the five teacher ratings, alpha = .85, which indicates a high degree of homogeneity among scales.

CHAPTER 6

Adaptational Styles

Adaptational style refers to the characteristic pattern of thoughts and behavior a person employs in order to mediate between goals and emotions and the demands of the enveloping social environment. These patterns of thought have been variously labeled by other investigators as defense mechanisms (e.g., Hauser, 1986) and ego processes (Haan, 1977); in the discussion that follows, I use the term *adaptational styles,* following Vaillant (1977), to emphasize the ubiquity and necessity of these patterns of thought in healthy development. Before turning to the findings of the longitudinal study, however, it will be useful to consider the history and current status of the concept of defense mechanisms (to be replaced with the term *adaptational styles* from this point forward).

There are two points of consensus among theorists and researchers of adaptational styles. The first is that modern conceptions of adaptational styles have their origins in Sigmund Freud's theorizing. In his 1905 work *Jokes and Their Relation to the Unconscious,* Freud described a range of adaptational styles such as repression, suppression, and isolation. Generally, Freud believed that adaptational styles are psychological processes that serve to regulate painful emotions arising from interactions with the social world (Paulhus, Fridhandler, & Hayes, in press). This is the point of departure for all work on adaptational styles. The second major contribution to the literature on adaptational styles is Anna Freud's 1966 *The Ego and Mechanisms of Defense.* This volume is noteworthy because it is the first systematic effort to catalogue the various adaptational styles that might be used by the individual. The implication of this enumeration is that there is a finite number of adaptational styles that are useful for understanding human behavior. Each of these adaptational styles manages painful affect in a unique way; consequently, the student of behavior will learn little about an individual from broad characterizations such as neurotic or psychotic; one needs to identify the individual's specific pattern of affect management in order to characterize his adaptational style.

That adaptational styles constitute identifiably discrete ways of managing affect is a well-accepted tenet. Unfortunately, there is little else in the field upon which theorists agree. The points of contention in the field are quite varied and are unlikely to be resolved in the near future. A brief outline of three of these schisms can provide the reader with a sense of the conflicted state of current research. Some theorists are quite insistent that adaptational styles must be unconscious (e.g., Vaillant, 1986) and consider conscious behaviors to be coping mechanisms or problem-solving strategies. Yet there are a few investigators who argue that little is gained by restricting the construct so as to prohibit the inclusion of strategies of which the person is aware (at least to a degree) that otherwise appear identical to adaptational styles (e.g., Erdelyi, 1990; Swanson, 1988). Researchers in this latter group argue that the conscious–unconscious distinction is increasingly difficult to maintain in light of recent findings from cognitive psychology and that to base definitions on it is to risk miring the field.

A second debate concerns the status of the adaptational styles. The traditional approach has been to assume that adaptational styles themselves are the mechanisms through which affect is managed. To characterize a person as utilizing projection, for instance, is to assert that the individual perceives his or her own emotions and conflicts as belonging to another, not as part of the self. This behavior occurs because acknowledging the presence of these emotions and conflicts within the self would be too painful; instead, the individual perceives these emotions in or projects them onto another person. Recently, however, some theorists who have been influenced by cognitive psychology (e.g., Haan, 1977; Horowitz, 1988) have argued that the various adaptational styles that have been catalogued are actually *products* of a much smaller collection of psychological *processes*. Projection, for example, is seen as a process involving the confusion of conceptions of self and other (Horowitz, 1988), a process that could be involved in other adaptational styles, such as altruism, as well.

For the purposes of this book, neither of these two debates need be resolved (although my opinion is that little is gained by insisting that defenses are always unconscious, and the process–product debate about the nature of defenses is more central to psychotherapy than to an analysis of lives over time [Horowitz, Markman, Stinson, Fridhandler, & Ghannam, 1990]). However, a third point of disagreement is particularly important for our purposes here, and it concerns whether adaptational styles are to be considered part of normal adaptation (e.g., Vaillant, 1977) or evidence of pathology (e.g., Blum, 1953; see Paulhus *et al.*, in press, for a discussion). Some theorists would consider the use of any adaptational style besides sublimation (through which instinctive drives are transformed into pleasure-producing, societally approved activities) to be evidence of pathology (e.g., Fenichel, 1945); in this view one would expect the healthy individual to make use of few adaptational styles. An alternative perspective, and the one followed here, is to assume that adaptational styles are adaptive; they serve a necessary purpose (Vaillant, 1977). According to this view, all adaptational styles help a person cope with the strains of social and emotional life. The healthy and happy person is characterized not by the absence of adaptational styles but by the use of relatively sophisticated and mature adaptational styles, which manage stress more successfully than the less sophisticated, immature ones. Vaillant's (1977) work on the life histories of men followed for 40 years is an elegant testament to the adaptive qualities of adaptational styles, and it is largely because of his work that researchers are beginning to recognize that adaptational styles are integral aspects of healthy personalities. To emphasize their necessity in development, I have chosen to use the term *adaptational styles,* which is free of the pathological connotations of *defense mechanism.*

Given the fractious debate on adaptational styles and the relative lack of empirical evidence for them (see Palhus *et al.*, in press), why are they included here? My answer is that an adequate account of the lives of the men considered in this book requires it. In the previous chapters the development occurring in the men in the study was considered primarily in terms of their aspirations and values and the meanings they construct for them: the constellation of social and occupational roles composing their ideal selves, the patterns of meaning composing their ego-ideals, which provide a sense of direction in life, and their characteristic perspectives on moral dilemmas. These different facets provide a sense of life as it is lived through by the men in the study, particularly of how they understand themselves and their relationships with others. To this point, then, the emphasis has been on men's conscious problem solving, theory making, and goals and to a lesser extent on the ways in which their relationships with others facilitate the development of these various components.

What is missing from the account of these men's lives, however, is a description of the biases, self-deceptions, and unusual adaptations that inevitably emerge in the course of development. These biases and unusual adaptations arise because the course of life brings with it obstacles and frustrations that cannot always be resolved and whose consequence is that an individual's goals—emotional, social, occupational—are not usually realized.

The frustration, tension, and stress arising from the discrepancy between one's reality and one's goals evokes different types of responses (Vaillant, 1986). The individual may seek help from others and utilize conscious problem solving. However, in many instances these conscious responses are ineffective in diminishing stress. There is then an involuntary deployment of adaptational styles, which "alter[s] perception of both internal and external reality, and often, as with hypnosis, the use of such mechanisms compromises other facets of cognition" (Vaillant, 1986, p. 200). Through the distortion and reorganization of reality, adaptational styles reduce stress and frustration.

Adaptational styles, as discrete patterns of thought and behavior that mediate between a person's goals or emotions and the demands of the enveloping social environment, provide a useful perspective from which to characterize the biases and distortions individuals manifest in adapting to the demands of life.

There are many different taxonomies of adaptational styles, but there is an emerging consensus for a core set useful for understanding development (Horowitz, 1988; Jacobson et al., 1986; Snarey & Vaillant, 1985; Vaillant, 1977, 1986, 1988). In a series of studies with diverse populations, George Vaillant (1977, 1986; Snarey & Vaillant, 1985) has offered a description of what he calls adaptational ego mechanisms. Vaillant (1977) reanalyzed interviews collected over long periods of adulthood in order to elucidate developmental trends in adaptational styles. The results of Vaillant's fascinating research suggest that the adaptational styles that an individual utilizes influence mental health (Vaillant, 1977) and social mobility (Snarey & Vaillant, 1985).

Vaillant's program of studies on adaptational styles is important in several respects. First, Vaillant has demonstrated the importance of adaptational styles for understanding psychopathology and successful adjustment in adulthood. Although the assessment procedures and statistical analyses reported in some of his studies (e.g., Vaillant, 1977) are less rigorous methodologically than is desirable, he has nevertheless presented considerable evidence that adaptational styles can be reliably identified through reanalysis of data originally collected for other purposes (McCullough, Vaillant, & Vaillant, 1986). Second, Vaillant (1977) has presented preliminary analyses suggesting that considerable change occurs in patterns of adaptational style from childhood into early adulthood. As Hauser (1986) has noted, however, the sparseness of the data from childhood and the lack of it for adolescence has precluded conclusions concerning changes and continuities in adaptational style prior to early adulthood.

In a series of studies Haan (1977, 1978; Haan, Aerts, & Cooper, 1985) has demonstrated that adaptational styles (1) can be reliably identified in different types of data, (2) change from childhood to early adulthood, and (3) may be related to moral judgment. Because Haan's scheme of adaptational styles is used in this study, it is described here in some detail.

Haan (1963) proposed 10 generic adaptational styles (or "ego processes"). Each adaptational style has two modes: mature (or "coping") and immature (or "defense"). In the mature mode the adaptational style enables the person to mediate flexibly among various intra-personal and environmental demands, to make full use of cognitive abilities, and to adjust to interpersonally defined reality. The same adaptational style in the immature mode results in impulsive expression of desires; rigid, maladaptive transactions with reality; and an inability to fully utilize cognitive abilities. For example, one generic adaptational style is *discrimination*. Discrimination is the "process of separating idea from feeling, idea from idea, and feeling from feeling by the utilization of cognitive functioning" (Haan, 1977, p. 300). The use of discrimination in the mature mode, labeled *objectivity*, allows the person to realistically assess a problem, as well as to recognize intrapersonal ambivalence about solutions to the problem. Immature discrimination, or *isolation*, however, results in a lack of coordination between ideas and emotions or between ideas and ideas. As a consequence, an optimal assessment and response to a problem is precluded.

Haan has arranged the generic adaptational styles into four groups according to their function: cognitive, reflexive-intraceptive, attention-focusing, and affective-impulse regulating. The *cognitives* adaptational styles are involved in solving problems arising in transactions with the world as well as in accommodating to interpersonal realities. *Reflexive-intraceptive* adaptational styles "reflect the person's assimilatory engagement with his own thoughts, feelings, and intuitions" (Haan, 1977, p. 38). There is only one generic adaptational style in the attention-focusing group, *selective awareness*, and it is involved in the person's deployment of attention to important problems. Finally, *affective-impulse regulating mechanisms* are means of transforming primitive emotions to allow their expression in an interpersonal context. A brief description of each of the 10 mature and 10 immature adaptational styles is presented in Table 6.1.

Haan (1977) has examined the development of the adaptational styles through an analysis of longitudinal data collected in the Berke-

TABLE 6.1.
Capsule Descriptions of Adaptational Styles

I. *Mature defenses*
  A. *Cognitive*
      Objectivity: separation of ideas from feelings, allowing objective evaluations in affect-laden situations
      Intellectuality: ability to let thoughts roam and to describe and symbolize feelings
      Logical analysis: identification and elucidation of causal chains of events which results in an accurate, nondistorted life history
  B. *Reflexive-Intraceptive*
      Tolerance of ambiguity: ability to deal with complexity and nuances; allows qualified judgments
      Empathy: sensitivity to another's feelings and perspective
      Playfulness: playful with ideas and feelings, relatively unconcerned with their apparent practicality
  C. *Attention-Focusing*
      Concentration: ability to put aside attractive or frightening thoughts in order to concentrate on task at hand
  D. *Affective-Impulse Regulating*
      Sublimation: the expression of relatively primitive emotions in societally endorsed fashion
      Substitution: fair, appropriate, and civilized behavior in difficult situations
      Suppression: control of emotions in situations in which their expression would be inappropriate
II. *Immature Defenses*
  A. *Cognitive*
      Isolation: an inability to synthesize thoughts and feelings
      Intellectualization: retreat from affect to abstract formulations
      Rationalization: superficial, self-serving justifications for behavior
  B. *Reflexive-Intraceptive*
      Doubt and indecision: inability of subject to resolve ambiguity
      Projection: attribution of one's own objectionable tendencies onto another
      Regression: dependent, immature behavior aimed at avoiding responsibility
  C. *Attention-Focusing*
      Denial: refusal to acknowledge facts that would be painful
  D. *Affective-Impulse Regulating*
      Displacement: the expression of an emotion or affect in a temporal or situational context different from the one in which it arose
      Reaction formation: the apparent transformation of an emotion into its opposite
      Repression: the unconscious but purposeful forgetting of emotion-laden events

Note. The capsule descriptions are based on Haan, 1977.

ley Guidance and Control Study. Adaptational styles were assessed through a combination of ratings and Q-sort measurements of interviews with the subjects during childhood, at age 30, and at age 40. The individual adaptational styles and a composite coping measure, formed by averaging the salience scores for all 10 adaptational styles, were examined for stability and change. Some evidence for both stability and change in ego processes was obtained, with stability generally higher for the coping modes than for the defensive modes. Over the age range of relevance here (from childhood to age 30), Haan found significant correlations over time for 10 ego processes in her sample of women but only 3 significant correlations over time for her sample of men. Haan speculated—although she was not able to test this hypothesis because the testing points are too widely separated in time—that this stability in coping modes may be disrupted during periods of transition (Haan, 1977, p. 101), during which there might be an increase in the use of defensive modes.

The discussion of adaptational styles to this point has been theoretical. In the next section the life of one man is examined against the backdrop of adaptational styles. As we shall see, important facets of Ronald Brown's life cannot be captured without reference to the sorts of self-deceptions and distortions to which the stresses in his life pushed him.

THE LIFE OF RONALD BROWN

A consideration of Ronald Brown's life can illustrate the value of adaptational styles for understanding development across adolescence and adulthood. In 1955, when he entered the study, Ronald was unremarkable by most of the measures that were used at that testing point. His parents both had some college education, and his father worked as an accountant at a large Chicago firm. Despite the educational background of his parents, Ronald's grades in high school were rather mediocre, as was his performance on the IQ test (which was slightly below average). The moral judgment, ego-ideal, and ideal-self scores all suggest that Ronald Brown was an average adolescent.

In terms of adaptational styles, Ronald as a 16-year-old was relatively average, too, with a coping score of 5.2 (these scores range between 1 and 9 and are discussed in detail in a later section) which put him almost in the middle of his age group. There was evidence of both mature adaptational styles and immature ones in his interview.

For instance, in his remarks about school Ronald revealed that he did not like school ("if we didn't have so much homework ... and if teachers didn't grade so much"), but he demonstrated an ability to put aside his negative feelings in order to evaluate the societal worth of teachers (objectivity). When he was asked if he could respect teachers, Brown laughed and answered as follows:

> That brings up a touchy subject. Well, we need them for education.
> *Can you respect a teacher even if you don't like him?*
> Yes, for the kind of work he's doing. You may just hate him something awful but say he gave a speech before an audience or something, and it's such a good one that you like it very much ... you respect him in the field he's in, but still hate him. You can respect the way he's teaching and still hate him.

Later in the interview Ronald was asked how much persons in different jobs should be paid and again revealed his ability to distinguish between his own feelings on an issue and the facts of the matter:

> *Should some jobs be paid more?*
> Yes. Take the school teacher, for instance. That is a touchy subject for me, but I think they should get more because they give up much more time than you usually think they do. It's quite important that you have them. Without them, you wouldn't get anywhere in the world.

Yet mixed in with the evidence for Ronald's employment of mature adaptational styles were signs of surprisingly immature modes of interacting with the world as well, particularly in his discussion of his interactions with persons with whom he had a complex relationship. For instance, when he was asked if he was a good son, Ronald Brown responded:

> Some of the time, I suppose—better than my brother and sister at times. And that is a proven fact. I can prove that.
> *In what ways?*
> They are the biggest stealers; I'm surprised the house isn't gone by now—or the garage or car or something.
> *How old are they?*
> Old enough to know they shouldn't do those things. My brother John has a little—he's down in the basement; my mother moved

him clear out of civilization finally. He steals cookies; he doesn't tell anybody—blames it on everybody else—me included.

As the interviewer continued to ask questions, it gradually became clear that the reason that Ronalds' brother lived in the basement had less to do with John's behavior and more to do with Ronald's inability to share a room with him:

> I just didn't want him in my room, to tell the truth, so I pushed him out. We both had the little room; it was about time we got by ourselves.

The unusual immaturity—"My brother stinks and is worse than me"— is evidence of regression, an adaptational style through which one attempts to avoid responsibility by failing to act in an age-appropriate way. For Ronald, acknowledging his responsibility for the poor state of his relationships with others was too shameful; consequently, he adopted the persona of a child who cannot be held responsible for the quality of his relationships (as is the case with most of the subjects, this immaturity was counterbalanced, to some extent, by an awareness of it—Ronald knew that he had forced his brother out). Although Ronald was perhaps unique in the extent of his regression, it should be noted again that the overall maturity of his adaptational styles is representative of the 16-year-old boys in this study.

By the third testing time, it was evident that Ronald Brown's adaptational styles were decidedly immature; in fact, his coping score was lower at age 28 (4.6) than it was at age 16. Three immature adaptational styles were characteristic of him at age 28: intellectualization, rationalization, and doubt and indecision. Consider first the evidence for intellectualization, which in the following example is revealed in the abstract, emotionless way that Brown discussed his relationships with women:

> I want to be a good son, because I would want my son to be a good son to me. This is the proper balance, because this is necessary and later on, for later on I might take the plunge [get married].

> *Are you thinking about taking the plunge now?*
> Oh, well, not now, but this will obviously come to pass someday and to keep a proper balance it is very necessary.

When do you think you will take the plunge?
Oh, it won't be for a while, I'm sure; I don't really know. I can't say.

Do you date now?
Not now, no.

Have you in the past?
Oh, I wasn't really a social climber, shall we say.

One senses in this excerpt the yearnings of a young man for a relation-ship with a woman, his relative lack of success toward achieving one, and the conflict that the distance between his desires and his reality must have aroused. Ronald Brown dealt with this conflict by describ-ing relationships with women as necessary for some abstract notion of balance, a perspective that obscured, even to himself, the distress he must have felt. The task of early adulthood, as Erikson noted, is the formation of intimate relationships, a task that probably cannot be resolved by any man without considerable stress (certainly, many men and women recall this period as a time of stress). Ronald's reliance on intellectualization is interesting because it characterizes his manner of adapting to stressful circumstances, not because he was alone in expe-riencing stress with this life task.

Rationalization is most frequently observed in the recounting of personal histories in ways that justify or explain away failures, mis-takes, and immoral behaviors. Everyone tends to formulate stories that are self-serving, of course, but for some persons the self-serving bias is particularly influential. For Ronald Brown, rationalization was employed to defend against the painful self-doubt arising from diffi-culties in finding a good job. His failure to find a good-paying job meant that he could not afford his own apartment and had to live with his parents. Difficulty finding a job was relatively unusual for a 28-year-old in 1966; the overall unemployment rate was only 3.8% and was lower still for those, like Ronald, with a college degree. After graduating from college with a biology degree, Ronald stayed in his college town in southern California in order to look for a job but had little success:

There was no market for anything down there at the time. Then it was coming up to the Christmas season, it was later October and November, but even then they didn't have a thing. Oh, there may have been interest in high school graduates for jobs as clerks in the big companies, that sort of thing, but if you wanted to get into something big, you just had nothing . . . . So I came back home, and I've been here ever since. I felt I really wasn't prepared for anything. You can't do much biology unless you have a master's degree or a Ph.D., or something like that, and you don't have the money you can't really do it, so I struck out to give it whatever I could and I could find nothing. I was all over the place, and man, there just wasn't anything. I think I have my name in every store and business in the city . . . I'll be 29 soon, and that's sort of late in the business world. You should have done something by age 17 or something like that, but better late than never. So it's going to take a little while.

Ronald defended against the awareness of occupational failure in his own life by weaving a tale in which he was the victim: he could not get a job because there were none available for college graduates in southern California or in Chicago; his college gave him an inadequate education; he could not be expected to succeed in business because he was now too old. Everyone who has searched for a job can sympathize with Ronald's difficulties and the resulting anguish; who, in the same position, has not questioned his own self-worth?

Ronald's justifications have a grain of truth to them. The job market for biology majors without advanced degrees is usually quite soft, and firms often prefer younger men for entry level positions. Yet from the vantage point of the observer it seems that Brown's account is overly self-serving. The stress and anxiety that permeated his life at that moment prevented him from acknowledging that virtually all of his peers who faced the same challenges were able to find jobs. His portrayal of himself as helpless victim may in fact have made it more difficult for him to pursue job leads, which in turn might have solidified his tendency toward rationalization.

Finally, there is evidence of doubt and indecision in Ronald's account of looking for work. He related that he had information about job openings in an oceanographic institute in California; "It's very interesting, I'm interested in this sort of thing . . . . It would be an excellent opportunity to do something like this." But Brown had not actually applied for the job. He considered becoming a flight controller, but his application was rejected because he did not get his college transcript in before the deadline. He also expressed interest in a job at the zoo:

I've always been interested in caring for animals, that sort of thing. There was an opening at the zoo; this may seem a little ridiculous, but I think it may be kind of interesting . . . . It's sort of a prestige builder in a way. You walk around with authority all over you.

Yet this interest never resulted in his applying for a job with the zoo. These examples suggest that Ronald was paralyzed by the variety of his interests and by his inability to decide which ones to pursue. He could not make up his mind.

By age 36 Ronald had succeeded in turning his life around. The overall maturity of his adaptational styles (as indexed by his coping score) placed him in the middle of his age group. Perhaps the biggest change in his life was that he had found a job with the circus and derived great pleasure from it:

> In high school I was a wallflower, shy and everything, and this job has got the most out of me, and done the most for me, and I have been greatly rewarded by being out and by being thrust into the public life and the public eye, and be forced into dealing with others. It has done the most in the world for me.

At age 27 Ronald had fantasized about getting a job with high prestige and far-reaching authority; by age 36 he was aware that he lacked the motivation to strive for such a position:

> I would like the power, a title, I'm on the periphery of these sorts of things in the circus. But it would be hard to take that responsibility. I used to think I might have what it takes, but now, with years of experience I have had working with people with high authority, I see that it is more of a headache than anything else and it can kill you.

Although the overall maturity of Ronald's adaptational styles was much higher at age 36 (6.7, placing him in the upper half of the sample) than at age 27, there remained, as with all the men, some immaturities. For Ronald, the issues that drew forth immature adaptational styles were family and women. He had recently been named in his brother's will to be the guardian of his niece in the event of the deaths of his brother and sister-in-law; in his discussion of this issue some immaturities are apparent:

> My niece and I get along extremely well. I was named the guard-

ian over my sister-in-law's sister, who is young and frivolous.
If something happened to my brother and sister-in-law, then I
would be the one to take over. They obviously feel that through
my experience dealing with my occupation and being thrust out
and being more open, that I could handle things better than my
sister-in-law's sister.

His comparisons of himself to his sister-in-law's sister suggest, to some
extent, rationalization. Certainly, his occupational success, competence
in managing his life, and self-confidence were evident to members
of his family; yet his belief that his brother and sister-in-law had chosen him to be the guardian of their child in the event of their deaths
based on their assessment of his public exposure with the circus seems
ill-considered. From the perspective of an observer, such a rationale
seems unlikely; one assumes that parents rely on other criteria in
addition to occupational success in choosing a potential guardian for
their child.

The contours of Ronald Brown's life characterize most of the
men in the study. There were periods of turmoil, which were accompanied by the employment of immature adaptational styles,
and periods of successful adjustment as well. The rough chapter in
Ronald's life occurred in his mid-twenties, when he had difficulty
finding a direction in life and was living at home. Yet he was able to
overcome those difficulties and had achieved a life that he found
satisfying by age 36. Like most of the men in the study, he continued
to manifest some immature adaptational styles in his thirties; this
reflects the difficulty of adapting to life, rather than shortcomings in
any individual man.

An account of Ronald Brown's life would be incomplete without
a description of the ways in which he dealt with stress. To say that he
experienced difficulties at some points in his life and was healthy at
other points would obscure the revealing details concerning his modes
of adaptation. Viewing Ronald Brown's life in terms of adaptational
styles permits a characterization of him that integrates much of the
richness of his life without sacrificing a framework within which individual differences can be understood.

In the next section the patterns of adaptational styles across the
age span of subjects in this study are examined. These analyses provide a view of how the men as a group changed in their adaptational
styles as well as indicate the extent to which their adaptational styles
remained stable.

LONGITUDINAL ANALYSES

Relationships of Age to Adaptational Styles

Curiously, there is very little research on the relationship between age and the salience of different adaptational styles, except for the research of Vaillant and Haan, reviewed earlier. Their research provided only the weakest of evidence for patterned changes in adaptational styles over time, because both studies had only a few testing points and these were separated by many years. Consequently, the work of Vaillant and Haan demonstrates that the adolescent's configuration of adaptational styles is different from a middle-aged adult's, but this hardly provides a differentiated portrait of the general relationship between age and adaptational style.

Theoretically, of course, the relationship between age and adaptational styles is important. Anna Freud (1966) claimed that adaptational styles

> have their own chronology . . . they are more apt to have pathological results if they come up too long after it. Examples are denial and projection which are "normal" in early childhood and lead to pathology in later years; or repression and reaction formation, which cripple the child's personality if used too early. (p. 177)

The emergence and transformation of particular adaptational styles have been related to such diverse factors as the acquisition of particular Piagetian stages (e.g., Haan, 1977) and age-related reorganizations of psychic structures and surging libido drives (Blum, 1953). Unfortunately, the data in this study will not allow a definitive statement as to the sources of transformations in adaptational styles (although some possibilities will be considered). Nonetheless, an accurate delineation of the age-related nature of adaptational styles can lead to improved theorizing on the underlying sources of development.

Stability of Adaptational Styles over Time

A second issue that is examined is the extent to which adaptational styles characterize an individual over time. Adaptational styles are, of course, presumed by all theorists to be somewhat stable over time; if they were not, they would offer little interpretative leverage for understanding the paths that lives follow. Yet within this general consensus, there are widely varying perspectives on the extent of stability (see Paulhus *et al.*, in press). This debate is best addressed through the use of longitudinal data in which testing points are relatively close in time. Closely spaced testing points, such as is the case in the study presented here, permit inferences about the rate of change over time (which is not possible in studies in which there are only a few testing points that are separated by decades, as was the case in the Haan, 1977, and Vaillant, 1977, studies).

Relationship to Moral Judgment

A final issue to be reviewed here is the relationship of adaptational styles to moral judgment, which is considered in considerable depth by Hart and Shmiel (1992). This work is reviewed here for several reasons: First, the work allows an assessment of the extent to which the facet of personality captured by adaptational styles interacts with a cognitive, problem-solving variable like moral judgment. For the most part, theorists have argued that moral judgment is a unique domain and that its sources of development are to be found in social interaction with others (Hart, 1988). If adaptational styles are related to moral judgment development, however, these claims would need to be revised in order to acknowledge that moral judgment development occurs in an individual with particular resources and stresses.

A demonstration of a relationship between adaptational styles and moral judgment development can also serve to confirm the value of the former. Relatively little evidence has been garnered to convince the field of developmental psychology of the value of adaptational styles for understanding development. If a convincing case can be made for the influence of adaptational styles on the development of a well-validated, widely accepted construct like moral judgment, it would be an important step forward toward the acceptance of the concept of adaptational style.

As discussed earlier, development in moral judgment derives from cognitive disequilibrium (an awareness of the inadequacies of lower stage reasoning for successfully resolving conflicting moral claims) and social role taking (an accurate understanding of others' perspectives and concerns). Adaptational styles are likely to influence moral judgment by regulating the extent to which individuals are (1) sensitive to the weaknesses of their own moral principles, and therefore experience cognitive disequilibrium, and (2) capable of understanding, and being empathic to, the perspective of others. It seems clear that individuals who are using mature adaptational styles will be more likely than those who rely heavily on immature ones to develop sophisticated moral judgment.

Several studies provide partial support for this predicted relationship between adaptational styles and moral judgment development. Haan (1978) found a relationship between adaptational styles and moral judgment development, as evidenced in both group discussions and moral judgment interviews. Researchers observed adolescents as they participated in various group activities designed to elicit moral discussions and then used a Q-sort procedure to characterize each adolescent in terms of a profile of adaptational styles. Generally, the results of the study suggested that adolescents for whom the mature adaptational styles were especially characteristic were most likely to use developmentally mature patterns of discussion with their fellow group members. Furthermore, one defense mechanism, objectivity, was positively associated with moral judgment development occurring between the pretest and the posttest.

In another study Haan (1977) compared the relative contributions of adaptational styles, cognitive level and socioeconomic status to the prediction of concurrently measured moral judgment development among middle-aged adults. Adaptational styles were assessed by rating clinical interviews that focused on the subjects' lives, both in the past and in the future. The complicated results of Haan's various analyses of the relationships between adaptational styles and moral judgment development are not easily distilled. This is because Haan formed many multiple regression equations, using scores for any one of the adaptational styles, taken by themselves or in combination with other adaptational styles, in the equations. The large number of variables allowed into the equations, along with the relatively small number of subjects, make the results suggestive rather than conclusive. Nonetheless, Haan's analyses found that adaptational styles were correlated with moral judgment scores even after controlling for IQ, cognitive level, and socioeconomic status. Surprisingly, Haan found that two immature adaptational styles, denial and intellectualization, were correlated with high moral judgment scores. Haan (1977) claimed on the basis of these results that those "who reach the higher levels of formal moral reasoning are verbally productive and nonrepressive but their denying and intellectualizing propensities suggest that they are evidently socially and emotionally illiterate" (p. 117).

Although Haan's findings suggest a relationship between adaptational styles and moral judgment development, they must be regarded skeptically, since Haan formed many multiple regression equations and calculated many correlations, leading to the possibility that some of her findings are artifacts. Further, her argument that persons at the higher stages of moral judgment in Kohlberg's sequence are "socially and emotionally illiterate" is contrary to theory and is perhaps more of a reflection of her interest in advancing a competing account of moral development than of the results of her studies.

In summary, the exploratory nature of the statistical analyses (multiple regression equations and correlations with many variables and relatively few significant findings) in combination with the cross-sectional design of Haan's studies leave unanswered questions concerning (1) the direction of influence between adaptational styles and moral judgment development and (2) the relationship of specific adaptational styles to moral judgment advance. In the sections that follow, some recent answers to these questions emerging from analyses of Kohlberg's longitudinal study presented by Hart and Shmiel (1992) are reviewed.

Method

The transcribed interviews were coded using Haan's Q-sort for Ego Processes (1977). This Q-sort consists of 60 different items, 3 for each of the mature and immature adaptational styles described in Table 6.1. Each item consists of a statement or two describing behavior characteristic of the defense it represents. The coder sorts these items, following a fixed 9-step distribution, according to how characteristic or uncharacteristic each item is of the individual as manifested in the interview. After the sorting process is completed, the number of the step at which each of the items is placed, ranging from 1 (very uncharacteristic of the person) to 9 (very characteristic), is recorded.

Extensive testing of the Q-sort prior to beginning this study suggested that some of the items could not be easily sorted by the raters; for these items, additional statements were added, all of them drawn from Haan's descriptions of the defense in question (the modified items are available upon request from the author). The Q-sort procedure offers several advantages for the purposes of the proposed study. First, because the Q-sort results in a description of the relative saliency of adaptational styles within the individual, rather than between individuals, it can be used with persons of widely varying backgrounds and developmental statuses, as well as with different sources of data. Haan (1977) has meaningfully applied the Q-sort to samples of children, adolescents, and adults, basing the judgments on different types of interviews as well as on observations of moral discussions. As Haan (1977) notes, any data that reveal issues of concern to the individual can serve as a basis for the Q-sort; the wide variety of topics considered in the interviews with the men in the Kohlberg study certainly tap such domains.

Two hundred and six interviews were coded in random order by a well-trained researcher who was unaware of the subject's age, moral judgment score, and performance on other interviews. Reading and coding each interview took approximately 2 hours.

The step scores for the three items for each defense mechanism were summed, resulting in a defense mechanism salience score, which ranges from 3 to 27, with low scores indicating the mechanism was not prominent in the individual's makeup and high high scores suggesting the mechanism was very prominent. The defense mechanism salience scores for the 10 mature adaptational styles (objectivity, intellectuality, logical analysis, tolerance of ambiguity, empathy, playfulness, concentration, sublimation, substitution, and suppression) were averaged to form a general Coping Score (CS). The CS provides an index of the maturity of the individual's defense mechanism profile.

Interrater reliability was assessed by having a second well-trained coder score seven randomly selected interviews. One measure of reliability is to correlate the step scores for the 60 items provided by one rater with the step scores from the other rater for each interview and then determine the median correlation. The median correlation for the two raters was $r = .78$. It is also possible to calculate correlations for the CS, the summary scores for the four types of adaptational styles, and for each defense mechanism salience score taken separately. The correlation between the two raters for the coping score was $r = .99$. The reliability for rating the various adaptational styles ranged from 0 to .99, with 13 of the correlations exceeding .60. The adaptational styles for which this acceptable level of agreement was reached were as follows: objectivity ($r = .96$), intellectuality (.99), logical analysis (.76), tolerance of ambiguity (.72), empathy (.62), playfulness (.87), isolation (.92), intellectualization (.87), rationalization (.73), doubt (.82), regression (.60), projection (.62), and denial (.91). Generally, then, the results indicate that the two raters coded the data reliably.

Results

Age Trends

The relationships between age and the salience of the overall coping score and each of the reliably scored mature adaptational styles are depicted in Figure 6.1; the relationships between age and the salience of the reliably scored immature adaptational styles are to be found in Figure 6.2. The statistical significance of these trends was confirmed by calculating correlations between age and the coping score and between age and the salience score for each of the depicted adaptational styles (these correlations between age and score were as follows: coping, $r = .60$; objectivity, $r = .56$; logical analysis, $r = .54$; playfulness, $r = .58$; tolerance of ambiguity, $r = .46$; isolation, $r = -.51$; rationalization, $r = -.45$; intellectualization, $r = .32$; regression, $r = -.53$; doubt, $r = -.57$; denial, $r = -.53$; regression, $r = -.30$; all with $p < .001$). Across the age span included in this study, then, there is abundant evidence for significant change in patterns of adaptational styles with age.

The patterns presented in Figures 6.1 and 6.2 suggest that the relationships between adaptational styles and age are strongest in adolescence; to test this prediction, correlations between age and adaptational style scores were calculated for adolescence (ages 10 to 20) and adulthood (ages 24 to 36). All of the associations between age and adaptational styles were significant for the adolescent period, but none of them were for early adulthood. This indicates that the age of an adolescent is likely to be revealing about the maturity of the adaptational styles he employs, while the age of an adult is not.

Stability and Change

The overall stability of a profile of adaptational styles can be assessed by correlating Q sorts at different ages. Higher correlations indicate greater stability whereas lower correlations suggest unpredictable change. The medians for correlations between Q sorts at adjacent ages were as follows (averages are presented in parentheses): age 10 to age 13–14, .60(.41); 13–14 to 16–18, .26(.18); 16–18 to 20–22, .44(.29); 20–22 to 24–26, .54(.45); 24–26 to 28–30, .70(.65); 28–30 to 32–34, .58(.54); and 32–34 to 36, .51(.53). This pattern indicates that the overall profile of adaptational styles is least stable between ages 13 and 16, with increasing stability thereafter.

A related issue concerns the extent to which the maturity of a

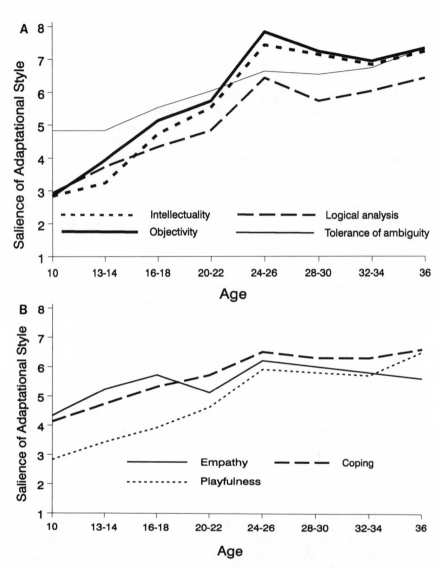

FIGURE 6.1. Salience of mature adaptational styles as a function of age. Part A shows relationship between age and use of intellectuality, objectivity, logical analysis, and tolerance of ambiguity. Part B shows relationship between age and use of empathy, playfulness and coping.

person's adaptational styles, reflected in his coping score measured at one testing time, is related to his relative maturity measured at another. Correlations between coping scores for the six testing times were

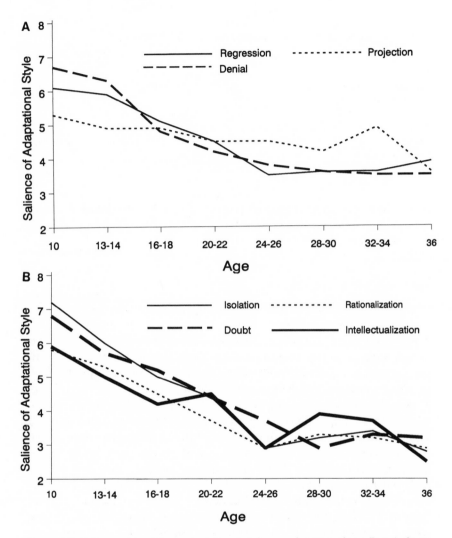

FIGURE 6.2. Salience of immature adaptational styles as a function of age. Part A shows relationship between age and use of regression, denial, and projection. Part B shows relationship between age and isolation, doubt, rationalization, and intellecutalization.

calculated and are presented in Table 6.2. Although there is no simple pattern evident in the correlations in Table 6.2, it is apparent that coping scores are rarely related to each other if separated by more than 6 years; furthermore, the correlations suggest that adulthood coping scores are more interrelated than are adolescent coping scores. This

TABLE 6.2.
Correlations among Coping Scores at the Six Testing Times

	Time 1	Time 2	Time 3	Time 4	Time 5
Time 1					
Time 2	.41(37)*				
Time 3	.51(20)*	.03(19)			
Time 4	.25(37)	.22(34)	.54(21)*		
Time 5	.05(33)	−.09(30)	.62(13)*	.19(30)	
Time 6	.18(28)	.24(25)	.58(11)	−.02(25)	.84(26)*

*p < .05, one-tailed.

latter finding makes sense, of course, given the evidence for con-siderable change in adolescent adaptational styles, especially in early adolescence.

Relationship to Moral Judgment

In their analyses of the relationship of moral judgment to pat-terns of adaptational styles, Hart and Shmiel (1992) found clear evi-dence that moral judgment development is influenced by patterns of adaptational styles in adolescence. They formed a series of multi-ple regression equations with MMS at each age in adulthood as de-pendent measures, with one set of equations using CS and MMS at ages 13–14 and IQ as predictors and a second set using the paral-lel measures at ages 16–18 as predictors. Briefly, the results indicated that CS (indexing the overall maturity of the individual's adaptational styles) was retained in the regression equations when predicting moral judgment scores at the older age ranges. Indeed, remarkably high multiple Rs were obtained for some of these equations; for instance, the multiple R for predicting MMS at ages 28–30 was .84 with IQ and ages 13–14 MMS and CS entered as predictors. These analyses (along with many others presented by Hart and Shmiel, [1992]; see that work for additional evidence) suggest that adaptational styles in adoles-cence may play a role in influencing moral judgment development into adulthood.

A second finding worthy of note in Hart and Shmiel's (1992) analyses was that Haan's (1977) claim that immature adaptational styles result in the attainment of higher moral judgment stages was not supported. It appears to be the case that Haan's finding that those who relied heavily on intellectualization and denial had higher MMSs than those who did not was an artifact of the many correlations that were calculated in her study.

Relationship to Other Variables

The longitudinal nature of the study permits an assessment of the influence of childhood IQ and social class on the development of adaptational styles, as well as an assessment of the contribution of adaptational styles to subsequent achievement. Table 6.3 reports the correlations between coping scores at seven of the eight age ranges and the aforementioned variables. It is clear that, for the most part, the social class status of the parents played little role in determining the overall maturity of adaptational styles, either in adolescence or adulthood (although the correlation between childhood social class at age 24 and coping is quite high, the failure to obtain a significant association at any other age cautions against interpreting it). This finding confirms Vaillant's (1977) finding that childhood social class by itself does not predict to the maturity of adaptational styles.

Snarey and Vaillant (1985) claimed that the maturity of adaptational styles predicts occupational success. In their study adaptational styles were measured concurrently with occupational success, and the authors were able to demonstrate that adaptational styles were correlated with adulthood social class even when the effects of childhood IQ and other variables were partialled out. This led to the authors' assertion that the maturity of adaptational styles determined, in part, the social class that the individual achieved. Although this is an intrigu-

TABLE 6.3.
Correlations between Coping Scores at Seven Ages and Childhood SES, Childhood IQ, and Adulthood SES

Age	Childhood SES	Adulthood SES	IQ
10	.02(16)	−.28(16)	−.26(16)
13–14	−.18(33)	−.07(31)	.12(32)
16–18	.21(39)	.16(38)	.23(39)
20–22	.05(30)	.20(28)	.21(19)
24–26	.87(24)*	.49(22)*	.45(29)*
28–30	.01(34)	.23(34)	.39(33)*
32–34	.07(22)	.66(22)*	.62(21)*

Note. Values for n are in parentheses. The age = 36 group is omitted because there were too few subjects.
*$p < .05$.

ing finding, an equally plausible interpretation is that the achievement of high-status positions resulted in the employment of mature adaptational styles.

A better means of examining these relationships is through longitudinal investigation, which permits an assessment of the extent to which the maturity of adaptational styles assessed at the transition to adulthood predicts to subsequent social class achievement in early adulthood. The pattern of correlations between coping and adulthood social class presented in Table 6.3 confirms Snarey and Vaillant's basic finding-that the maturity of adaptational styles is correlated with social class, but there is no clear evidence of causality. This is because the first significant relationship does not emerge until ages 24–26, by which time most men were on a relatively stable career path (all the men had completed high school, most of those who attended college were in the work force, and even those who had pursued graduate education were done or nearly done with their training, with a few exceptions). Consequently, there is little evidence to support the claim that adaptational styles determine (even in part) social class achievement.

Finally, it is worth noting that the association between coping and IQ increases with age. There is no association between IQ and coping during childhood and adolescence. This may be a reflection of the demands of these periods of life; intense emotions, powerful peer and family conflicts, and an inadequately developed personality structure may be pressures on the adolescent that demand more in the way of control of emotions than in thoughtful consideration of possibilities. As I noted in Chapter 1, Block (1971) found that the transition from early adolescence to late adolescence is marked by a decrease in internal conflicts and an increase in a cognitive, reflective approach to life. The data presented here tell a similar story, with the reflective intelligence tapped by IQ tests important for coping in adulthood but not in adolescence.

CONCLUSION

This chapter explores the characteristic biases that pervade men's lives. These biases, labeled here as adaptational styles (but called defense mechanisms, ego processes, and ego defenses by various investigators), were first considered in the context of Ronald Brown's life. The distortions and reorganizations of reality that were apparent in

Brown's life were explored using the framework of adaptational styles developed by Norma Haan. I argued that an account of Brown's life would be incomplete without a description of the patterns of adaptational styles he employed at various points in his life.

Ronald Brown's life also illustrated some of the findings emerging from the longitudinal study. For instance, although the general trajectory of Brown's life was toward greater maturity in his adaptational styles between ages 16 and 36, there were stresses that occasionally resulted in regression to less satisfactory adaptational styles. For Brown, the stress that brought on his retreat to less mature adaptational styles was the transition from college to the adult world; in particular, his difficulty in finding a job and entering into relationships with women was sufficiently painful so as to require the employment of adaptational styles that distort the perception of reality. Once these stresses were reduced, Brown once again moved toward a reliance on the more mature adaptational styles.

These same patterns were found in the sample as a whole. The salience of the mature adaptational styles increased from childhood to early adulthood, with little evidence for age-related change thereafter. The salience of the mature adaptational styles during adulthood appeared to derive from, not lead to, the social class status of the men. Those men who entered the highest social classes were more likely to deploy the mature adaptational styles than were the men at the lower end of the social class hierarchy, who were likely to be under greater stress. Finally, there was little evidence that individual differences in patterns of adaptational styles were stable from childhood through adulthood, although there was considerable evidence for periods of stability over 3 to 4 years; those who had the highest coping scores in adolescence were not necessarily the men with the most mature patterns of coping in adulthood. These findings suggest that the developmental tasks that occur across adolescence and adulthood are sufficiently diverse so as to prevent an individual from successfully employing a single pattern of adaptational styles throughout life. For instance, the low stability in patterns of adaptational styles between ages 13–14 and 16–18 suggests that the changes in relationships with peers and parents in combination with cognitive and emotional development result in a thorough reorganization of adaptational styles, the success of which can be only weakly predicted from the maturity of adaptational styles in early adolescence.

Finally, the analyses of the relationships between adaptational styles and moral judgment development provide one demonstration of the value of a multifaceted perspective on lives across time. The results of these analyses indicate that moral judgment development can be best understood against a backdrop of other personological variables. In combination with the results presented in Chapter 5, the results presented here demonstrate the value of understanding the development of a problem-solving skill like moral judgment within the context of an individual person with limitations and biases who is developing in a specific family environment.

None of the various disputes about the nature of adaptational styles that divide the theoretical community have been resolved here. Whether adaptational styles are conscious or unconscious, processes or products, necessary for adaptation or unnecessary are questions that cannot be answered in the context of the longitudinal study. The contribution of the longitudinal study to this field is in its findings concerning development, stability, and relationships to other variables. To a field badly in need of replicable findings, the results presented here are perhaps more useful than yet another theoretical account grounded in clinical observations.

In the future it may come to pass that the concept of adaptational style is replaced by more precise variables that allow more precise measurements; the increasingly experimental orientation of personality research leads one to suspect that psychologists will attempt to purge the field of constructs, like adaptational style, that retain any vestige of grounding in clinical practice and psychodynamic theory. Before embarking on this study, I was doubtful of the usefulness of such constructs for understanding development. However, once I began reading the interviews, I realized that the lives of the men could not be understood without reference to the distortions and biases that permeated their lives. Use of the construct of adaptational style is one valuable means for interpreting these distortions and biases and for gaining a better grasp on the lives of the men who participated in this study.

CHAPTER 7

The Study in Perspective

This book has presented a personological investigation of the transition from adolescence to adulthood. The goal has been to develop an account that answers important questions about men's lives. The focus has not been on proving one answer to be better than another but on developing an account that retains the richness of men's lives as they are lived. The different chapters suggest that there is wisdom in each of the three approaches to the study of lives described in Chapter 1; at issue is discovering where in the study of lives that wisdom is valuable.

QUESTIONS AND ANSWERS IN THE STUDY OF LIVES

Stability and Change

Consider first the issue of stability versus change in the course of development. The findings presented in Chapters 3 to 6 indicate that there is both in the course of life from adolescence to adulthood. For instance, the following were found to be stable individual differences: the ego-ideal through late adolescence; coping in late adolescence and early adulthood; and the ideal self and moral judgment over the 20-year span of the study. There is little question, then, that there is considerable continuity in the course of development. The claims for stability made by personality trait theorists are confirmed by these results.

But there is evidence for change as well. Individual differences in developmental levels of the ego-ideal apparently are not stable in early adulthood. The value criteria that men use to judge their aspirations are not clearly related (in a developmental sense) to those they used as adolescents. What seems to be the case is that the tasks

187

encountered during the transition from late adolescence into adulthood—leaving home, finishing school, entering the work place, marrying, forming a family—are sufficiently powerful to engender developmental discontinuity. Men who at age 22 valued fidelity to personal values and responsibility to society (Ego Ideal Level 4 concerns) were not necessarily the ones with these values at age 30. This sort of finding, although in need of replication, is consonant with the claims of crisis-transformational approaches like those of Erikson, Vaillant, and Levinson.

Even within those domains with stable individual differences there is evidence for developmental transformation. In the ideal self this is reflected in the decreasing salience of the active roles and the increasing desirability of the professional ones. That is, the 33-year-olds find the professional roles more desirable than do the 13-year-olds, although the 13-year-olds who desire most to hold professional roles become the 33-year-olds who find the same roles extremely attractive.

Developmental transformation within the context of stable individual differences is clearest in moral judgment scores. The correlations among moral judgment scores taken from the different testing times are routinely high; one can predict with confidence that an individual who has a high moral judgment score relative to others measured at the same time will retain that advantage at later testing points. However, it is important to note that the advantage may not be reflected in the same *way* at the later testing time. The 13-year-old who consistently appeals to interpersonal expectations in defending moral judgments (Kohlberg's Stage 3 reasoning, which is seldom the modal stage for this age) in resolving a moral dilemma rejects the adequacy of that reasoning as an adult in favor of arguments based on obligations and commitments (Stage 4) or a hierarchy of rights (Stage 5). This means that the developmental advantage evidenced at age 13 is maintained at age 30, but its manifestation is quite different at the later age.

Rate of Change

Three of the facets of lives (ideal self, moral judgment, adaptational styles) show a similar pattern with respect to their developmental trajectories (the ego-ideal is much less predictable). Generally, the pattern is one of decreasing change with increasing age, which is reflected in two ways. First, the most consistent correlations with age were found for the adolescent era (age 10 to age 22); few significant correlations were found between age and any of the constructs of interest for the adulthood years (age 24 to age 36). Second, the rate of change between adjacent testing times is greatest in adolescence. Figure 7.1 charts the rate of change between adjacent testing times for the ideal self, moral judgment, and adaptational styles. Of course, calculating differences between ordinal scores such as the moral judgment stages (MMS) can be misleading (it is not clear if, from a developmental perspective, Stage 3 is equidistant from Stages 2 and 4), but the pattern of the curves for moral judgment, the ideal self, and adaptational styles is nonetheless suggestive. The rate of change is substantially lower in adulthood. Together, these trends suggest that development has slowed dramatically by the third decade of life (the age at which, some trait psychologists argue, adulthood begins, e.g., McCrae & Costa, 1990).

Sources of Stability and Change

Unfortunately, the data collected in this study do not permit powerful inferences about the contributions of genes, culture, and family

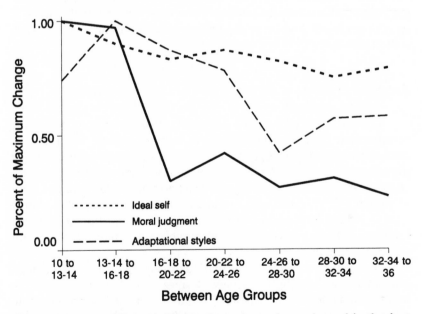

FIGURE 7.1. Amount of change (relative to the maximum change observed for that facet over the entire study) for each age range.

to the development of lives. Some evidence for the influence of culture on the ideal self was presented in Chapter 3. The comparison presented there between the youth of 1955 and 1988 suggests that historical setting and sex roles, both complex cultural phenomena, affect the aspirations of adolescents. In Chapters 4 and 6 there was some evidence that social class, yet another complex cultural variable, influences ego-ideal development and the extent to which individuals manifest mature adaptational styles. Although these relations indicate that cultural influences on lives can be discerned, more revealing analyses about the contributions of specific aspects of these complex cultural variables were not possible.

A stronger and more interesting case was made for parental influences on moral judgment development (unfortunately, because of the incompleteness of the records for some men, it was not possible to conduct parallel analyses for the other variables). The pattern of results in Chapter 5 suggests that fathers are particularly important in facilitating the moral judgment of their sons. Those boys who identified with their fathers and whose fathers were highly involved with them achieved the highest stages of moral judgment in adulthood. Although these findings are based on a small number of subjects, they are consonant with recent findings from other longitudinal studies of ego development (Dubow *et al.*, 1987) and empathic concern (Koestner, *et al.*, 1990).

Facets of Lives

Central to the perspective developed throughout the book is the position that there are different facets to lives, each of which has its own developmental trajectory. Each of the detailed examinations of individual lives presented in the preceding chapters aimed at elucidating the value of a particular facet for understanding development. Each facet—ideal self, ego-ideal, moral judgment, adaptational styles—offered new information about the man and the path his life followed. Together they offer considerable interpretive leverage for understanding lives.

One of the most important findings to emerge is that these facets interact. Again, the best evidence derives from the analyses of the moral judgment data. In Chapter 5 moral judgment development into adulthood was found to be influenced by an adolescent personality variable, namely, conscience strength (as assessed through teacher and parental ratings). The analyses presented in Chapter 6 demonstrated that adolescent coping scores also influenced moral judgment development into adulthood, with those adolescents high in coping achieving the higher moral judgment stages in adulthood. Particularly interesting about the contributions of adolescent personality (conscience strength and coping) to adulthood moral judgment is the fact that the relationship is stronger for measurements of moral judgment more distant from adolescence than for those close to it. Several complementary interpretations of this phenomenon are plausible. The first is that the nature of moral judgment development is different in the years immediately following adolescence than in later years. For instance, most men in their early twenties are in the process of consolidating their moral judgment at Stage 3. Development in the late twenties and thirties is less a matter of consolidation and more one of discarding Stage 3 and elaborating Stage 4. Perhaps personality factors contribute to the elaboration process but not to consolidation. This could explain why conscience strength and coping, as measured in adolescence, are predictors of moral judgment at the more distant measurement points; that is, these personality factors are relevant for the distal, but not proximal, developmental tasks.

This interpretation rests on the assumption that conscience strength and coping, as measured in adolescence, remain stable attributes of the person through adulthood. Although this is true to some extent, it is not the full story. An examination of the coping scores suggests that, in general, the stability from adolescence to adulthood is not high (unfortunately, conscience strength was not measured in adulthood, so its stability cannot be assessed). Furthermore, the correlations between adolescent coping scores and adulthood moral judgment are greater in magnitude than those between adulthood coping scores and adulthood moral judgment. Together these findings suggest (but certainly do not prove) that the influence of adaptational styles on moral judgment development may be an age-specific phenomenon of adolescence. Perhaps a particular configuration of factors in adolescence (conscience strength, coping) sets the stage for later development in moral judgment by guiding the commitments and decisions that prepare the way for adulthood. Once these commitments and decisions are made, it may be that the factors no longer have an effect on moral judgment development. This admittedly speculative interpretation is in need of confirmation but, if verified, might be a prototype of how the interaction of different facets occurs.

Conscious and Unconscious Facets of Lives

Much of past and contemporary psychological research seems dedicated to the proposition that consciousness, self-reflection, and one's own interpretations are dispensable (or even dangerous) elements in a scientific account of persons. The dismissal of consciousness was, of course, true of behavioristic psychology but, surprisingly, continues to characterize much current research in an era in which constructs like self-concept, self-monitoring, self-discrepancies, and theories of mind are in vogue. Frequently, these constructs are studied from the perspective of cognitive psychology, in which the methodology of choice is a reaction time experiment of one sort or another. The goal in these experiments is to infer the organization of different constructs and the ways in which various cognitive processes operate without depending upon the subjects' introspections. As critics have pointed out (e.g., Searle, 1984), the results of these experiments tend to be inconclusive and often fail to shed light on issues of significance.

Ignoring individual's own perspectives on their lives, however, seems unlikely to result in genuine psychological understanding. Certainly, one could offer only an impoverished account of the lives of Bob Eagleton and Frank Jones (Chapter 4) without describing each man's view on what is of value in life. Despite their many similarities (SES, IQ, ideal self, even moral judgement stage), the case analyses revealed an important difference between the men: Jones valued roles that provided him with an opportunity for individual success and recognition while Eagleton quested for fidelity to personal values. It seems implausible that an account of lives would be complete without this sort of information: a genuine psychology of persons must "take seriously human construction of experience as more than merely countable 'responses' or 'verbal reports' " (Carlson, 1971, p. 215). This information, of course, is available only by allowing the individual to express his own conscious perspective on life.

Summary of Research Findings

An overview of the relationship of the different facets of lives traced in the preceding chapters to the issues posed in Chapter 1 and elaborated in this chapter is presented in Table 7.1. The cells of the table are based on the review of literature in Chapter 1 and the analyses presented in Chapters 3 to 6. An inspection of the table reveals that

TABLE 7.1.
Overview of Relationship of Several Facets of Lives to Various
Issues Addressed in This Study

Issues	Ideal self	Ego-ideal	Moral judgment	Adaptational styles
Paradigmatic orientation Methodology usually used to investigate the facet	Personality traits Structured inventory	Structural-developmental Interview	Structural-developmental Interview	Crisis-transformational Observer ratings
Extent of stability in the facet during adolescence and adulthood	High	Low/Moderate	High	Low/moderate
Extent of transformation in the facet during adolescence and adulthood	Low	High	High	Moderate/high
Correlation found with	Social class achieved during adulthood	Moral judgment stage; social class in adulthood	Ego-ideal level; IQ; adaptational styles	Moral judgment achieved in adulthood; IQ; social class in adulthood
Underlying sources of stability and change in the facet				
Genetic	Low-moderate	Low	Low/moderate	Low
Family	Moderate	Moderate	High	Low
Cultural	Moderate	Moderate	Moderate	Moderate
Acceptance of the individual as an active interpreter	Low/moderate	High	High	Moderate

the description of life that emerges from a consideration of any single facet is different from one drawing upon all four. For instance, the transition from adolescence to adulthood might be characterized as involving little change and high stability if the ideal self alone is considered (indeed, such claims emerge from studies of self-esteem that use structured inventories; e.g., Bachman *et al.*, 1978; Dusek & Flaherty, 1981). Quite a different depiction of the passage from adolescence to adulthood is suggested by the research on adaptational styles, which indicates considerable change and transformation during this time. The point is that the view of the passage of lives is profoundly affected by the perspective the researcher assumes; a full three-dimensional characterization of lives demands that the researcher look at lives from multiple perspectives.

Cautions and Limitations

The subjects who have been followed longitudinally in this study are not representative of Americans in any meaningful sense. They are men; none of them is black; all lived at one point in suburban Chicago; each was born and raised during a unique slice of American history. The extent to which these specific characteristics of the sample influenced the lives studied in this book is largely unknown.

Gender, for instance, has profound implications for development. The results presented in Chapter 3 indicate that there are sex-role typical differences in aspirations between boys and girls. Boys in 1988 aspire more to peer roles (e.g., being a good friend) and active occupations (e.g., pilot); girls are more interested in family (becoming a good mother) and professional (e.g., doctor) roles. It seems reasonable to infer that the differences between boys and girls would have been greater back in 1955 when the study began, which means that the developmental trajectory for the ideal self sketched in Chapter 3 would be quite different if Kohlberg's original sample had been composed of girls instead of boys.

The extent to which the descriptions of development in adaptational styles and the ego-ideal apply to women remains largely unknown; similarly, there is a dearth of information on how parenting differentially influences the lives of boys and girls. Perhaps future investigations will provide a consistent account for these facets of life and the factors that influence them (e.g., the Blocks ongoing longitudinal study of personality development is one of the best prospects for discovering the different effects parents have on boys and girls; see

Block & Block, 1980). Although research can shed light on the extent to which there are gender differences in the facets of life of interest in this book, debates in related fields (e.g., moral judgment) have raged hotly for years and frequently are of ideological rather than scientific origin (e.g., Mednick, 1989). It is unlikely, then, that research findings alone will lead to a consensus on the extent of similarity between males and females.

It would also be foolish to claim that the path traversed by a sample of men from a single historical cohort is universal. Chapter 2 presented an outline of some of the significant historical events that these men experienced; it is difficult to imagine that World War II, the civil rights movement, and the Vietnam War did not leave their imprints on the men. History had its influence on the parents of the men as well. Frank Jones's (Chapter 4) rejection of his father's occupational passivity in favor of success and achievement may be a choice that was not available to his father as a youth; those who experienced the hardships of the Great Depression became converts to the importance of job security (Elder, 1974).

Chapter 3 presented results indicating that the aspirations of today's youth are different from those of the men followed in this study. In the 1950s and 1960s adolescents aspired more to being good sons and good sports than was true for adolescents in 1988; working hard to get ahead was also viewed more favorably. Why these differences emerge cannot be answered from the data of this study. My own guess is that it is a combination of cultural and economic forces, rather than any single one, that has produced this change. It would indeed be rash to assert that adolescents becoming men today are identical to the men in this study.

One can point not only to the sorts of subjects that were not included in the study but also to the measures that were left out. No single study can possibly examine all that is of interest in the study of lives (Carlson, 1971), and the investigation presented in this book is no exception. There are many limitations to the account of lives over time that has been presented in these pages. As I noted in Chapter 2, it is terribly unfortunate that more information was not collected about the relationships the men had with their parents, children, and spouses. Without this information, the facets of development traced out in this book's chapters seem naked, stripped of the interpersonal context within which they derive much of their meaning.

Regretful, too, was the omission of standardized cognitive and personality measures. These measures would have allowed more certain assessment of the interaction of broad, stable facets of personality with those that evidence more change and transformation. If these measures had been included, augmented by more observer data (additional parental, peer, and teacher ratings as well as observations by children, wives, and fellow employees), a fuller depiction of development would have emerged.

Finally, the study is hampered by the small number of subjects, most of whom did not participate at every testing point. Furthermore, complete sets of data are not available for each subject; for instance, only a few of the fathers completed the parenting questionnaires at the second testing time. Consequently, it was impossible to do many of the statistical analyses that would have been desirable.

Despite the many limitations of the study, I believe that progress has been made toward understanding men's lives. This can be seen readily by examining the different facets of lives in the context of a single individual.

THE LIFE OF DAVID VOST

Age 13

David Vost entered the study as a 13-year-old. His parents were well educated (they had graduated from Columbia University), and his father held a good job as a manager at a large Chicago company. He was both academically talented (his IQ was in the top quarter of the sample) and popular among his peers. The initial interview with David suggests that he was typical of the subjects in this study, with areas of relative maturity and immaturity. The overall index of the maturity of his adaptational styles, his coping score, was in the top quarter of scores in his age group. More specifically, he used the adaptational styles of objectivity and intellectuality far more frequently than did his peers, which indicates that he was capable of making unusually full use of his cognitive abilities in emotional situations.

David's ability to utilize his sophisticated cognitive capacities in difficult situations was related to, and reflected in, his moral judgment (as one would predict on the basis of his coping score, David was relatively advanced in this domain, with an MMS in the top half of the sample). For instance, when he was asked by the interviewer if a man whose duty is to protect the city in time of crisis could leave his post to check on his family, David offers a response characteristic both of intellectuality and Stage 3 moral judgment:

> I don't think he should go to see his family. They might be all right and someone else might get hurt who he could have saved. If everybody went off to see his family, there wouldn't be much cooperation and the city might be destroyed.

David was also in the top quarter of the age cohort in terms of the orientation of his ideal self toward professional roles. More than most 13-year-olds, David aspired to be a head of a company, a judge, or a doctor; he also ranked working hard to get ahead as one of the most desirable roles. To tap the source of this orientation toward success, he was asked if his parents would be disappointed if he didn't get ahead in life. David replied "Yes, they want me to be successful and get a good education." David seemed oriented toward both the success and the money that would accompany a professional position. His ego-ideal reasoning (his ALEI score placed him in the bottom quarter of his age cohort) was a mixture of Level 2 (the acquisition of material goods, exchange of favors) and Level 3 (differentiation from the surrounding social context). For instance, when he was asked if he would like his father's job, he emphasized differentiation through educational achievement: "I wouldn't mind that, being an office worker. But I would still like something you study more for." When asked to compare the positions of office worker and head of a company, David said, "Well, you just make lots of money when you own a chain of stores. You are doing pretty good."

There was considerable evidence of Level 2 (exchange of favors) reasoning in his discussion of social roles:

> *Why do you want to be a good sport?*
> Sometimes you are in trouble, and your friends could help you out of it.

> *Why do you want to make your family proud of you?*
> When they like you, you will have lots of help.

Briefly, then, David Vost valued status and material rewards quite highly (he perceived his parents as emphasizing these, too); and he found social roles desirable, in part, because they offered the opportunity to acquire favors from others.

Age 17

The passage into middle adolescence was characterized by considerable continuity in David's life. He remained in the upper half of his age cohort in the maturity of his adaptational styles (with a coping score of 5.9) and in moral judgment (MMS of 302). He continued to be well regarded by others: for example, his teacher rated him "reliable," "very fair," "very obedient," "independent," and a "very hard worker" (the composite teacher rating places David in the upper quarter of the sample). This rating is to be expected, of course, because teacher ratings are related to moral judgment; they are also predictive of moral judgment development into adulthood (Chapter 5). Both his mother and father concurred with the judgments of David's teacher. They perceived him to be a trustworthy, responsible young man (their ratings of his conscience strength put him in the upper half of the sample). His mother related the following anecdote:

> He has always been trustworthy and has shown leadership in this field when his friends were hesitant about the proper road to take. For instance, he went to Springfield for the state championships. He stayed in a fancy hotel with practically no supervision. Some of the boys went out into the town and got into deep trouble; David did not.

Like many adolescents, David had a complex and somewhat ambivalent relationship with his parents. At 17 he no longer wished to be like his father (a possibility he rated as undesirable); his interests were different from those of his parents (he was in the bottom half of the sample in the extent of involvement he had with them), and his parents judged him to be quite unlike either of them (maternal and paternal identification scores were in the bottom half of the sample). Yet their influence on him continued to be particularly evident in his ideal self. As at age 13, David continued to aspire to professional roles (particularly that of doctor) more than did his peers. These aspirations reflected those his parents held for him. His mother wrote that her "fondest dream" for David was that he would become "a successful doctor." Mr. Vost's fondest dream for David also emphasized success and included social roles as well: "I hope that he will live a long, happy, and healthy life; a good-paying job; a nice wife and family (as satisfactory as mine); and on top of all this, that he be a good citizen and a moderately religious person."

David was certainly aware that his parents hoped he would become a physician, but, in keeping with his disengagement from them, he denied that their expectations played a significant role in his occupational aspirations:

What do your parents want you to be?
A doctor. Not because they are; my father's cousin was about the only one. But that's not why I picked it out. They wanted me to be anything I wanted.

As was true for the other adolescents in his age bracket, David was less interested at age 17 in being like his father than he had been at age 13:

I like my father, but it always struck me that you should have a little initiative of your own, and not just copy somebody else. You should copy good things, but I wouldn't want to do what my father does.

The theme of initiative in David's explanation for not wanting to be like his father was broadened later in the interview into a consistent Level 3 ego-ideal concern, with achievement and success.

Why is it important to you to work hard to get ahead?
You'd always take the initiative, and I think in the long run you'd end up happy and successful.

How about being head of a company, why is that something you'd like?
Well, if you were doing pretty well, moneywise. I don't think it would be real interesting, but if you were a success . . .

The big pay is the main thing.
Yeah, you want to be successful. I'm not saying that money is the mark of success, but I would like a lot of money.

Age 25

David Vost was next interviewed at age 25. His adolescent goal (and the one his parents held for him) of becoming a doctor was becoming a reality. His academic success in high school led to his acceptance at Columbia University, where he excelled as both an undergraduate and a medical student. He listed going to medical school, getting married, and moving to New York as the three most important events occurring since his last interview at age 17. He felt very much in charge of his life and believed that he had achieved an identity of his own making:

> It is easier to adhere to something that you feel and you have arrived at yourself than something that is not just given to you. You may not really like it and may not believe it as to your right and wrong values.

Although there was much about David's life that had changed—a sense of identity, marriage, an occupation, a new home—there was continuity as well. At age 25 David was still in the upper half of his age cohort in coping and moral judgment (although the latter was now a mixture of Stage 3 and Stage 4, rather than the pure Stage 3 at age 17). There was also continuity in the evaluative criteria forming his ego-ideal. At age 25 David was as oriented to individual achievement and success as he was as a 17-year-old:

> *Why is it important to you to work hard to get ahead?*
> I think you have to have goals that you want to reach. A lot of trouble with people is that they just don't have any motivation at all. They want to sit around and do nothing. I think if people have something they are working for, they are much happier. They are frustrated, I'll admit that, if they can't reach it; maybe their goal is too high. With me, I like to have something to shoot for and then work fairly hard at it. That's a quality I like as long as it doesn't get to be the only thing in life. You can overdo it. I admire that quality, wanting to achieve your goal, whatever it is.

David shared his orientation toward success with his wife, who had recently left her job as an accountant in order to attend law school.

Although David was centrally concerned with achievement, his marriage had resulted in an increasing concern with beginning a family of his own and with social roles in general. At ages 13 and 17 he was less interested in social roles than were most of his age-mates; at age 25 social roles had become much more central. For instance, he wanted very much to be a good father:

> I'm about at the age of starting a family, and you see so many families that aren't close; to me that is something I would like to have. One way to do it is to be a good parent. You are really responsible for the way your kids are going to turn out, and I

would like to be a good influence. That's important to me right now; I doubt if it was ten years ago.

Overall, David's ego-ideal reasoning was a mixture of Level 3 and Level 4, which placed him in the upper half of the sample.

Age 29

David at age 29 was still recognizably the person he had been at age 25 (e.g., his moral judgment score was the same), but he had changed to some degree. His coping score had slipped (putting him in the bottom half of the sample), as had his ego-ideal scores (bottom quarter) and his interest in social roles (bottom quarter). It seems that his full entry into the medical profession and the birth of his first child had resulted in some revisions in David's ideal self, ego-ideal, and ability to make use of mature adaptational styles. At age 25 the role working hard to get ahead had been very desirable; at age 29 it no longer was. The problem for David was that he was not sure what sorts of values constituted his core. His search for values had stranded him between what he used to believe in (material success) and another set of evaluative criteria that he had not yet elaborated. Consequently, in the interview he relied on intellectualization, making vague gener-alizations about the values to which he did and did not subscribe. These broad statements lacked the clarity and self-awareness that had characterized his beliefs at earlier ages. For instance, David explained in a contradictory way his rejection of material success as the criterion by which he measured his life:

> I think of working hard to get ahead as just being material success and I think that is sort of dying out now. I think that was more my parent's generation, trying to accumulate a lot money, things like that.
>
> *What does getting ahead in life mean to you?*
> Success for me. In medicine, success, I think, is saving difficult patients, being recognized in the medical community as being competent and things like that. I think that would be success.
>
> *Is that important to you?*
> Oh yah, I am competitive, as far as I like to win, but I don't—money to me is not all important. I like to spend money, but I don't have an all-consuming type of obsession with it.

In this interview David's claims seem unpersuasive; one still senses that he had yet to fully reject material success (although he attributed a concern for money to his "parents' generation," he had apparently "forgotten" how important money was for him (as the excerpts from earlier interviews suggest), and he admitted to a continuing desire for recognition. This hollowness, in combination with such generalizations as linking the desire to "accumulate a lot of money" with his parents' generation, is characteristic of intellectualization. Apparently, the difficulties associated with adapting to a wife, a family, and full entry into the world of work resulted in David's reliance on intellectualization, for this adaptational style was never characteristic of him at earlier points in his life—nor was it descriptive of him at the next.

Age 33

By the age of 33 David Vost had resolved the difficulties evident in his life at age 29. He now had three children, his wife had graduated from law school, he was involved in a range of community activities, and he had found new meaning in being a physician.

David's scores on the various facets reflect his adjustment. His score in moral judgment is in the top half of the sample, as one would expect based on his high coping and conscience strength scores as an adolescent (although the low levels of identification and involvement with his father in adolescence mediate against extremely high scores). His profile of adaptational styles is very mature, with empathy being particularly characteristic of him; his coping score is in the top quarter of the age cohort. Finally, his ego-ideal score and the composite social and professional scores are now all in the top half of his group. Together these findings suggest that David has rebounded from the difficulties he experienced in his late twenties.

At age 33 there was a greater sense of self-awareness in David's reflections on his life. At earlier ages he had explained his lack of interest in becoming like his father in terms of a need of all men to be "different" and not "copy" their elders. At age 33 he admitted that he just did not like his father. This does not mean that his reasons for disliking his father were reasonable. His new insight was limited to his own feelings and those of his patients, children, and wife. Although he was quite empathic, he continued to lack insight into the motives of his father:

Yah, I don't like my father that much, his lifestyle, so I wouldn't want to pattern myself after him.

Could you say what it is about his lifestyle that you don't like?
Well, he does not relate to people very well. He worked for a long time on a job that he didn't like and to me you have to enjoy what you are doing.

At age 29 David could not offer a clear account of what was of value in his profession and what was not. At age 33 he recognized that his original motivations for becoming a physician were no longer operative:

Why did you become a doctor?
My dad told me that doctors make a lot of money, so I originally got the idea to be a doctor for that, and that is the wrong reason. I also thought being a doctor would have some prestige in it; besides, it just sounded like an appealing thing to do. It turned out that I have enjoyed it thus far. I don't think that when I went into it, that I knew what I would be doing when I got out of medical school.

Earlier in his life David enjoyed medicine because of the money, the prestige, and the opportunity it offered him to compete (age 29) in the contest of who is the best doctor. As he entered his thirties, however, he began to recognize that medicine has a human side as well (one that, sadly, many physicians never learn of):

Do you have any philosophy about how you go about your work?
I think you've got to know how to work with people, you've got to be a psychologist. You've got to know people's problems, you've got to be able to read them, to know what they are saying when they don't, or can't, say anything. There is an intellectual side to it, too, where you have to know medicine, and you especially have to know when you are in trouble.

David's appreciation of the human side of medicine was emerging along with a deeper commitment to personal relationships. When he was asked to explain why he aspired most to be a good father, he replied:

To me family relationships are the most important thing in life, even if you are a total failure in everything else. I think that is really most important. I value my family more than anything. I want to be a good parent and that is very important to me.

Ironically, David rejected his father's values but had become what his father had hoped for: a successful physician, a good citizen, and a man whose family provides him with genuine satisfaction.

Summary

David Vost's life between the ages of 13 and 33 can be understood, in part, in terms of the facets of lives and the influences on them considered throughout this book. These constructs provide a framework within which the continuities and transformations evident in his life can be understood. Although the framework does not encompass all that is important in his life, it does preserve much of the richness.

CONCLUSIONS

The account of lives that has been developed in this chapter and the preceding ones has relied heavily on traditional theoretical constructs. Adaptational styles (defense mechanisms), parental identification, moral stages, the ego-ideal, and the ideal self all have long histories in psychology, though they seem less prominent in current developmental and personality research. The movement in developmental and personality psychology toward laboratory studies has led many investigators (e.g., a trend noted by Carlson, 1971) to abandon and deride broad constructs like those elaborated in this book. Although the precision with which sophisticated laboratory procedures can test complicated models of "new" constructs of personality is beguiling, lost is the sense of how the findings contribute to an understanding of persons. Perhaps the enterprise of studying many facets of real persons over long periods of time—like the one presented in this book—will reveal that the psychology of earlier eras had much to say about lives and life (see also Westen, 1991, for a similar viewpoint); I am convinced that will be so.

References

Anastasi, A. (1976). *Psychological testing*. New York: MacMillan.

Appelbaum, M., & McCall, R. (1983). Design and analysis in developmental psychology. In W. Kessen (Ed.) *Handbook of child psychology* (Vol. 1, pp. 415–457). New York: Wiley.

Armon, C. (1984). Ideals of the good life and moral judgment: Evaluative reasoning in children and adults. *Moral Education Forum, 9*, 1–27.

Armon, C. (1991, April). *The development of reasoning about the good life*. Paper presented at the meeting of the Society for Research on Child Development, Seattle.

Bachman, J., O'Malley, P., & Johnston, J. (1978). *Adolescence to adulthood: Change and stability in the lives of young men*. Ann Arbor, MI: Institute for Social Research.

Baldwin, J. M. (1902). *Social and ethical interpretations in mental life*. New York: Macmillan.

Baumeister, R. (1988). Should we stop studying sex differences altogether? *American Psychologist, 43*, 1092–1095.

Bellah, R., Madsen, R., Sullivan, W., Swidler, A., & Tipton, S. (1985). *Habits of the heart*. New York: Harper & Row.

Blasi, A. (1988). Identity and the development of the self. In D. Lapsley & F. Power (Eds.), *Self, ego, and identity: Integrative approaches* (pp. 226–242). New York: Springer-Verlag.

Blasi, A. (1980). Bridging moral cognition and moral action: A critical review of the literature. *Psychological Bulletin, 88*, 1–45.

Block, J. (1971). *Lives through time*. Berkeley, CA: Bancroft.

Block, J. H., & Block, J. (1980). The role of ego-control and ego-resiliency in the organization of behavior. In W. A. Collins (Ed.), *Minnesota symposia on child psychology* (Vol. 13, pp. 39–101). Hillsdale, NJ: Lawrence Erlbaum Associates.

Bloom, B. S. (1964). *Stability and change in human characteristics*. New York: Wiley.

Blum, G. (1953). *Psychoanalytic theories of personality*. New York: McGraw-Hill.

Bouchard, T., Lykken, D., McGue, M., Segal, N., & Tellegen, A. (1990). Sources of human psychological differences: The Minnesota study of twins reared apart. *Science, 250*, 223–228.

Bray, D., & Howard, A. (1983). The AT&T longitudinal studies of managers. In K. W. Schaie (Ed.), *Longitudinal studies of adult psychological development* (pp. 266–313). New York: Guilford Press.

Broughton, J. (1978). The cognitive-developmental approach to morality: A reply to Kurtines and Greif. *Journal of Moral Education, 7*, 81–96.

Broughton, J., & Zahaykevich, M. (1988). Ego and ideology: A critical review of Loevinger's theory. In D. Lapsley & F. Power (Eds.), *Self, ego, and identity: Integrative approaches* (pp. 179–208). New York: Springer-Verlag.

Brown, R., & Herrnstein, R. (1975). Moral reasoning and conduct. In Brown & Herrnstein (Eds.), *Psychology* (pp. 289–340). Boston: Little, Brown.

Bruner, J. (1990). Culture and human development: A new look. *Human Development, 33,* 344–355.

Burke, K. (1945). *The grammar of motives.* New York: Prentice-Hall.

Buss, A. H. (1989). Personality as traits. *American Psychologist, 44,* 1378–1388.

Campbell, D. (1971). *Handbook for the Strong Vocational Interest Blank.* Stanford, CA: Stanford University Press.

Carlson, R. (1971). Where is the person in personality research? *Psychological Bulletin, 75,* 203–219.

Carroll, J., & Chang, J. (1970). Analysis of individual differences in multidimensional scaling via an *n*-way generalization of "Eckart-Young" decomposition. *Psychometrika, 35,* 238–319.

Caspi, A., Elder, G., & Bem, D. (1987). Moving against the world: Life-course patterns of explosive children. *Developmental Psychology, 23,* 308–313.

Cohn, L. (1991). Sex differences in the course of personality development: A meta-analysis. *Psycyhological Bulletin, 109,* 252–266.

Colby, A., & Kohlberg, L. (1987). *The measurement of moral judgment* (Vol. 2). New York: Cambridge University Press.

Colby, A., Kohlberg, L., Candee, D., Gibbs, J., Hewer, A., & Speicher, B. (1987). *The measurement of moral judgment: Vol. 2. Standard issue scoring manual.* New York: Cambridge University Press.

Colby, A., Kohlberg, L., Gibbs, J., & Lieberman, M. (1983). A longitudinal study of moral judgment. *Monographs of the Society for Research in Child Development, 48*(1–2, Serial No. 200).

Costa, P., & McCrae, R. (1978). Objective personality assessment. In M. Storandt, I. C. Siegler, & M. F. Elias (Eds.), *The clinical psychology of aging* (pp. 119–143). New York: Plenum Press.

Costa, P., & McCrae, R. (1987). On the need for longitudinal evidence and multiple measures in behavioral-genetic studies of adult personality. *Behavioral and Brain Sciences, 10,*22–23.

Costa, P., McCrae, R., & Arenberg, D. (1980). Enduring dispositions in adult males. *Journal of Personality and Social Psychology, 38,* 793–800.

Costa, P., McCrae, R., & Holland, J. (1984). Personality and vocational interests in an adult sample. *Journal of Applied Psychology, 69,* 390–340.

Costa, P., McCrae, R., Zonderman, A., Barbano, H., Lebowitz, B., & Larsen, D. (1986). Cross-sectional studies of personality in a national sample: 2. Stability in neuroticism, extraversion, and openness. *Psychology and Aging, 1,* 144–149.

Cottle, W. (1950). A factorial study of the Multiphasic, Strong, Kuder, and Bell inventories using a population of adult males. *Psychometrika, 15,* 25–47.

Cronbach, L. (1951). Coefficient alpha and the internal structure of tests. *Psychometrika, 16,* 297–334.

Cronbach, L. (1957). The two disciplines of scientific psychology. *American Psychologist, 12,* 671–684.

Damon, W. (1983). *Social and personality development.* New York: Norton.

Damon, W., & Hart, D. (1986). Stability and change in children's self-understanding. *Social Cognition, 4,* 102–118.

Damon, W., & Hart, D. (1988). *Self-understanding in childhood and adolescence.* New York: Cambridge University Press.

Duberman, Martin. (1989). *Paul Robeson: A Biography.* NY: Ballantine Books.

Dubow, E., Huesmann, L., & Eron, L. (1987). Childhood correlates of adult ego development. *Child Development, 58,* 859–869.

Dusek, J. B., & Flaherty, J. F. (1981). The development of the self-concept during the adolescent years. *Monographs of the Society for Research in Child Development, 46*(4, Serial No. 191).

Elder, G. (1974). *Children of the great depression.* Chicago: University of Chicago Press.

Erdelyi, M. (1990). Repression, reconstruction, and defense: History and integration of the psychoanalytic and experimental frameworks. In J. Singer (Ed.), *Repression and dissociation: Implications for personality theory, psychopathology, and health* (pp. 1–31). Chicago: University of Chicago Press.

Erikson, E. (1956). The problem of ego identity. *Journal of the American Psychiatric Association, 4,* 56–121.

Erikson, E. (1963). *Childhood and society.* New York: Norton.

Erikson, E. (1968). *Identity: Youth and crisis.* New York: Norton.

Erikson, E. (1982). *The life cycle completed.* New York: Norton.

Fenichel, O. (1945). *The psychoanalytic theory of neurosis.* New York: Norton.

Fowler, J. (1981). *Stages of faith: The psychology of human development and the quest for meaning.* San Francisco: Harper & Row.

Freud, A. (1966). *The ego and the mechanisms of defense.* New York: International Universities Press.

Freud, S. (1957). On narcissism: An introduction. In J. Strachey (Ed. and Trans.), *The standard edition of the complete psychological works of Sigmund Freud* (Vol. 14, pp. 73–102). London: Hogarth Press. (Original work published 1914)

Freud, S. (1969). Jokes and their relation to the unconscious. In J. Strachey (Ed. and Trans.), *The standard edition of the complete psychological works of Sigmund Freud* (Vol. 8, pp. 1–258). London: Hogarth Press. (Original work published 1905)

Freud, S. (1961a). The ego and the id. In J. Strachey (Ed. and Trans.), *The standard edition of the complete psychological works of Sigmund Freud* (Vol. 19, pp. 3–66). London: Hogarth Press. (Original work published 1923)

Funder, D. (1991). Global traits: A neo-Allportian approach to personality. *Psychological Science, 2,* 31–39.

Gardner, H. (1983). *Frames of mind.* New York: Basic Books.

Gardner, H. (1981). *The quest for mind: Piaget, Levi-Strauss, and the structuralist movement* (2nd ed.). Chicago: University of Chicago Press.

Gardner, J. (1985). *The art of fiction.* New York: Random House.

Gibbs, J., Clark, P., Joseph, J., Green, J., Goodrick, T., & Makowski, D. (1986). Relations between moral judgment, moral courage, and field independence. *Child Development, 57,* 185–193.

Gibbs, J., & Schnell, S. (1985). Moral development "versus" socialization: A critique. *American Psychologist, 40,* 1071–1080.

Gilligan, C. (1982). *In a different voice: Psychological theory and women's development.* Cambridge: Harvard University Press.

Gilligan, C., & Murphy, J. (1979). Development from adolescence to adulthood: The philosopher and the dilemma of the fact. In D. Kuhn (Ed.), *New directions for child development: Intellectual development beyond childhood* (pp. 85–99). San Francisco: Jossey-Bass.

Glick, M., & Zigler, E. (1985). Self-image: A cognitive-developmental approach. In R. Leahy (Ed.), *The development of the self* (pp. 1–53). New York: Academic Press.

Gottfredson, G., & Holland, J. (1975). Vocational choices of men and women: A comparison of predictors from the self-directed search. *Journal of Counseling Psychology, 22,* 28–34.

Grotevant, H., & Cooper, C. (1985). Patterns of interaction in family relationships and the development of identity exploration in adolescence. *Child Development, 56,* 415–428.

Haan, N. (1963). Proposed model of ego functioning: Coping and defense mechanisms in relationship to IQ change. *Psychological Monographs, 77*(8), 571.

Haan, N. (1977). *Coping and defending: Processes of self–environment organization.* New York: Academic Press.

Haan, N. (1978). Two moralities in action contexts. *Journal of Personality and Social Psychology, 32,* 255–270.

Haan, N., Aerts, E., & Cooper, B. (1985). *On moral grounds: The search for practical morality.* New York: New York University Press.

Halverson, C. (1988). Remembering your parents: Reflections on the retrospective method. *Journal of Personality, 56,* 435–443.

Hanson, G. (1974). *Assessing the career interests of college youth: Summary of research and applications* (Report No. 67). Iowa City, IA: American College Testing Program.

Hart, D. (1988). A longitudinal study of adolescents' socialization and identification as predictors of adult moral judgment development. *Merrill-Palmer Quarterly, 34,* 245–260.

Hart, D., & Damon, W. (1986). Developmental trends in self-understanding. *Social Cognition, 4,* 388–407.

Hart, D., Kohlberg, L., & Wertsch, J. (1987). The social developmental theories of James Mark Baldwin and George Herbert Mead. In L. Kohlberg (Ed.), *Child psychology and childhood education: A structural developmental view* (pp. 223–258). New York: Longman.

Hart, D., Maloney, J., & Damon, W. (1987). The meaning and development of personal identity. In T. Honess & K. Yardley (Eds.), *Self and identity* (pp. 121–133). New York: Routledge & Kegan Paul.

Hart, D., & Shmiel, S. (1992). The influence of defense mechanisms on moral judgment development: A longitudinal study. *Developmental Psychology, 28,* 722–730.

Harter, S. (1983). The development of the self and the self system. In M. Hetherington (Ed.), *Handbook of child psychology: Socialization, personality, and social development,* (4th ed., Vol. 4, pp. 285–385). New York: Wiley.

Hauser, S. (1986). Conceptual and empirical dilemmas in the assessment of defenses. In G. Vaillant (Ed.), *Empirical studies of ego mechanisms of defense* (pp. 62–72). Washington: American Psychiatric Press.

Hauser, S., Powers, S., Jacobson, A., Noam, G., Weiss, B., & Follansbee, D. (1984). Family contexts of adolescent ego development. *Child Development, 55,* 195–213.

Havighurst, R., Robinson, M., & Dorr, M. (1946). The development of the ideal self in childhood and adolescence. *Journal of Educational Research, 50,* 241–257.

Hoffman, M. (1971). Identification and conscience development. *Child Development, 42,* 1071–1082.

Hoffman, M. (1976). Empathy, role-taking, guilt, and development of altruistic motives. In T. Lickona (Ed.), *Moral development and behavior* (pp. 124–143). New York: Holt, Rinehart & Winston.

Hoffman, M. (1982). Affect and moral development. In D. Cicchetti & P. Hesse (Eds.), *Emotional Development* (pp. 83–105). San Francisco: Jossey-Bass.

Hoffman, M., & Saltzstein, H. (1967). Parent discipline and the child's moral development. *Journal of Personality and Social Psychology, 5,* 45–47.

Holland, J. (1973). *Making vocational choices: A theory of careers.* Englewood Cliffs, NJ: Prentice-Hall.

Horney, K. (1950). *Neurosis and human growth: The struggle towards self-realization.* New York: Norton.

Horowitz, M. (1988). *Introduction to psychodynamics.* New York: Basic Books.

Horowitz, M., Markman, H., Stinson, C., Fridhandler, B., & Ghannam, J. (1990). A classification theory of defense. In J. Singer (Ed.), *Repression and dissociation: Implications for personality theory, psychopathology, and health* (pp. 61–84). Chicago: University of Chicago Press.

Hyde, J., & Linn, M. (1988). Gender differences in verbal ability: A meta-analysis. *Psychological Bulletin, 104,* 53–69.

Inhelder, B., & Piaget, J. (1958). *The growth of logical thinking from childhood to adolescence.* New York: Basic Books.

Jacobsen, A., Beardslee, W., Hauser, S., Noam, G., Powers, S., Houlihan, J., & Rider, E. (1986). Evaluating ego defense mechanisms using clinical interviews: an empirical study of adolescent diabetic and psychiatric patients. *Journal of Adolescence, 9,* 303–319.

James, W. (1890). *The principles of psychology.* New York: Holt.

Jessor, R. (1983). The stability of change: Psychosocial development from adolesence to young adulthood. In D. Magnusson & V. Allen (Eds.), *Human development: An interactional perspective* (pp. 321–341). New York: Academic Press.

Johnson, R., & Nagoshi, C. (1987). Secular change in the relative influence of G, E1 and E2 on cognitive abilities. *Behavioral and Brain Sciences, 10,* 27–28.

Kagan, J., & Moss, H. (1962). *From birth to maturity.* New York: Wiley.

Kitchener, K., & King, P. (1990). The reflective judgment model: Ten years of research. In M. Commons, C. Armon, L. Kohlberg, F. Richards, T. Grotzer, & J. Sinnot (Eds.), *Adult development: Vol. 2. Models and methods in the study of adolescent and adult thought* (pp. 63–78). New York: Praeger.

Koestner, R., Franz, C., & Weinberger, J. (1990). The family origins of empathic concern: A 26-year longitudinal study. *Journal of Personality and Social Psychology, 58,* 709–717.

Kohlberg, L. (1958). *The development of modes of thinking and choices in years 10 to 16.* Unpublished doctoral dissertation, University of Chicago.

Kohlberg, L. (1963). The development of children's orientations toward a moral order: Sequence in the development of moral thought. *Vita Humana, 6,* 11–33.

Kohlberg, L. (1969). Stage and sequence: The cognitive developmental approach to socialization. In D. A. Goslin (Ed.), *Handbook of socialization theory and research* (pp. 347–480). Chicago: Rand McNally.

Kohlberg, L. (1976). Moral stages and moralization: The cognitive developmental approach. In T. Lickona (Ed.), *Moral development and behavior* (pp. 31–48). New York: Holt, Rinehart & Winston.

Kohlberg, L. (1981). *The philosophy of moral development.* New York: Harper & Row.

Kohlberg, L. (1984). *The psychology of moral development.* New York: Harper & Row.

Kohlberg, L. (1987). *Childhood development and childhood education: A structural developmental view.* New York: Longman.

Kohlberg, L., & Kramer, R. (1969). Continuities and discontinuities in children and adult development. *Human Development, 12,* 93–120.

Kramer, D., & Woodruff, D. (1986). Relativistic and dialectical reasoning in three adult age groups. *Human Development, 29,* 280–289.

Kurtines, W., & Greif, E. (1974). The development of moral thought: Review and evaluation of Kohlberg's approach. *Psychological Bulletin, 81,* 453–470.

Lasch, C. (1979). *The culture of narcissism.* New York: Norton.

Lee, L., & Snarey, J. (1988). The relationship between ego and moral development: A theoretical review and empirical analysis. In D. Lapsley & F. Power (Eds.), *Self, ego, and identity: Integrative approaches* (pp. 151–178). New York: Springer-Verlag.

Levinson, D. (1986). A conception of adult development. *American Psychologist, 41,* 3–13.

Levinson, D., Darrow, C., Klein, E., Levinson, M. & McKee, B. (1978). *Seasons of a man's life.* New York: Knopf.

Loevinger, J. (1976). *Ego development: Conceptions and theories.* San Francisco: Jossey-Bass.

Loevinger, J. (1983). On ego development and the structure of personality. *Developmental Review, 3,* 339–350.

Loevinger, J., & Wessler, R. (1970). *Measuring ego development: Vol. 1. Construction and use of a sentence completion test.* San Francisco: Jossey-Bass.

Lowenthal, M., Thurner, M., & Chiriboga, D. (1975). *Four stages of life.* San Francisco: Jossey-Bass.

Luria, A. R. (1979). *The making of mind: A personal account of soviet psychology.* Cambridge: Harvard University Press.

MacCallum, R. (1981). Evaluating goodness of fit in nonmetric multidimensional scaling by ALSCAL. *Applied Psychological Measurement, 5,* 377–382.

Maccoby, E. (1980). *Social development: Psychological growth and the parent–child relationship.* New York: Harcourt Brace Jovanovich.

Maccoby, E., & Jacklin, E. (1974). *The psychology of sex differences.* Stanford: Stanford University Press.

Maccoby, E., & Martin, J. (1983). In M. Hetherington (Ed.), *Handbook of Child Psychology* (Vol. 4, pp. 1–101). New York: Wiley.

Marcia, J. (1966). Development and validation of ego identity status. *Journal of Personality and Social Psychology, 35,* 551–558.

Marcia, J. (1980). Identity in adolescence. In J. Adelson (Ed.), *Handbook of adolescent psychology* (pp. 159–187). New York: Wiley.

Markus, H., & Nurius, P. (1986). Possible selves. *American Psychologist, 41,* 954–969.

McAdams, D. (1985). *Power, intimacy, and the life story: Personological inquiries into identity.* Chicago: Dorsey Press.

McCrae, R. & Costa, P. (1980). Openness to experience and ego level in Loevinger's sentence completion test: Dispositional contributions to developmental models of personality. *Journal of Personality and Social Psychology, 39,* 1179–1190.

McCrae, R., & Costa, P. (1981). Openness to experience and ego level in Loevinger's sentence completion test: Dispositional contributions to developmental models of personality. *Journal of Personality and Social Psychology, 39,* 1179–1190.

McCrae, R. & Costa, P. (1983). Psychological maturity and subjective well-being: Toward a new synthesis. *Developmental Psychology, 19,* 243–248.

McCrae, R., & Costa, P. (1987). Validation of the five-factor model of personality across instruments and observers. *Journal of Personality and Social Psychology, 52,* 81–90.

McCrae, R., & Costa, P. (1988). Recalled parent–child relations and adult personality. *Journal of Personality, 56,* 417–434.

McCrae, R., & Costa, P. (1990). *Personality in adulthood.* New York: Guilford Press.

McCullough, L., Vaillant, C., & Vaillant, G. (1986). Toward reliability in identifying ego defenses through verbal behavior. In G. Vaillant (Ed.), *Empirical studies of ego mechanisms of defense* (pp. 62–72). Washington: American Psychiatric Press.

Mednick, M. (1989). On the politics of psychological constructs: Stop the bandwagon, I want to get off. *American Psychologist, 44,* 1118–1123.

Moss, H., & Susman, E. (1980). Longitudinal study of personality development. In O.G. Brim & J. Kagan (Eds.), *Constancy and change in human development* (pp. 530–595). Cambridge: Harvard University Press.

Nisbett, R., & Wilson, T. (1977). Telling more than we know: Verbal reports on mental processes. *Psychological Review, 84,* 231–254.

Noam, G. (1988). The theory of biography and transformation. In S. Shirk (Ed.), *Cognitive development and child psychotherapy* (pp. 273–317). New York: Plenum.

Norman, W. T. (1963). Toward an adequate taxonomy of personality attributes: Replicated factor structure in peer nomination personality ratings. *Journal of Abnormal and Social Psychology, 66,* 574–583.

Nozick, R. (1981). *Philosophical explanations.* Cambridge, MA: Belknap Press.

Parikh, B. (1980). Development of moral judgment and its relation to family environmental factors in Indian and American families. *Child Development, 51,* 1030–1039.

Paulhus, D., Fridhandler, B., & Hayes, S. (in press). Psychological defense: Contemporary theory and research. In S. Briggs, R. Hogan, & W. Jones (Eds.), *Handbook of personality research.* San Diego: Academic Press.

Peabody, D. (1987). Selecting representative trait adjectives. *Journal of Personality and Social Psychology, 52,* 59–71.

Perry, W. (1968). *Forms of intellectual and ethical development in the college years.* New York: Holt, Rinehart & Winston.

Piaget, J. (1929). *The child's conception of the world,* London: Routledge & Kegan Paul.

Piaget, J. (1965). *The moral judgment of the child.* New York: Free Press. (Original work published 1932)

Plomin, R., & Daniels, D. (1987). Why are children in the same family so different from one another? *Behavioral and Brain Sciences, 10,* 1–60.

Rawls, J. (1971). *A theory of justice.* Cambridge, MA: Harvard University Press.

Rest, J. (1983). Morality. In J. Flavell & E. Markman (Eds.), *Handbook of child psychology* (4th ed., Vol. 3, pp. 556–629). New York: Wiley.

Runyan, W. (1982). *Life histories and psychobiographies.* New York: Oxford University Press.

Saltzstein, H. (1976). Social influence and moral development: A perspective on the role of parents and peers. In T. Lickona (Ed.), *Moral development and behavior* (pp. 253–265). New York: Holt, Rinehart & Winston.

Sandler, J., Holder, A., & Meers, D. (1963). The ego ideal and the ideal self. *The Psychoanalytic Study of the Child, 18,* 139–158.

Scarr, S. (1991, April). *Developmental theories for the 1990s.* Presidential address, Society for Research in Child Development, Seattle.

Schuerger, J., Zarrella, K., & Holtz, A. (1989). Factors that influence the temporal stability of personality by questionnaire. *Journal of Personality and Social Psychology, 56,* 777–783.

Schulenberg, J., Goldstein, A., & Vondracek, F. (1991). Gender differences in adolescents' career interests: Beyond main effects. *Journal of Adolescent Research, 1,* 37–61.

Searle, J. (1984). *Minds, brains and science.* Cambridge: Harvard University Press.

Selman, R. (1980). *The growth of interpersonal understanding.* New York: Academic Press.

Shweder, R. (1982). Liberalism as destiny (Review of Lawrence Kohlberg's *Essays on moral development: Vol. 1. The philosophy of moral development. Contemporary Psychology, 27,* 421–424.

Simpson, E. (1974). Moral development research: A case study of scientific cultural bias. *Human Development, 17,* 81–106.

Snarey, J. (1985). Cross-cultural universality of social-moral development: A critical review of Kohlbergian research. *Psychological Bulletin, 97,* 202–232.

Snarey, J., Kohlberg, L., & Noam, G. (1983). Ego development in perspective: Structural stage, functional phase, and cultural age-period models. *Developmental Review, 3,* 303.

Snarey, J., & Vaillant, G. (1985). How lower and working-class youth become middle-class adults: The association between ego defense mechanisms and upward mobility. *Child Development,* 889–910.

Stevens, G., & Featherman, D. (1981). A revised socioeconomic index of occupational status. *Social Science Research, 10,* 364–395.

Stewart, A., & Healy, J. (1989). Linking individual development and social changes. *American Psychologist, 44,* 30–42.

Strong, E. K. (1943). *Vocational interests of men and women.* Stanford, CA: Stanford University Press.

Strong, E. K. (1955). *Vocational interests: 18 years after college.* Minneapolis, MN: University of Minnesota Press.

Swanson, G. (1988). *Ego defenses and the legitimation of behavior.* New York: Cambridge University Press.

Thoma, S. J. (1986). Estimating gender differences in the comprehension and preference of moral issues. *Developmental Review, 6,* 165–180.

Vaillant, G. (1977). *Adaptation to life.* Boston: Little, Brown.

Vaillant, G. (1986). A brief history of empirical assessment of defense mechanisms. In G. Vaillant (Ed.), *Empirical studies of ego mechanisms of defense* (pp. viii–xx). Washington, DC: American Psychiatric Press.

Vaillant, G. (1988). Defense mechanisms. In A. Nicholi (Ed.), *The new Harvard guide to psychiatry* (pp. 200–207). Cambridge, MA: Belknap Press.

Van den Daele, L. (1968). A developmental study of the ego-ideal. *Genetic Psychology Monographs, 78,* 191–256.

Vaughn, B., Block, J., & Block, J. (1988). Parental agreement on child rearing during early childhood and the psychological characteristics of adolescents. *Child Development, 59,* 1020–1033.

Veroff, J., Douvan, E., & Kulka, R. (1981). *The inner American: A self-portrait from 1957 to 1976.* New York: Basic Books.

Walker, L. (1983). Sex differences in the development of moral reasoning: A critical review. *Child Development, 54,* 1103–1141.

Walker, L., & Taylor, J. (1991). Family interactions and the development of moral reasoning. *Child Development, 62,* 264–283.

Westen, D. (1985). *Self and society: Narcissism, collectivism, and the development of morals.* New York: Cambridge University Press.

Westen, D. (1991). Social cognition and object relations. *Psychological Bulletin, 109,* 429–455.

White, R. W. (1952). *Lives in progress.* New York: Dryden Press.

Wilson, J., & Herrnstein, R. (1985). *Crime and human nature.* New York: Simon & Schuster.

Winnicott, D. (1971). *Playing and reality.* New York: Basic Books.

Index